D1474916

Software Engineering Environments

CONCEPTS AND TECHNOLOGY

Robert N. Charette

Intertext Publications, Inc.
McGraw-Hill, Inc. New York, NY

Dedication

To Mo.

Library of Congress Catalog Card Number 86-81063

10 9 8 7 6 5 4 3 2 1

ISBN 0-07-010645-2

Intertext Publications, Inc.
McGraw-Hill Book Company
1221 Avenue of the Americas
New York, NY, 10020

Ada is a registered trademark of the United States Government (Ada Joint Program Office)
Leonardo is a registered trademark of Microelectronics and Computer Technology Corporation.
PSL/PSA is a registered trademark of ISDOS, Inc.
SADT is a registered trademark of SofTech, Inc.
SREM is a registered trademark of TRW Corporation.
STEP is a registered trademark of GTE Corporation.
Teamwork, Teamwork/RT, Teamwork/SA, and Teamwork/SD are registered trademarks of Cadre Technologies, Inc.
UNIX is a registered trademark of Bell Laboratories.

The figures displayed on pages 118, 120, 121, 122, and 123 are reprinted with the permission of Cadre Technologies, Inc.

TABLE OF CONTENTS

ACKNOWLEDGEMENTS

It is a very difficult thing to write out the acknowledgement section of this book because so many people have been involved in its making. One always risks leaving someone out. Therefore, I want to thank first all those unnamed, but important people who have contributed ideas and have argued with me over the last few years to help clarify my thoughts on the subject. Individual members of the SEEWG, of NSIA, of NASA, of STARS, and SofTech, Inc. have provided the most help. It really has been you people that have shaped and developed the core contributions of this book, and deserve the majority of the credit.

I want to thank Paul Fortier of the Naval Underwater Systems Center for giving me the opportunity to write this book, and for commenting on and giving advice on how to improve many sections of it. I want to thank also Tom Conrad of the Naval Underwater Systems Center and Bob Converse of Computer Sciences Corporation for dedicating a tremendous amount of their precious free time also reviewing some of the initial drafts, and for setting me on the straight and narrow whenever I would craft some dubious idea.

I especially wish to thank Dr. Charles McKay of the University of Houston at Clear Lake City. Dr. McKay has been very instrumental in forcing a rethinking of many of my thoughts about environments, and for making me understand the problems of building software engineering environments for extremely large software systems like NASA's Space Station.

Special thanks go out to Commander Kate Paige, USN and Hank Stuebing of the Naval Air Development Center who have been the most influencial people in my thinking about environments. It would be difficult to find two people that have contributed more to the present direction of software engineering environments than Kate and Hank.

Finally, I want to thank a very special friend who kept me going throughout the agony of writing this book. She was the one who patiently listened to my complaints, encouraged me when I felt overwhelmed, and kicked me when I needed it. Books don't get written without those people around. To Maureen Albrecht of SofTech, my greatest thanks. Thanks, Mo.

Robert Charette
1 June 1986

1. SOFTWARE ENGINEERING

"Software is like entropy. It is difficult to grasp, weighs nothing, and obeys the Second Law of Thermodynamics; i.e., it always increases."

Augustine's Laws[1]

1.0 Introduction

Imagine, for a few minutes, that the time is the early 1990s. Your job, if you decide to accept it, is to determine the software support requirements of a new, computer-intensive system that a company you are interviewing with has just won a competition to build. This means you will be responsible for specifying all the computer-related elements required by the engineers, scientists, technicians, managers, etc. involved in the project. They will use these elements to create, maintain, and manage the application software that is going to be developed and used within the new system. To help you understand the nature of the job, a brief description of the system envisioned has been provided.

First, the proposed system architecture will contain several dozen heterogeneous computers networked together, but dispersed geographically across thousands of miles. Moreover, the system will possess a large, as yet undetermined, number of space-based elements continuously communicating with the network via ground and satellite links.

The system's reliability requirements are severe. No individual failure of a computer-based component of the system can keep a software task in execution from completion, nor can two such failures result in damage to life or property. Furthermore, when any software updates are inserted into the system, the system must continue to execute; i.e., the system cannot be brought

[1]

down during system regenerations. Once the system is made operational, it must continue to be operational throughout its lifetime.

Since the system will likely evolve over the next twenty years or more, easy technology insertion for both hardware and software is mandatory. First estimates are that somewhere around 100 million new lines of high-level code will be necessary for the system to fulfill its currently prescribed mission, and up to 300 million additional needed to support currently foreseen missions.

The system must be built within seven years, on time, within a tight budget under public and congressional scrutiny, and any failure of the system will be described in excrutiating detail by the world's press. And it better be fully documented. And, oh yes, there will be over 4,000 personnel, in thirty major companies, and countless minor ones, involved in the total software development. These companies will be located across the United States, and possibly Europe and Japan, and must be able to "share" the support system you are specifying.

Although grossly simplified, the system described above represents some of the requirements that will have to be met if NASA's Space Station Project is to meet its initial operational capability in the mid-1990s. Ambitious? Most definitely, but it is not alone in sheer size, cost, complexity, schedule, or necessity. For instance, WIS and the Strategic Defense Initiative (SDI) also fall into this category of "ambitious" systems, as do many others currently on the planning boards of both the commercial and government sector.[2]

Although the systems mentioned above are on the larger side of the size and complexity spectrum, many computer systems currently in everyday use are of similar scope. The financial transaction systems used at banks, the billing systems used by telephone companies, typical company payroll systems, and the Social Security and Veteran's Administration check distribution systems are only a few examples that twenty-five years ago would have been considered as ambitious as the Space Station, WIS, and SDI systems are today. The airline reservation system is a prime example of a system most of us take for granted, but which, on reflection, is rather impressive. Travel agents from anywhere in the United States can call into a computerized network to buy a ticket on almost any airline on one of thousands of specific flights to hundreds of domestic and international cities, select your seat (smoking, non-smoking, window, or aisle), order special assistance such as meals or wheelchairs, if necessary, and get your boarding pass — all within a few minutes without your ever having to set foot inside an airline terminal. And if it takes more than a few minutes, we get annoyed!

Both national security and domestic tranquility have become highly dependent on our computerized systems. However, increasingly there is something disquieting about this same level of dependence. Airplane crashes (e.g., the 1979 Air New Zealand crash in Antartica), aborted space launches (e.g., the Space Shuttle on its first two launch attempts in 1981), ghost trains (e.g., the San Francisco Muni Metro train that "wasn't there" in 1983), and runaway missiles (e.g., the Soviet cruise missile that "got away" over Norway and Finland in 1985) are only a few examples of what can happen when a computer system doesn't work correctly. Less spectacular events may result only in the nuisance of lost time or money as when your automatic bank teller swallows your bankcard because it wasn't reprogrammed to accept old bankcards when the new ones were issued. On the other hand, computer system failure can be potentially catastrophic to hundreds of millions of people. That's because now even our concept of national defense is predicated on what is achievable through the capabilities provided by computers. Some don't believe that is necessarily good.

For instance, Dr. David L. Parnas, recognized as one of the United States' leading computer scientists, does not believe that systems like the SDI, a cornerstone in our defense policy for the twenty-first century, can be built with the reliability necessary to accomplish its objective of protecting the United States from nuclear attack. This, he believes, is in large part because we neither understand enough about the system requirements nor the process of software creation to implement it [PARNAS85]. If this view is correct, the result is wasted money at best and, as others argue, possibly reduced national security.

Whether or not these specific views about SDI are totally valid — and many believe they are not — Parnas does point out some concerns that few will argue with. It seems most software development efforts are plagued by the fact that we don't know exactly what we are building, nor how to build it successfully. More specifically, if new systems such as the Space Station are ever going to be successfully realized, a number of serious problems that confront the current state of the practice of building computerized systems must be overcome. We can summarize the current situation with three points:

- *The High Cost of Software* — Software costs, in both financial and human terms, are increasing rapidly as computerization of society spreads. Software in large systems may approach $4 billion in initial costs alone, while a computer error in an accounting system may mean immeasurable anguish to an elderly person denied a much needed check. Software costs are the dominant costs of software-based systems today.

- *The Variation in Practice*—There is a wide range of software practices exercised both within and across government and commercial sectors. These practices may lag the state of the art by as many as fifteen years. As a result, software is difficult to manage and varies widely in cost, reliability, and maintainability.

- *The Need for Increased Productivity*—Based upon analysis of projected software requirements over the next two decades, demand will outstrip the resources for the production of software. The only viable answer is to increase productivity, which can be accomplished on the scale required only by increasing the productivity of the process as a whole. Failure to increase productivity tends to increase the severity of the two problems above.

Attacking these problems and creating successful software systems is the theme of this book. But before we explore this theme in detail, it would be beneficial to review a condensed history of how these software problems came to be. To paraphrase Santayana, if we don't understand our past, we are condemned to repeat it.

1.1 Setting the Stage: "The Software Problem"

In the early days of digital computing, software development was aimed primarily at getting a single specialized program to work. Computers, then as now, were meant to save large amounts of manual labor. First generation computers and programs in the 1940s were mainly targeted to the completion of the massive astronomic navigation and ballistic tables used primarily by scientists and the military. In the 1950s, as second generation computers provided more power and flexibility, and made it cost effective to use computers, the trend shifted away from the purely scientific and military usage of computers to the processing of business data.

In both the 1940s and 50s, a program was considered increasingly successful if it: a) executed; b) executed quickly; c) gave an acceptable answer. Regardless of the success criteria the quality of the program was highly dependent on the skill of the programmer. Because of the lack of resources provided by the computer to work with, there was great admiration for an individual programmer's ingenuity at providing the maximum computation using the least amount of resources.[3]

New memory technology spawned the third generation computers. These computers allowed even larger programs to be executed, and many programs to be executed concurrently. This additional capability moved the trend in software development in the late 1950s and early 1960s away from single programs or sets of small programs to large assemblages of programs linked to do one integrated system function. Large-scale use of software was probably first attempted in the SAGE (Semi-Automatic Ground Environment) air defense system. It contained a computer with 58,000 vacuum tubes, consumed 1.5 megawatts of power, executed a real-time application program of 100,000 instructions, and had a support system of 112 million instructions [AUGUSTINE83].

The creators of the SAGE system were the unfortunate first, but by no means the last, to experience the problems surrounding the development of large-scale software systems. Most of the problems they faced are still familiar to those creating software systems today.

For example, the application program was too large and complex to be created by a small group of programmers, instead requiring large teams of programmers. The increased number of personnel, along with their required logistical support (notice the large support system — much larger in fact than the system being built), rapidly boosted the cost of the project. The problem of scale also appeared. A large program just didn't seem to work all that well [YEH84]. It became clear that as the program size increased, the probability for error increased even faster. Although reliable statistics aren't available, SAGE probably also used most of the programmers then in existance, thus depleting the numbers available for other programming jobs in the commercial sector and driving up labor costs. Finally, a larger program and a more capable computer allowed the programmers to be even more "ingenious" than before.

However, the problems and lessons learned in the encounter with the SAGE system development were to be quickly dismissed as a period of great fervor and optimism swept the computer field in the mid and late 1960s. Newer, more capable computers and software techniques promised to make any lessons learned obsolete or marginally transferable to new system developments.

It was widely believed — or at least the marketing people claimed — the advent of the fourth-generation machines would allow the distribution of programs across networks to form systems magnitudes larger than those ever envisioned by the SAGE designers. Moreover, the costs of the hardware systems were constantly going to be reduced, and what were previously scarce resources (processing speed, memory, etc.) were going to become everyday items. Additionally, to handle the software development of these large systems, it was recognized that some discipline would have to be brought to the software field. But here, too, progress seemed to be making rapid headway.

After all, research efforts were reporting results in the areas of software design disciplines, problem abstraction, and notations for software representations. These factors would allow a rational approach to software development. Simultaneously, high-level programming languages first developed in the 1950s were finally gaining acceptance by the programming community as the code generated by the compilers became ever more reliable and efficient. The issues of programmer productivity and software quality, although still not completely solved, were seen as things of the past. The age of functional programming as seen in the 1940s, '50s, and early '60s would be replaced by the new age of structured programming [PETERS80]. The problems brought out by the development of the SAGE system would soon be solved.

However, by the late 1960s, this confidence was beginning to wane as more and more software system developments were encountering exactly the same problems as the SAGE system. So in 1968 and 1969, at two exciting and controversial NATO conferences held in West Germany, new ways were discussed to solve the "software problem," typified by expensive, unreliable, and unmaintainable software. A new term was coined to help express what was thought to be the solution: Software Engineering.

SOFTWARE ENGINEERING. The beginnings of software engineering, given some literary license, could make a great mythological tale in the tradition of Wagner. It began with the creation of a brother to hardware engineering, whose highly developed discipline was able to create systems that, unlike software, worked within design constraints. Envious, a rebel group of computer scientists sought to combine into a disciplined engineering approach the magical techniques used by the self-styled programming artisans who then controlled the creation of software. In 1969, these disciples of the engineering approach met in Europe and created the term "software engineering," which was to change forever the way of developing software. Software engineering was to mean "the establishment and use of sound engineering principles in order to economically obtain, software that is reliable and works efficiently on real machines" [NAUER69]. However, many opposed this view, calling it a fabrication that took away the uniqueness and magic of programming. So the great debates over whether the creation of software was an art, science, or discipline ravaged the land for almost twenty years [HOARE84].

Over the last few years the debates have died down as those who believe in the engineering approach seem to have won the battle for converts. Some cynical observers blame it on better public relations, although others say that since software still doesn't work well, neither those favoring the science or art approaches want to take the blame. Nevertheless, the term "software engineering" has received a certain level of acceptance throughout the software community and is the current thrust. However, exactly what it means is still somewhat fuzzy, and this is probably why everyone accepts it. It seems to mean whatever one wants it to mean.

This shouldn't be surprising to anyone either, as software engineering hasn't yet reached its twentieth birthday, and like most teenagers, still can't decide on what it wants to be. The IEEE Standard Glossary on Software Engineering Terminology [IEEE83] defines it as, "the systematic approach to the development, operation, maintenance, and retirement of software." Software is then defined as "computer programs, procedures, rules and possibly associated documentation and data pertaining to the operation of a computer system."[4]

In Fairley's text [FAIRLEY84] on software engineering concepts, software engineering is defined as "the technological and managerial discipline concerned with systematic production and maintenance of software products that are developed on time and within cost estimates." A software product includes the system-level software, application software, and all associated documentation. Some typical items making up a software product are shown in table 1-1. Rather than adding a new definition to the list, we will be content to use Fairley's definition as our operational one. However, we do wish to add one more element to the discussion.

The above definition of software engineering describes what it is, but only implicitly its goals. Pressman [PRESSMAN82] states them very succinctly: "The key objectives of software engineering are (to define, create, and apply[5]) (1) a well-defined methodology that addresses a software life

• Requirements Document	• Specification Document
• System Description Document	• Test Specification
• Software Development Plan	• Test Procedures
• Functional Design Document	• Test Reports
• Detailed Design Document	• User Manual
• Verification Plan	• Source Code Listing
• Trouble Reports	• Object Code Listings

Table 1 - 1   **Typical Components of a Software Product**

cycle of planning, development, and maintenance; (2) an established set of software components that documents each step in the life cycle and shows traceability from step to step, and (3) a set of predictable milestones that can be reviewed at regular intervals throughout the software life cycle." The combination of both these definitions allows the derivation of some of the goals/objectives of the software engineering process, which are shown in table 1-2.

So with the combination of these two thoughts still fresh in our minds, let's look at software engineering as it appears today.

1.2 Software Engineering Today

As has been amply documented elsewhere [BOEHM76, WEGNER78, REDWINE84] advances in software engineering technology have occurred on all fronts: requirements analysis, implementation strategies, cost models, etc., to name just a few. Each advance has been aimed at reducing one of the three problems we mentioned earlier: (1) the high cost of software, (2) the variation in practice, or (3) the lack of productivity. In reality, each problem is coupled tightly to the other, and solutions to one usually help to make the solutions to the others more feasible. For instance, the movement toward

Goals/Objectives of the Process of Software Engineering

- To improve the accuracy, performance, and efficiency of the overall product under development
- To apply well-defined methodologies for the resolution of software/system issues
- To provide rational resolution of conflicts and documentation of differences when resolution is not possible
- To provide for product change in response to new or modified requirements
- To provide an understanding of the role of all stakeholders in the resolution of complex issues and the differing sets of constraints under which they operate
- To provide clear communication among management and the members of the system/software engineering teams
- To provide the understanding of how current systems and the evolution of future products are impacted by present day decisions
- To provide explicit identification and consideration of all normally implicit tradeoffs, assumptions, constraints, and intentions, and recognition of what is, and is not, important for planning and decision making purposes
- To provide anticipation of contingencies and identification of the impacts of proposed situations
- To document decisions, the rationale behind decisions, and the actions taken; create and maintain a corporate memory
- To provide explicit descriptions of schedules and milestones, and an understanding of the effects of time upon issues under consideration

Table 1 - 2

using high-level languages in software development instead of assembly language can be traced primarily to improving programmer productivity. Although taken for granted now, even just ten years ago this was a major change of operating practice in some industry organizations. This single change has accounted for billions of dollars saved in software costs, the

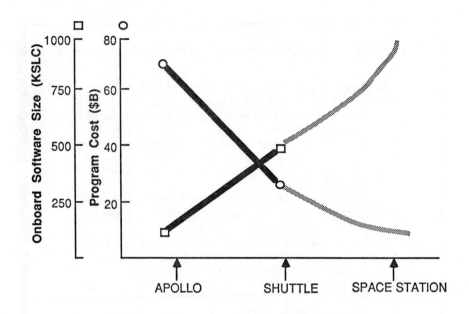

Figure 1 -1   **Software Cost ratio vs. Space Flight Software Trends**

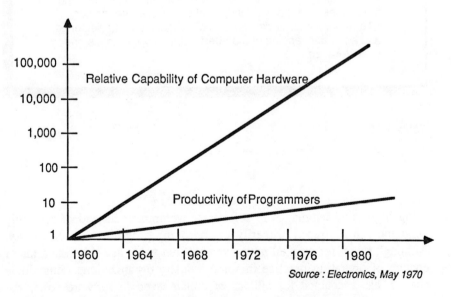

Source : Electronics, May 1970

Figure 1 - 2   **Relative Capability of Computer Hardware over Time**

capability for many different organizations to work together on the same project from remote sites, and the increased productivity of programming staffs many-fold.

Figure 1-1 helps illustrate this by showing the cost trends for some NASA programs compared to the size of onboard software in constant dollars. Apollo was written in assembly language, Shuttle is using a combination of assembly and high-level languages, and the Space Station will be almost totally done in high-level languages. Note that as more functionality was obtained, fewer real software dollars were expended than fifteen years ago.

Some argue that many of the cost advantages can be attributable to more capable (and cheaper) computers (see figure 1-2), yet all in all, software costs in constant dollars have gone down compared to the capability provided. This is exactly the trend one wants to see. Yet, if one were to compare the comments about the state of the software field twenty years ago and today, one would be struck by the fact that nothing seems to have changed except the terminology [MYERS78, GLASS80]! Software costs remain excessive, schedules are unpredictable, and quality is suspect. Why, then, is there this paradox of seeming to win the battles, but constantly losing the war? In the next several sections, we will examine in more detail the individual issues confronting software engineering today.

1.3 The High Cost of Software

Developing and maintaining software in the United States is a growth business. It was estimated that in 1980, approximately $40 billion was spent on software [BOEHM83]. If one totals all aspects of computing and data processing, the totals were closer to $130 billion [FAIRLEY84], with this figure likely doubling by 1990. Over $250 billion dollars may be the current value of existing software [MUNSON81]. The Electronics Industry Association, which publishes forecasts of the Department of Defense's use of computers, estimates a tripling of software costs in DoD alone between 1980 and 1990.

Most of the money spent on software is on maintenance, which is typically two to four times the original development costs. In fact, anywhere from 60 to 80 percent of all software costs are related to maintenance, and will likely remain so for the indefinite future.

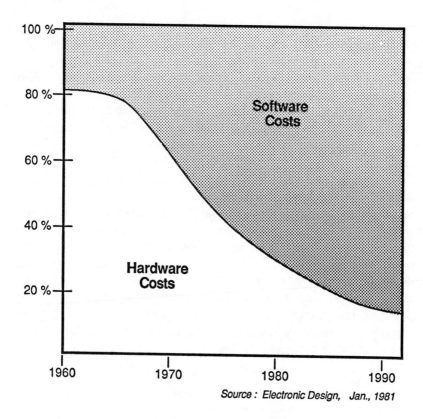

Source : *Electronic Design,   Jan., 1981*

Figure 1 - 3   **Hardware vs. Software Cost Analysis
of Typical Computer System**

Software costs also amount to almost 80 percent of all computer expenditures in 1980, and will probably reach 90 percent by 1990. Figure 1-3 shows the changing ratios of expenditures for hardware and software over the last twenty-five years.

The demand for software, too, is increasing at a pace that far exceeds the ability to provide it. There will be an estimated million person shortfall in trained personnel by 1990. With the average burdened cost of a programmer close to $100,000 today [WASSERMAN82], the law of supply and demand will push this cost up also.

The numbers above are some of the results of trying to develop software today, but what are some of the causes? One is the massive size of computer programs being built, and the effort involved. The development of the IBM 360 operating system required over 5,000 programmers five years to create the million instructions necessary for it to run [BROOKS75]. When one starts to add in the costs for all the support personnel (managers, secretaries, librarians, etc.) and logistics (computer equipment to support the development, space, computer paper, etc.) over a five year period, the high cost becomes obvious. The trend in operating systems for data processing applications is predicted to be 4 to10 million bytes of code by 1990, so costs will only increase [BROWN84].

System size is an insidious cost driver. The larger the system size, the longer it takes to create. Ergo more cost. Also, the larger it is, the more unreliable it is. Therefore, more time and people are necessary to make it reliable, which is usually done by the addition of checks in the software. This drives up the size of the system, which then requires more time, which then makes it less reliable, ad infinitum. The bottom line is more cost.

The size of software systems being created has increased rather rapidly over the last few years as demonstrated by table 1-3a. Boehm [BOEHM81] listed some "average" sizes of systems in 1981, and Fairley did the same in 1984. It is interesting to note that the categories are roughly similar, except Fairley now includes Very Large and Extremely Large on the list. The next categories after that we believe should be "Ambitious," which are systems in the 25 to 100 million range, and "Probably Won't Work Today," which is anything larger.The trend will continue to be towards ever larger systems, and the range of what is considered a large system will inevitably change as time goes on. We postulate the "typical sizes" will approach those shown in table 1-3b by 1995.

DOD SOFTWARE. To further help illustrate what has happened to drive up software costs, we will examine a special creator and user of application software, namely the Department of Defense. The DoD, and its contractors, constitute the largest single developer of software in the United States followed by the Department of Energy, NASA, and then the rest of the commercial market [GARMAND85].

Department of Defense software is divided into two categories: Mission Critical Computer Resources (MCCR) and non-MCCR software. Basically, the division is roughly along the traditional lines of Automated Data Processing (ADP) and non-ADP computing, although elements of MCCR

BOEHM 81		FAIRLEY 84		CHARETTE 86	
Category	Source Lines	Category	Source Lines	Category	Source Lines
Small	1-2 K	Small	1-2 K	Small	1-2 K
Intermediate/ Medium	8-32 K	Intermediate/ Medium	5-50 K	Intermediate/ Medium	5-100 K
Large	32-128 K	Large	50-100 K	Large	100 K - 1 M
Very Large	512 K	Very Large	1 M	Very Large	1 - 10 M
		Extremely Large	1 - 10 M	Extremely Large	10 - 25 M
				Ambitious	25 - 100 M
				Probably won't work today	100 M -?

(a)

(b)

Table 1 - 3 **Size categories for Software Products**

software may have an ADP flavor. MCCR software includes that found in communication systems, intelligence systems, combat systems, etc.

REQUIREMENTS. MCCR software is the dominant type in DoD, and its requirements are not unlike those used by many commercial systems, such as power or process control plants, or that by the Department of Energy or NASA. The requirements for MCCR software fall into three broad categories. First, it must execute in real-time. It does one very little good to detect an incoming missile two minutes after it has impacted due to slow computer processing of reflected radar signals. Response times for a typical system may be in the microsecond range.

MCCR software is also subject to extreme support requirements. The software must be able to be, and usually is, supported in operational locations far from where they are developed and tested. It is not uncommon in the Navy to send maintenance personnel by helicopter to a ship on patrol to fix a computer bug. Moreover, it is not unusual that the system is supported by an entirely different organization than the one that originally created it.

The final requirement for MCCR software is its stringent maintenance needs. It is usual to find many military platforms having the same computer system but not having identical software. One squadron of F-14s may have one version of software for its computer-based avionics suite, while another squadron on the same base may have a slightly different version. Tight configuration management in such an atmosphere is a must.

CHARACTERISTICS. MCCR software can be characterized as massive in size, requiring frequent modifications, and having long life spans. Sizes for MCCR software can vary greatly, but a system aboard a submarine or surface ship may be as large as 750,000 lines of real-time application code, with many such systems executing and communicating simultaneously. The total WIS system, for example, may exceed 25 million lines of code initially.

The extremely long lifetimes of MCCR systems is also typical. A system may have 15 to 20 years from inception to deployment, and then twenty years of service after that. The Navy, which was the first service to go digital in a big way, still has in operation computer systems that were deployed in 1956. Unlike old soldiers, military software systems neither die nor fade away, they just keep computing.

MCCR software also undergoes frequent modifications and enhancements. The constantly changing nature of defense requires a rapid response to a new threat. One Navy system the author is familiar with started as a 100,000 line program running on uniprocessor and has grown through over a half-dozen modifications to a million line program running on a multiprocessor in less than ten years, with plans to make it a 4 million line program executing on a distributed system in another five. Needless to say, keeping everything working is a non-trivial matter.

CONSTRAINTS. Developing MCCR software is constrained, not only by the sometimes extreme technical difficulties involved, but also contractually. The government tries to stringently control and constrain the development process. Regulations and policy guidelines describe how the software is to be developed and what is to be delivered. These guidelines can be contractually imposed on both in-house government developers and outside contractors. Deviations from the standard usually must be obtained through an official waiver process. The reasons for imposing these guidelines are to allow the

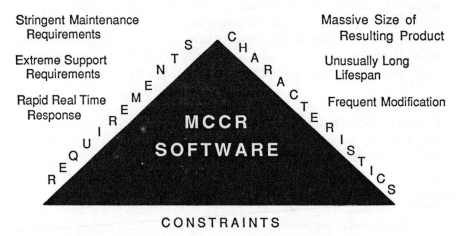

Stringent Maintenance Requirements

Extreme Support Requirements

Rapid Real Time Response

Massive Size of Resulting Product

Unusually Long Lifespan

Frequent Modification

MCCR SOFTWARE

CONSTRAINTS

Stringently Controlled and Constrained Development Process

Failures Impact a Large Population

Catastrophic Cost of Failure

Figure 1 - 4   **Typical MCCR Software Requirements, Characteristics, and Constraints**

government to have some insight into progress of the system development, as well as to ensure that the delivered product possesses a desired level of quality. After all, if these software systems don't work well, peoples' lives are at stake, not to mention the country's security. If a "glitch" in say the launch-control program for a nuclear-tipped missile causes it to launch accidentally, the results are rather nasty to contemplate.[6] The net total effect of all these constraints, no matter how noble the reason, is an increased contribution to the software cost.

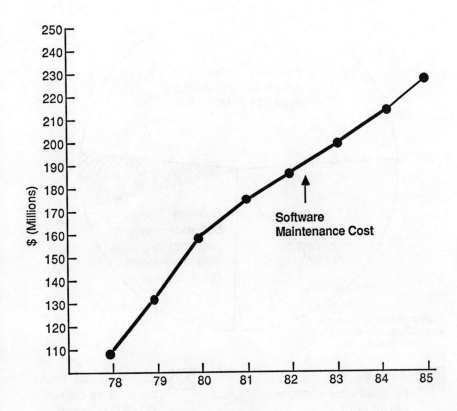

Figure 1 - 5   **Growth in Cost of Ownership**

END RESULTS. Figure 1-4 summarizes the requirements, characteristics, and development constraints of MCCR software. It is easy to see how each of these elements helps contribute to increasing a software system's cost. For example, real-time programming is probably the most difficult to perform, so one needs the best (and highest paid) programmers available. The long life spans and frequent modifications of the systems mean that continual increases in funding are required for maintenance as more and more systems join, and few leave, the inventory. This drives up the cost of ownership. Figure 1-5 illustrates the rising cost of maintaining DoD systems. What holds true for

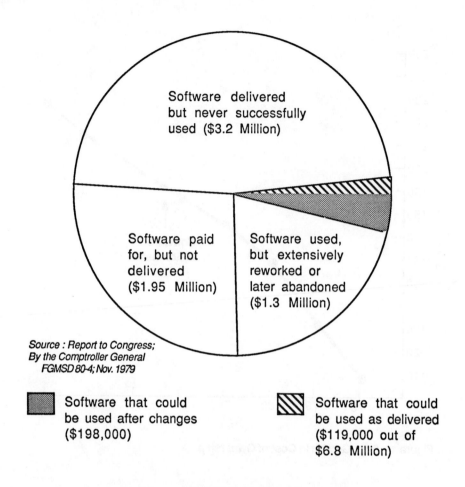

Figure 1 - 6   **Nine Software Development Contracts totaling $6.8 Million: Where the Money Went**

military systems also tends to hold true for commercial systems, although probably not to the same degree.

One last reason why software costs so much lies in the fact that much of what is built doesn't work, regardless of size or complexity. A particularly gruesome tale is told in a Report to Congress by the Comptroller General [COMP79]. Reviewing an admittedly small number of government projects, some of which were examined precisely because they were in trouble, the

Comptroller General found that only about two percent of the software contracted for could work on delivery, three percent more could work after some reworking, over 45 percent was delivered but never successfully used, 20 percent was used but either extensively reworked or abandoned, and 30 percent was paid for, but not delivered[7] as shown in figure 1-6. No general conclusions can be inferred from this one report, but we are sure that everyone has their own favorite horror story about money spent for software that never was used. Most of the time and money spent on maintenance is there for a good reason.

Why don't software systems work? That brings us to the next problem: the variation in software practice.

1.4 The Variation in Practice

As was discussed earlier, most of the money being spent on software is not on the initial creation process, but on the enhancement or maintenance of it. And as the Comptroller General report illustrated, there seem to be good reasons why this is true. However, one does suspect that if a system could be built right the first time, the overall costs might start to drop. A good question to ask is, where do we spend our time and money right now when we build systems, and is there a better way of making use of it?

Figure 1-7 is a composite of a number of studies [PRESSMAN82, BOEHM84a, FAIRLEY84] that have been conducted on this issue, and demonstrates the typical distribution of time spent on the initial creation of a software system. As one can see, most of the time is spent on the actual implementation of the system. In contrast, other studies [BOEHM75, YEH84] have shown that requirements, specification, and design errors are the most numerous in a system, averaging 64 percent compared to 36 percent for coding errors as illustrated in figure 1-8. Moreover, most of the errors are found not by the developers, but by the testers and users of the system. The resulting cost to fix these errors grows with the time lag in finding them. In other words, a requirements error found at requirements time costs only about one-fifth of what it would if found in acceptance testing, and one-fifteenth of what it would if it is found after the system is in use [BOEHM81]. The direction to take seems pretty clear.

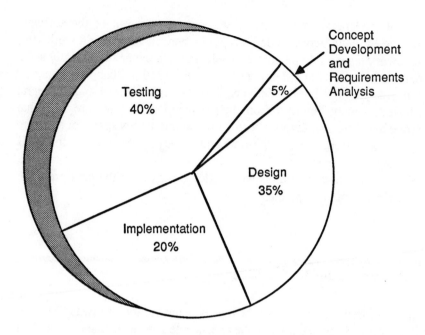

Figure 1 - 7 **Distribution of Effort for Product.   Initial Development**

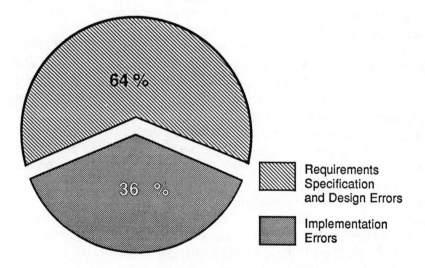

Figure 1 - 8   **Typical Errors in a Product**

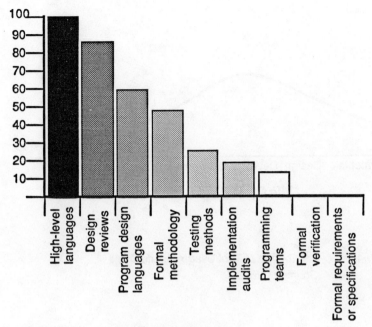

Figure 1 - 9   **Practices Currently Used**
Source : [ZELKOWITZ85]

APPROACHES. Has software engineering failed to provide the support necessary to attack these problems? Hardly. What has not been in short supply are the "solutions" to the software problem. Literally hundreds, if not thousands, of techniques, some automated, some not, exist to help the software manager, developer, or maintainer do his/her job better and save money. One can obtain catalogs with descriptions of various techniques that may be of use [REIFFER80, HOUGHTON80]. In fact, at first glance, one might be suspicious that with all these techniques around, the rising cost of software is really attributable to all the efforts going into the creation of them. See for instance [SOFTTOOLS85].

A good first question to ask is whether any of these techniques work. The answer is an emphatic, if qualified, "Yes." Studies [HECHT82, YEH85, PARNAS85a] have shown reductions in software cost and more reliable systems by the application of some of these techniques. However, the problem is that few organizations bother to use them. It is rather startling to find how little software engineering technology really is used. Zelkowitz [ZELKOWITZ85] has conducted a number of studies that show that most

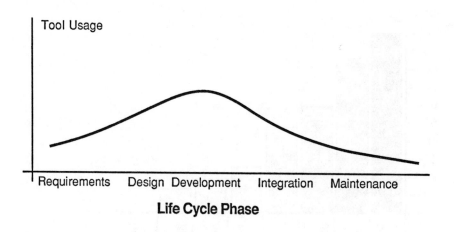

Figure 1 - 10   **Distribution of Tool Usage vs. Life Cycle**
Source : [YEH85]

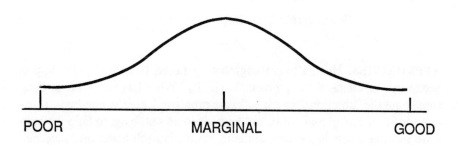

Figure 1 - 11 **Software Engineering Practices of U.S. Companies**
Source : [ZELKOWITZ85]

organizations use some type of software techniques internally, but they don't apply very many of them. Figures 1-9, 1-10, and 1-11 illustrate the breakdown of what techniques are used, the distribution over the software life cycle and the performance of companies in applying software engineering methods. Notice that most of the software efforts are concentrated on the implementation phase of the life cycle, even though the previous studies show the highest rate of return is to concentrate on the phases before that point.

WHAT'S THE PROBLEM? It would seem that either no one reads the studies or there isn't very much incentive to use the techniques where they can benefit most. We will examine the reasons why in detail in Chapters 11 and 12, but we will outline some of the issues here. First, not everyone believes that applying software engineering techniques, especially automated ones, does indeed save money. After all, software is expensive, automated tools are software, therefore tools are expensive [NASSI80]. And then there are the questions of all the training costs, automated support the techniques require (they need maintenance, too), etc., that make decision makers balk at using them.

Second, the efforts involved in the research, development, and application of the techniques are very fragmented. Yes, there are many techniques available, but each is usually unique, cannot be used in conjunction with any other technique, or is a "research technique;" i.e., it works well on toy programs but not on real problems.

Conrad [CONRAD82] has suggested the real problem is software tool pollution, and what is really needed is a good "software ecology movement." Be that as it may, for the most part, much of the technology developed in software engineering hasn't made the transition from the research community to the general practioner. The reasons are well discussed in [MYERS85, ROUSE85], with the main conclusion being that the research community has little incentive to make the transition with the technology. The result has been that the state of the practice follows the state of the art by as much as 15 years. While the practioner claims the researcher doesn't understand his problem, the researcher claims he has already solved it. What further aggravates the problem is that it takes typically 17 years (+/- 2) from concept inception to commercialization for an automated software technique [RIDDLE84]. It is small wonder why industry hasn't kept up.

The Department of Defense has taken action to try to correct this problem by the creation of The Software Engineering Institute (SEI) at Carnegie-Mellon University in Pittsburgh. There, the primary goal is to test out, evaluate, and transition much of what has been behind closed doors in the academic arena and make it available to industry for use on real projects. They will also undertake the effort to educate the practitioner on what is useful and what is not. With the mass of techniques available, no single individual can possibly learn more than a few, and so most unfortunately never even try. U.S. industry is also getting into the act, with a number of consortia being instituted, and European, Asian, and South American countries are also getting involved. Chapter Ten discusses these efforts in more depth.

LACK OF CONSISTENCY. Another problem is that software engineering does not possess a single, agreed upon vocabulary to discuss the problems confronting the field. This is good in that it shows the field is still maturing, but it also gets in the way. For example, there is no common software development model or process that everyone (or anyone) agrees upon. Some believe in the "Waterfall" model, some in the "Rapid-Prototype," and some in the "Operational." We will discuss some of these in the next chapter, but the problem is at the heart of software development. For instance, recently the Department of Defense spent six years developing DoD STD 2167, "Defense System Software Development," as a standard model of its development process. Less than a year after it was released, and after the defense industry commented on the previous draft versions at numerous reviews and conferences, a new version called DoD STD 2167A is being worked on because the first was still found wanting in a number of areas.

Every organization has developed its own unique way of producing software, and although if one were to examine descriptions of each, the upper levels might all appear the same. However, the details and emphasis would differ greatly. These details change with and after each system development as more experience is gained, as it should be. But it does make it difficult to communicate between organizations, or even within organizations. Everyone has a different opinion on how to improve the process, and it is colored by where one sits in the company hierarchy [FAIRLEY84, BOEHM84b].

Finally, building software products is not particularly easy. Or maybe it should be rephrased as: Building quality software products isn't particularly easy. Producing software is very easy. In fact this is probably the second biggest bane of the whole computer industry, next to the fact that we as a nation can afford not to be efficient in software development, even though we know how to be. Two facts stand out. First, high-level languages allow almost anyone to program, whether they have had any formal training or not. The demand for programmers, and the high pay, have attracted many into the computer field from non-technical areas whose skills are not as refined as they would be with more formalized training. Some are good, many are not. Second, programmers like to code, coding shows one is busy and making progress, and managers like progress. Combine the two elements

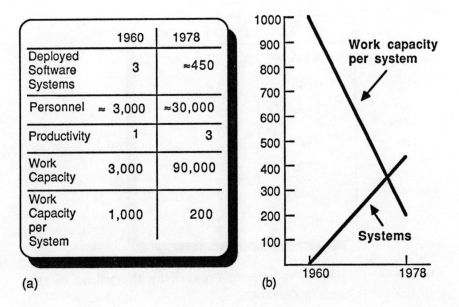

	1960	1978
Deployed Software Systems	3	≈450
Personnel	≈ 3,000	≈30,000
Productivity	1	3
Work Capacity	3,000	90,000
Work Capacity per System	1,000	200

(a)   (b)

Figure 1 - 12   **Trends in Resources Applicable to
                      Deployed Software Systems**

and one has the makings of a problem. As Brooks noted, programmers will deliver programs as complex as one wants, they just won't guarantee they will work as advertised [BROOKS75].

With these thoughts in mind, let's turn our attention to the third problem: the lack of productivity.

1.5 The Lack of Productivity

Productivity, at least in the software industry, is a rather nebulous term. Typical definitions state that productivity is: "abundance or richness in output" or "the effectiveness in utilizing labor and equipment." Depending on whether one is in management, or a programmer, or somewhere in between, this could mean: increase the amount of code produced per person; lower the

YEAR	PRODUCTIVITY
1955	1.0
1960	1.6
1965	2.0
1970	2.3
1975	2.7
1980	3.1
1985	3.6

Table 1 - 4   **Relative Programmer Productivity Normalized to 1955**
Source : [DOLOTTA76]

cost of the software product; increase the "quality" of the product; make the scheduled milestones; etc. None of these are particularly satisfying in themselves, and productivity should probably be viewed as the sum quantity of measures of each one of these. Studies to measure and quantify productivity have been carried out by numerous groups and one, IBM [WATSON77], has a method that takes into account over 30 variables.

A number of examples, however, can serve to illustrate the point indirectly. Figure 1-12a shows the number of deployed systems (not individual units) using computers in DoD in 1960 and in 1978, and the number of personnel being used to program them. If we say that the 3000 personnel in 1960 had a productivity factor of one, then their capacity to do work ("work capacity") on those three systems was 3,000, or 1,000 per system. In 1978, the work force available was increased by a factor of ten, as was their productivity by a factor of three (i.e., their ability to produce code), but the number of systems also increased by a factor of 150. The work capacity per system, or resources that could be used on developing a system in 1978, was only equivalent to 20 percent of what was available in 1960, as shown in figure 12-b.

The trend above has continued over the last six years and will continue. Table1-4 shows the relative programmer productivity compared to total

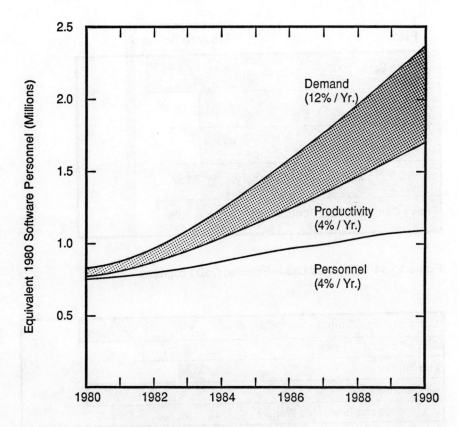

Figure 1 - 13   **Trends in Software Supply and Demand**

yearly code production normalized to 1955 while figure 1-13 shows the demand for software compared to the number of available programmers. Most researchers [DOLOTTA76, MUSA85] point to about a 4 percent average increase in programmers per year, with somewhere around 12 percent required to stay even. It is not uncommon in the computer industry to have projects delayed or abandoned because the personnel were not available to perform the job. This backlog of software projects is uncounted, but probably very costly to the economy.

THE NEED FOR SOFTWARE. The problem is not easy to solve. One reason is that many systems don't exist without a computer system being involved. A

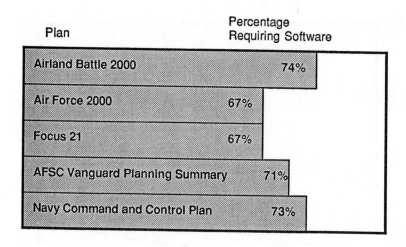

Figure 1 - 14   **Projected Use in Selected DoD Programs**

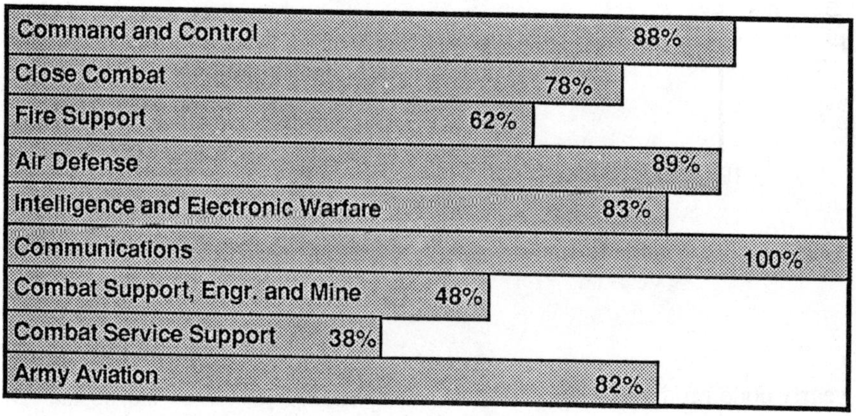

Figure 1 - 15   **Airland Battle 2000 : Summary of Military Mission Areas Requiring Software**   *Source : [REDWINE84]*

prime example is the X-29 Forward Swept Aircraft. The aircraft promises to bring a revolution to aviation as its lower drag, higher lift, and better maneuverability makes it well suited to numerous DoD and commercial roles. There are two slight problems, however. It is structurally unstable (at high speed, the wings have a tendency to fall off), and aerodynamically unstable (in pitch at subsonic speeds). New composite materials have solved the structural problem, and a computer system has solved the aerodynamic problem.

The reason a computer system is needed is that unlike previous aircraft in which the pilot could compensate for pitch problems, the pilot can't compensate rapidly enough in the X-29. The compensations needed are so fine and required so quickly (in tenths of a second) that it is literally impossible for a human to fly the aircraft — well, at least for more than half a second before needing to bail out if the computer fails.

More systems then ever are requiring this type of computer dependence. A recent study [REDWINE84] investigated some major projected DoD programs and found that 70 percent of the technologies, functions, systems and actions required software. Figure 1-14 depicts the percentage of software required in a number of DoD programs, with figure 1-15 illustrating one of the program software requirements in detail.

TRADEOFFS. Another reason the problem of increasing productivity is not easy to solve is because of what is termed the "plurality of goals" [BOEHM81]. Little benefit is derived if the software project personnel are productive enough to meet the scheduled delivery date, but the reliability of product is so poor that it is useless, or will require tremendous amounts of money in maintenance fees to fix it [FLECKSTEIN83]. A software project has many, often contradictory, goals, which pushes and pulls at the software development, as shown in table 1-5. It is difficult to make a product reliable, affordable, efficient, usable, maintainable, etc., simultaneously. In one system, increasing reliability may mean adding in redundancy checks which adds execution overhead, and also requires a more flexible software design. These may add to the cost, and schedule, and make the system a little harder to maintain. Not always, but enough times that a designer, user, or buyer will think twice about adding it in as requirement to the system. To paraphrase Boehm, the most important software engineering skills that must be learned are the tradeoffs required by the plurality of goals, and their coordination with the plurality of the means available to carry them out. Each provides a degree of help or hindrance in achieving a given goal in a given situation.

Boehm's ideas are important because certain techniques do help build better software products and increase the productivity of software developers. High-level languages and development environments seem to improve productivity [BOEHM81, ALBRECHT83, BEHRENS83]. Smaller

Correctness	Usability	Flexibilty	Interoperability
Acceptability	Operability	Adaptablity	Complexity
Completeness	Human Factors	Extensibility	Modularity
Consistency	Communicativeness	Accessibility	Structuredness
Expression	Convertability	Expandability	Uniformity
Validity	Documentation	Augmentability	Time
Performance	Understandability	Modifiability	
Reliability	Clarity	Testability	
Availability	Legibility	Accountability	
Accuracy	Self-descriptiveness	Cost	
Robustness	Maintainability	Portability	
Precision	Stability	Transferability	
Tolerance	Manageability	Compatibility	
Efficiency	Conciseness	Reusability	
Integrity	Repairability	Generality	
Security	Serviceability	Utility	
Privacy		Self-Containedness	

Table 1 - 5   **Goals of Software Development**

projects also seem more productive than larger ones [BOEHM84], thus pointing a way to possibly structure large projects. Reusing existing code has been estimated to save up to 80 percent of the effort required to develop new code [ZELKOWITZ83] (more about software reuse is discussed in Chapter Seven).

Boehm has also investigated 63 software projects for different factors affecting productivity and cost [BOEHM81]. Although too extensive to discuss in depth here, figure 1-16 does list some of the results and their relative importance to increasing productivity. Notice that good personnel can positively affect productivity and decrease software cost the most. Boehm notes that poor management can also reverse any gains the quickest. This leads one to believe using common sense is still the best way to increase productivity.

One final note. An interesting study by Bell Laboratories [FAIRLEY84] showed that only about 13 percent of a programmer's time actually is spent on

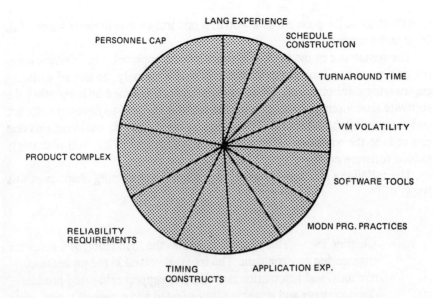

Figure 1 - 16   **Relative Product Multiplicative Factors**

"programming." Where is the other time spent? Boehm has estimated that 33 percent of a programmer's time is spent on documentation. If one wanted to increase productivity rapidly, this is a very ripe area to explore [BOEHM 81].

1.6 What to Do Next?

So far, we have quickly examined some of the problems confronting the practice of software engineering today. We have seen there is a wide variation in practice, with most practioners using only a small portion of the available technology. Research efforts appear fragmented and aren't effectively reaching the practicing community. We've seen that there is low productivity in producing software caused by a lack of trained personnel and an ever increasing demand for more software. Each element contributes to the rise in software costs.

Solving or controlling any one of the three problems will help tremendously, but it will not be enough to solve the software problem as a whole.

One must solve the problem as a whole, if one truly wants to build successful, large software products.

The remainder of the book will examine one approach that is now evolving as a means to control the software problem, namely the use of software engineering environments. These environments are aimed at integrating the software development process with the techniques used to develop software and automating the result. It is hoped that by creating these environments one can reduce the variation in practice, increase productivity, and ultimately reduce software costs.

The following is a brief description of each the remaining chapters of this book:

- Chapter Two – This chapter examines the foundation of a software engineering environment. The issues involved in the processes, methods, and automation necessary to support mid-sized product developments and larger are investigated and a general model of an environment developed.

- Chapter Three – This chapter investigates the Requirements Analysis Phase of a product development. The generic processes, methods, and automation used in the phase are examined, and the activities that can be supported by a software engineering environment listed.

- Chapter Four – This chapter investigates the Specification Phase of a product development. The generic processes, methods, and automation used in the phase are also examined, and the activities that can be supported by a software engineering environment listed.

- Chapter Five – This chapter investigates the Design Phase of a product development. The generic processes, methods, and automation used in the phase are examined, and the activities that can be supported by a software engineering environment listed.

- Chapter Six – This chapter investigates the Implementation, Testing, and Evolution Phases of a product development. The generic processes, methods, and automation used in each phase are examined, and the activities that can be supported by a software engineering environment listed.

- Chapter Seven – This chapter investigates the Management Activities that span the life-cycle of the product development. Aspects of management including resource management, product assurance, and reusability are investigated, and the activities that can be supported by a software engineering environment listed.

- Chapter Eight – This chapter investigates the linkages necessary to tie together the various activities identified during each lifecycle phase into a software engineering environment. The issues of the database, support functions, and physical architectures are examined.

- Chapter Nine – This chapter brings together all the previous chapters and describes an "ideal" software engineering environment which can be used to support mid-sized and larger product developments.

- Chapter Ten – This chapter reviews some of the software engineering environment efforts that are taking place in the U.S., Asia, Europe, and South America.

- Chapter Eleven – This chapter examines some of the technical issues confronting the construction of software engineering environments such as that described in Chapter Nine.

- Chapter Twelve – This chapter examines some of the issues confronting the introduction of a software engineering environment into an organization, and some of the possible impacts it will have on the organization.

FOOTNOTES:

1. Augustine's Laws, Norman R. Augustine, American Institute of Aeronautics and Astronautics, New York, New York, 1983
2. WIS is a prime example of government double-level acronyms- World Wide Military Command and Control System (WWMCCS - i.e., the 'W') Information System.

3. Unfortunately, this "Lone Ranger" trait is still admired today [ENOS81].

4. Note, many software engineers and scientists would disagree vehemently with the latitude implied by the word "possibly" in the above definition.

5. Adding these three words to the definition defines the true meaning of software engineering. Software engineering practice is to apply the methodologies, create the documents, and define the milestones.

6. The first ICBMs, which were not particularly reliable, had the nickname Into Cuba By Mistake [AUGUSTINE83].

7. Another study showed that 75% of computer projects started were never used or completed   [BLUM85].

2. SOFTWARE ENGINEERING ENVIRONMENTS BASIC REQUIREMENTS

When One Automates a Mess, One Gets an Automated Mess
— Various

2.0 Introduction

In Chapter One, we examined in detail the three major problems plaguing current software development: the high cost of software, the variation in practice and the lack of productivity of the developers. Solving any one of these problems is highly dependent on concurrently solving the other two, thus making it necessary to attack the process of developing software as a whole, rather than in a piecemeal fashion.

Almost since software was first developed, efforts have concentrated on improving the tasks surrounding coding. The state of the practice is now expanding past this narrow view of software development to encompass the totality of effort involved. It is realized that the processes involved in software creation include much more than producing the code itself, but also includes items such as documenting and managing the effort as well. As has been shown, over one-third of a development effort is devoted to the documentation effort. Although documentation has little to do with the actual production of code,[1] if it isn't done correctly or is incomplete it will eventually severely impact code reliability, maintainability, and cost. Management, on the other hand, requires visibility into and control of the development process itself. A software project gets behind one day at a time, and management needs to realize when and why it is happening [BROOKS75].

The solution is more than just better documentation and management, however. It has been demonstrated that increasing the efforts in the front end of the development process, where the descriptions of the requirements and specifications of the software are made, will eventually decrease the cost of the software by reducing the cost of errors. Moreover, integrating the efforts to attack issues such as those identified as software cost drivers shown in figure 1-15 can increase developers' productivity by factors of two in five years, and four in ten [BOEHM84a]. The question is how all these diverse solutions to the software problem can be brought together simultaneously?

The general agreement is that the solution to the problems of software development lie in the direction of software engineering environments [MYERS78, WASSERMAN81, SEEWG82, BOEHM83a, DEMILLO84, MCKAY86] . Most researchers and experienced practioners believe that by using environments the quality of software will increase, productivity will be enhanced and the cost of software will decrease. There is less agreement, as we shall see, about the specific ways in which these goals can be accomplished.

2.1 Software Engineering Environments – A Definition

The term "environment," when used in conjunction with software engineering is, needless to say, not very well defined. Just as in the case of the term "software engineering," there is no generally agreed upon definition. Some argue that a software engineering environment is any set of techniques, automated or not, which helps with the production of software. Others argue that it is the complete, formal, rigorous and robust set of methods and their complete automation that forms an environment. Still others argue it is somewhere in between. Dictionaries don't clarify matters much either. The verb "environ" is typically defined as "to surround or enfold with a condition, atmosphere, or other intangible thing : surround permeatingly." The term "environment" is then defined as "something that environs" or "the surrounding conditions, influences or forces that influence or modify." Terms like "intangible things" or "influences" are not helpful in the pursuit of being precise.

SOME SHORTCOMINGS OF CURRENT SOFTWARE DEVELOPMENT PRACTICES

- Inconsistent, incoherent, incomplete specifications and designs
- Designs fail to provide for change
- Unreusable software and software designs
- Responsibilities, duties and accountability are poorly defined and controlled
- Developed product hard to operate
- Poor performance of resulting product
- No provision to perform impact analysis in relation to specific parameters
- Completion criteria are poorly defined
- Histories are unavailable
- No metrics are available to test overall system quality
- No effective means to manage complexity
- Ineffective communication/feedback between development and personnel
- "Team" efforts are not coordinated
- Performance assessment done after the fact
- No effective documentation aids
- No assistance available for the resolution of conflicts or issues
- Excessive development costs and schedule
- Unreliable and unmaintainable products
- Low effect of resources

Table 2 - 1 **Shortcomings of Current Software .   Development Practices**

However, the above definition does point out the basic difficulty one has in arguing over what constitutes a desirable software engineering environment. The fact is, everybody's view is correct. We can illustrate what we mean by this with an example.

Soon after writing his or her first program, a person quickly forms an opinion of how software can be developed better. As the individual gains more experience, this opinion becomes (hopefully) more refined and tempered, the thoughts about burning down the computing center having all but disappeared by then. Regardless of the specific software project worked on, this person will encounter one or more of the common problems listed in table 2-1. Thus, when he or she says an appropriate environment is one which must support, say, better automated design (because the project currently being worked is always having design problems), this individual is correct. An environment is one that helps solve this particular problem. The same is true of another who argues for better automatic documentation aids. The perceived need as to what is required to correct the problem thus varies from one individual to another, and so does the environment required to solve it. Unfortunately what this also ends up meaning is that an environment, to satisfy everyone's needs, has to become all things to all people. This is not easy to accomplish.

Given this as a context, we choose then to simply define a Software Engineering Environment as being:

"The process, methods, and automation required to produce a software system."

ENVIRONMENT SCOPE. For this book, we will limit our scope and interest in software engineering environments to those which can be used in developing medium-sized and larger software systems (as defined in Chapter One). Thus the "influences," "intangible things," and problems encountered in producing these types of software systems will define our environment's range and domain. We are specifically interested in such projects because they represent the dominant trend in the software efforts currently taking place in the United States and elsewhere.2

The purpose of a software engineering environment is to provide the context for the rational, orderly, and manageable evolution of a software system in the face of all the influences and intangibles that can act upon it. These influences and intangibles can range from the people assigned the job to an organization's way of doing business to the tradition of the company. Additionally, this means that one is concerned not only with the development of the system (i.e., pre-delivery), but with its existence after it has been delivered, up until the time it has been retired. An environment is in some ways more important for the support of the post-delivery stage, which consumes 80 percent of a total system's cost and consists of 90 percent of its lifetime.

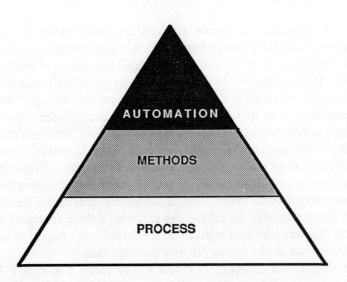

Figure 2 - 1 **Model of Software Engineering Environment**

2.2 A Software Engineering Environment Description

A software engineering environment can be depicted as consisting of three individual layers as illustrated in figure 2-1. At the bottom is the process of developing software, above which are software engineering methods, and finally above that, their automation. The **process** of developing a software system is the foundation of the environment. Its basic function is to describe the chain of events required to create a particular software product. Typically it is a sub-model of a much larger model that describes all the activities, such as hardware development, required to produce the total system. The **methods** in a software engineering environment include all those which are required to define, describe, abstract, modify, refine, and document the software product, and are defined by the development process below it in the illustration. The use of the computer to implement the methods necessary to develop the software product we term **automation**. A software engineering environment consists of each of these elements, and the degree to which each layer is integrated with the one above or below it will determine its class and type.

In most respects, a software engineering environment is directly analogous to a compiler (refer to figure 2-2). Roughly speaking, a compiler's job is the translation of one type of input (logical) into output of another type (physical). This translation is defined by a series of well-defined steps (lexical analysis, syntactic analysis, code generation, etc.) each performing a "sub-translation" with its own input and output descriptions. The output descriptions of one step are reused as inputs to the next. Certain methods are used to implement each of these steps, and each step is in turn fully automated. The specific steps and methods used are dependent on both the original input description (the language used) and ultimate output description (the target computer), as well as the "outside influences" that define the requirements on the execution of the output. For example, if there are tight memory constraints, the compiler may need an added optimization step in its translation process to reduce the quantity of output description.

If we started with the compiler model and extended it to include higher and higher levels of abstraction as input, we would be creating software engineering environments of varying capability in much the same way as what happened as more front end capabilities were added to the first assemblers to make them into compilers. An ideal software engineering environment is analogous to the compiler model where everything is automated except the initial input description.

To clarify these ideas, the following sections will examine each aspect of a software engineering environment in more detail.

2.2.1 The Software Engineering Environment Process

When we talk about a software development process, we are simply describing a model of what is expected to be occurring during the development of a software product. This model provides a certain view of the development process and the mechanisms that influence it. It also provides the common vocabulary by which all the participants involved can communicate.

The process model of software development describes what will be done, how it will be accomplished, when it will be finished, and who will use what to implement it. A poor model of the process can lead to confusion about the goals of the project as well as a misapplication of the resources to accomplish them. Unfortunately, our confidence in today's process models is no better than our confidence in New England weather predictions. Formulating a

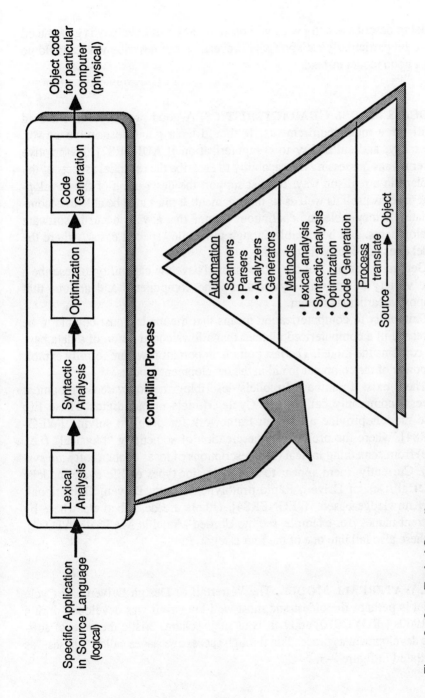

Figure 2 - 2   Typical Compiler

model to describe exactly what will occur on any particular day is guaranteed not to be particularly satisfying. However, we can describe what should go into a good model instead.

PROCESS MODEL CHARACTERISTICS. A good process model should fulfill three main requirements. It should have good descriptive power, generality, and suitability to computerization [LAUBER82]. Descriptive power means possessing the capability to describe the essential aspects of the problem in a realistic way. It must support the description of the development process itself as well as its management. It must also be able to accommodate the inevitable and continuous change that always occur in software developments, and be flexible enough to handle "special cases" where the model does not fit especially well.

Generality means that the model should have the capability to describe a wide variety of software systems and the components and actions that compose a particular system.

Suitability to computerization means that the model must be able to be expressed in a computerized manner that allows construction of a data base that contains the model. The last point is important if we are to fully exploit the power of the computer to aid in the development process.

There exist a number of models describing the software development process, commonly called **Life Cycle Models** or paradigms. These life cycle models provide a uniform framework for problem solving [WEGNER84], where the problem is the creation of something "physical" (i.e., code) from something logical (i.e., descriptions of ideas about a software system). Currently, there appear to be four major types of life cycle models: Waterfall/Design Driven, Rapid-prototype/Strategy Driven, Operational, and Knowledge-based [WEGNER84]. Others are described elsewhere by different names [for example, see the Unified Model in MATSUMATO84], but these also fall into one of the four categories.

THE WATERFALL MODEL. The Waterfall or Design Driven Life Cycle model is perhaps the oldest and most well-known. It was developed during the 1960s [ROYCE70] and has as its major characteristic the view of software development as proceeding through successive stages called "phases, "as illustrated in figure 2-3.

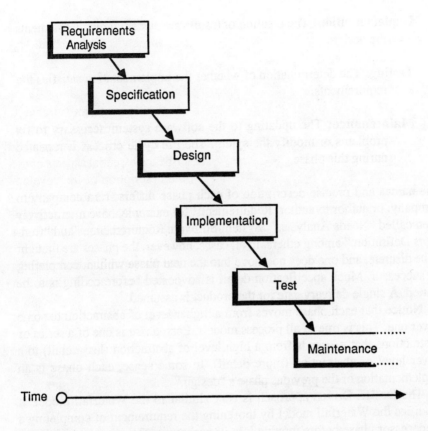

Figure 2 - 3   **Waterfall Model**

The phases generally are categorized in the following fashion [SEEWG82]

Requirements Analysis: The definition and analysis of the users' needs.

Specification: The translation of requirements into a precise description of the externals of the software system.

Design: The creation of an abstraction of a software system that is consistent with the specification and provides a reasonable decription for implementation.

Implementation: The creation of a software system which implements the design.

Testing: The determination of whether the implementation satisfies the requirements.

Maintenance: The updating to the software system necessary to fix problems or modify the sytem. The life cycle process is repeated during this phase.

The names and precise description of each phase differs from company to company, or author to author. Requirements, for example, have alternatively been called "Needs Analysis," "System/Software Requirements," and "Concepts Definition," among others. In all cases, however, the phases are thought to be discrete, and one does not move into the next phase without completing its successor. Much specification detail is advocated before coding is to be started. A single delivery date for the product is assumed.

Notice that each phase moves from a higher level of abstraction to some lower one. This is true of all process models. Each phase is one of a series of abstractions that proceeds from a high level of abstraction (less detail) to a lower level of abstraction (more detail). In some sense, each phase is an implementation of the previous phase's "design."

The Design Driven approach is very similar to the Waterfall model. It modifies the Waterfall model by loosening the requirement of completing a predecessor phase before moving into its successor. The change was needed because it was quickly realized that trying to define everything before moving on to the next step was unreasonable in practice where not everything is known or described or can change. This modification allows a project to be in two or more phases simultaneously. Note, however, that this does not mean any steps can be skipped.

ADVANTAGES AND DISADVANTAGES. There are a number of advantages to the Waterfall/Design Driven model. Conceptually, it describes intuitively how most feel software development should take place. One should define everything before moving on to the next step to make sure nothing is lost or forgotten. Boehm has shown [BOEHM81] that overall, the model does match fairly well to how software is actually developed in practice. Reordering of the steps also proves to be sub-optimal. Moreover, one always knows what one is producing at any particular time, and where one is in the development process. Finally, there exists a large body of experience, tradition, and success in applying the model, which makes it very attractive to use.

However, there are a number of problems with the Waterfall/Design Driven model as well. First, it doesn't possess enough descriptive power. It fails to realistically integrate "activities" that span life cycle phases, such as resource management, quality assurance, configuration management, or verification and validation. These activities sit "outside" this model and are not integrated into it. This makes the management of the development difficult.

The model also lacks generality in two areas. First, the model assumes a near-perfect process will take place, and when problems occur, the model has a hard time accounting for them. For instance, it is the nature of the software business is to change requirements during development, based on schedule, cost, or some other influence. Since making an error in a requirement or specification may not be found until design time or later, iterating back to the requirement phase is necessary to correct the problem, as well as fixing anything that followed in subsequent phases that depended on that requirement. Because this is not easy to do, great pressure is placed on defining the requirements only once, which then often leads to poorly defined requirements, and poorly implemented systems. It also leads to poorly documented software because new changes are not rippled back in at all the appropriate places. "Fix it in maintenance" is the oft heard cry when using this process model. Second, the model was developed when the problem of small systems with a monolithic nature was the dominating influence. The model does not scale up very well to large system developments where the unknowns in the front end of the development cycle are much greater than in small systems.

Finally, the model lacks suitability to computerization. It was developed during the period of time when computer-aided engineering was not well understood. Thus, the model is geared toward and is usable primarily by humans, not computers.

Overall, the Waterfall/Design Driven model works well on small software development projects. However, when scaling up to larger projects, the creation of a monolithic system becomes inappropriate, with the disadvantages of using the model outweighing the advantages.

RAPID-PROTOTYPING MODEL. The Rapid-prototype model [SEEWG82, GARMAND85] was created to overcome the perceived deficiencies of the Waterfall/Design Driven model. These deficiencies had been noted for some

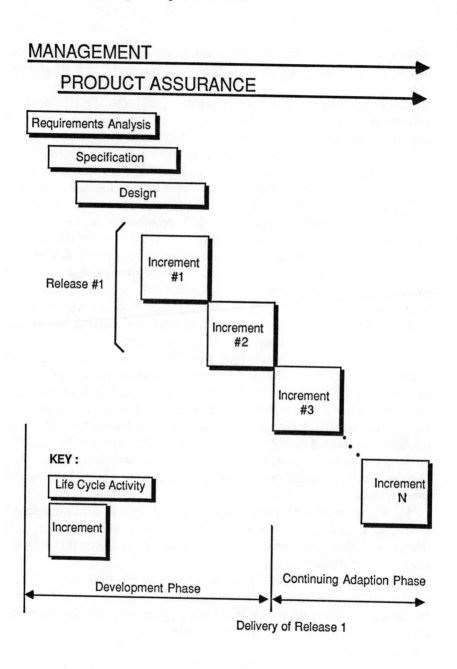

Figure 2 - 4   **Incremental Development Model**

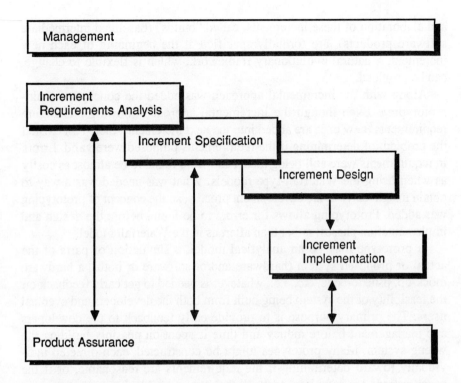

Figure 2-5   **An Incremental Sub-Model**

time [BASILLI75, PARNAS76, MILLS76, BOEHM81]. It closely resembles the Waterfall model in appearance, but possesses significant differences. The first of these is that it supports the concept of incremental development.

Incremental development is the creation of a software system in small, manageable increments, where each new increment is the old "system" with additional functionality as illustrated in figures 2-4 and 2-5. The software product is not viewed as a monolithic entity with a single delivery date, but as an integration of the outputs of successive steps of each iteration. Only at the end is the "complete system" available, although each increment is a working system in and of itself.

The incremental development approach is meant to eliminate the necessity to possess a set of requirements, specifications and designs for the system before the start of the software product implementation. Because refinement and elaboration of these increments, called "builds" (baselined intermediate software products), are formally specified at the beginning of each new increment, a natural evolutionary framework, which is flexible to change, can be provided.

Along with the incremental approach was added the concept of rapid-prototyping. Even though the incremental approach allows for changing requirements (new ones are added into the next increment), there still existed the problem of determining if the requirements proposed were valid. Errors in requirements were still being made, and were found to be almost as costly as when using the Waterfall-type models. What was needed was a way to obtain insight early in the development process, so the concept of prototyping was added. Prototyping allows for errors to be found before the design and implementation phases, rather than after, as in the Waterfall model.

A prototype may be an analytical model, a simulation of parts of the actual or proposed system (hardware and/or software or both), a hardware mock-up, psuedo-code, etc., i.e., whatever is needed to get early feedback on the feasibility of the system being built from both the developers and eventual users. The primary purpose is to provide early feedback to the developers and management before money and time is spent on possibly building the wrong system. Many prototypes might be constructed, each directed individually toward determining if the requirements are reasonable, or if the specifications are complete, or the design even possible. The prototype may or not form the basis of the final system, although the general rule is to plan to throw it away [BROOKS75].[3]

Another aspect of the Rapid-prototyping model is the integration of the resource management, configuration management, verification, and validation activities into the model. As previously noted, these activities span all the life cycle phases. Resource management is concerned with making decisions about the project from both a day to day viewpoint (i.e., have we met this week's milestones, is everybody available for a meeting, etc.), and from a more global perspective as well (i.e., will the project be on time, within budget, etc.).

Configuration management is the ability to provide a controlled and baselined version of the software system currently being built. This is necessary to insure that the following incremental version is built as a successor to the current version and not an "unauthorized," and therefore suspect, modified version. Only those changes which do not detrimentally affect the development of a current or future product are approved.

Verification is the establishment of the correspondence between what is being built and what was specificied. Validation is the establishment of whether the system built meets the operational goals. Each of these will be discussed in detail in Chapter Seven.

ADVANTAGES AND DISADVANTAGES. The major advantages of the Rapid-Prototyping model are that it enhances the descriptive power of the process model. It more closely resembles the reality of the development process, and allows for the usual iteration of a system to take place more naturally than in the Waterfall model. Combining the elements of incremental development with rapid prototyping also provides the capability to implement the concept of "Build a little, test a little," which is necessary to build large systems successfully.

Additionally, the Rapid-Prototyping model allows for better control of the process by incorporating the aspects of resource management, configuration management, verification and validation. The control is accentuated by being able to build larger systems with smaller development teams, thus increasing overall developer communications and productivity [BOEHM84]. The model also promotes getting the user inputs early in the system development process.

There are some disadvantages to using the Rapid-Prototyping model as well. First, the coupling between the management aspects and the development aspects of the life cycle process is not clear. This coupling is usually made through the configuration management activity [BOEHM81], which intermixes the two. The management and development aspects are distinct (but related) processes, as will be shown later in this chapter, and require separate treatment.

Incremental development also acts as a double-edged sword. While allowing for smaller parts of the total system to be created, if a problem is encountered in one construction, everything later must wait for its resolution. The problem is the same as that found on a car assembly line if the winch to hold transmissions were to break. Everything from that step on would be delayed. Practically speaking, if an error goes undiscovered in one of the first increments to be delivered, then that error is in the system "forever." The cost to change it is extremely high as every increment with the error either has to be fixed, or resolved in the next increment to be started, or the error lived with. Either way, the baseline is destroyed and at least one incremental build must be changed.

Also, allowing many "systems" to be built simultaneously, each in different stages of the life cycle, significantly increases the management overhead. It becomes hard for management to estimate the resources needed to perform the development at any particular moment since many systems are in a partially completed state. Resource juggling taxes management's abilities and becomes an unwanted added "influence" on the development. Finally, the model is not very suitable for complete computerization.

OPERATIONAL MODEL. A somewhat different approach from that of the Rapid-prototype model suggested to alleviate the problems of the Waterfall/Design Driven model is the Operational model [ZAVE82]. This model varies from the previous ones by concentrating on operational rather than behavioral abstractions of the system being developed. The implementation mechanisms are not hidden, but are instead used as a basis to specify behavior. In other words, the Operational model creates executable specifications (called operational specifications) that are successively transformed into efficient implementations as depicted in figure 2-6. Thus, the external behavior of the system is implicit in the specification, while the internal structure is not.

Paraphrasing [ZAVE84], the Operational model description of a system makes the operational specification appear to be very close to a design in previous models. However, designs refer to specific runtime environments whereas the structures provided by the executable specification language are independent of resource allocation strategies or configurations. Moreover, unlike the previous models discussed which place great emphasis on separating requirements (i.e., their external behavior) from the internal structure of the system, the operational model interleaves the two. This interleaving is necessary to achieve an executable form, but also expresses inseparably what the system is doing from how it is to be accomplished. This makes the operational specification structure then, problem-oriented, rather than implementation-oriented.

ADVANTAGES AND DISADVANTAGES. There are a number of advantages to the Operational model. First, it has great descriptive power directed at solving a software system problem. The descriptions are formal, rigorous, and can be analyzed. The user and developer have an executable model (i.e., a rapid-prototype) from which to evaluate possible system solutions very early in the system development. These rapid-prototypes come for "free" upon specification definition. The greatest benefit is that the model is very suitable to computerization, and most research efforts in this area are aimed at automating the transformations of the operational specifications.

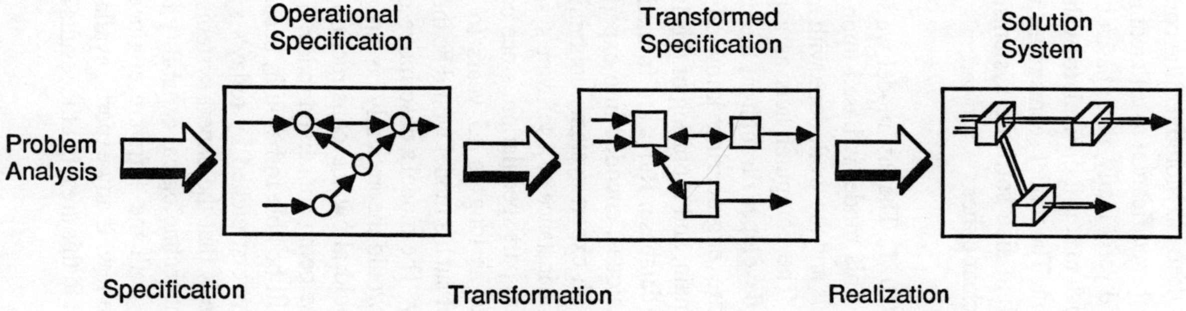

Problem
Analysis

Specification

Operational
Specification

Transformation

Transformed
Specification

Realization

Solution
System

* Based on [ZAVE84]

Figure 2 - 6   Operational Model

The disadvantages of the Operational model also lie in its powerful descriptive nature. Since one needs to transform the external behavior to internal structures before specifying them, the result may be overconstrained and prematurely produced designs. Moreover, the complete set of transformations from an operational specification to efficient implementations hasn't been completely determined yet. Finally, there hasn't been widespread use of the Operational model, which makes it difficult to evaluate, especially for use in large system development. The model seems more aimed at the process of developing small to medium size software systems. How it supports the management process isn't clear either.

KNOWLEDGE-BASED MODEL. The last model we wish to examine is the Knowledge-based model. This model is based upon a combination of the previously discussed models and the work done with artificial intelligence in the expert system realm. The computer acts as a partner in the system development, guiding the developer throughout the process. The key is the separation of the software engineering knowledge domain from the application knowledge domain, and capturing of this information along with the process paradigm in a database. Rules are formed based upon accepted software engineering techniques, encoded into expert systems, which then are used in conjunction with expert systems containing application knowledge rules to form a specific instance of a software system [FRENKEL85].

The above description is part speculation, since complete systems don't exist today, and may take as long as 15 years to create [BALZER83]. However, the advantages of such a model would be the tremendous potential for increasing productivity. The model's descriptive power, generality, and suitability for automation would theoretically be integrated into one, generating a capability that would allow the construction of systems orders of magnitude larger than those being conceived today. This model may be the only way these systems will be able to be built, because the complexity of today's models is being overstretched by today's systems' requirements. The potential disadvantage is that the expert systems needed to be created may be beyond our present technological capability to build them. Experts are still needed to create both the software engineering and application domain rules, and there are few, if any experts, available. Some specialized research is being conducted in this area, but the results are still tentative.

MODEL COMPARISON. Note that each process model described has some good points. The Waterfall/Design Driven model represents a model that is

Life Cycle Model	Category		
	Descriptive Power	Generality	Automation Suitability
Waterfall	L	L	L
Rapid-Prototype	M	M	M/H
Operational	M/H	M	H
Knowledge-Based [1]	H	H	H

KEY: H - High;   M - Medium;   L - Low;

NOTES: 1 - Results are Speculation

Table 2 - 2   **Comparison of Life-Cycle Models**

intuitively attractive, and has an experienced user base behind it. The Rapid-prototype model improves upon that model by including life cycle activities like management, develops the system incrementally, and provides rapid feedback to the developers and users. The Operational model produces specifications that are executable, increasing the role of automation, and tightens the link between what is specified and what is implemented. The Knowledge-based model helps separate the software engineering knowledge from the application knowledge, and has the potential of building very large systems. Table 2-2 provides a relative rating of each process model against the categories of descriptive power, generality, and suitability to automation.

No perfect or ideal life cycle process model exists. For starters, one requires an understanding of the fundamental process of software development [OSTERWEIL82]. This is very difficult since the question of whether the origins of the processes discussed are observed or imposed is still being argued [BLUM85].[4] Moreover, there are too many intangibles for a model to encompass them all. For instance, the project may start with a customer having some very vague concept of what the system will be, and when it is partially completed, may decide that isn't what was wanted after all. The "I don't know what I want, but I know what I don't want" which is very prevelant in real software developments, is hard to model. Another problem is that each software development is unique, and therefore no model will be able to encompass them all. Some developments will inevitably be short-changed by use of certain models.

What should one do? Perhaps the best advice is to "fake it" [PARNAS-86].What is important is not that a process model isn't perfect, but that one is used. It is better to use an incomplete model than none at all [DEMARCO78, HOWES84]. This way project participants can at least communicate, and management can have some measurement of project schedule and success. And using a model does work [BOEHM81]. Also, using a model, and finding its weaknesses moves one closer to the ideal. This is amply illustrated by the fact that each process model above is an attempt to overcome past deficiencies, and the resulting models are, over time, becoming more robust.

Each of the life cycle models described has some deficiency that makes it difficult to use as is as a foundation for a software engineering environment, however. The Waterfall/Design Driven model is very restrictive in its monolithic approach to building software. It fails to specifically include activities that occur across the life cycle such as project or configuration management, nor does it provide for feedback to the users or developers on the quality of the system being built. It also fails to account for the changes that inevitably occur in system development. The Rapid-prototype model overcomes most of these deficiencies, but includes some of its own. The primary one is that it interweaves the process of management and development. There is no clear separation of the two. Further, like the Waterfall model, it wasn't designed specifically for automation. On the other hand, the Operational and Knowledge-based models are specifically geared for automation, but focus primarily on the process of developing a software system. The management aspect is implicit rather than explicit, just as in the Waterfall model.

2.2.2 An "IDEAL" Process Model-Requirements

For a comprehensive software engineering environment to be built, each of the problems inherent in the life cycle models previously described must be addressed in some form. Although this author doesn't pretend to have the final solution to the problem of the ideal life cycle process model (many more years of research and practical experience are required just to get the state-of-the practice to a very reasonable, workable, and comprehensive model), it appears that intermediate solutions that are closer to this ideal model exist. And to satisfy Parnas Lamant [PARNAS74], we will advance some arguments why we believe this is true.

Toward this end, we will describe some of the requirements for an "ideal"[5] life cycle process model using Lauber's characteristics of a good life cycle model. Unfortunately, there isn't room in this text to describe in detail a complete model that meets these requirements but the salient points can be illustrated.[6]

CHARACTERISTICS OF A GOOD LIFE CYCLE. First, and foremost, the ideal life cycle model must be suitable for automation. Only by gearing the total process toward the idea of being eventually automated will the power of a software engineering environment be realized. This means knowing what we are building, i.e., the "products" of the total development process. Typical products include not only the software developed but the documentation that describes the software system itself, how the software works, its relationship to the total system, and how it was built. These products are the outputs of the environment and must be explicitly defined, as does the information contained in them. Moreover, the information contained in each of the products must be reusable and traceable from one product to another. All the information describing the products must be integrated and manipulable. This is termed the active integration of information [APPLIX-85, CHARETTE85], and follows the compiler analogy used earlier.

The ideal life cycle model must also be very general. This means having a model which is amenable to change, but also is repeatable. Repeatability is important to understanding the model and changing it. A way of accomplishing this requirement is to separate the model into small pieces using the concept of the separation of concerns and information hiding. In other words, only that which must be known at one time is seen, and all which might be affected by a change is grouped together. This implies a dynamic, rather than static process model. Given this requirement and the requirement to build products, the descriptive power of the life cycle model must be enhanced significantly.

The descriptive power of the previous process models studied are their weakest points. Three main areas need improvement: separating the management aspects of the development process from the development process itself; a means to separate the software engineering knowledge from the application knowledge; and the need to make explicit the relationships among the various information required to develop a software product and the management of that product.

MANAGEMENT. Management is the most influential and difficult aspect of developing a software system. Bad management can affect the success of a project more than any other factor. But surprisingly, it also seems to be the least understood in the context of developing a software process model. It is common to all the previous life cycle models to see no distinct management model, but instead to see management as a part of or indistinguishable from the software development itself. There appear to be two main reasons why this has happened.

First, the temporal nature of management has not been recognized as separate from the non-temporal nature of developing a system, and secondly, the lack of recognition that phases in a life cycle process model are arbitrarily defined.[7] To help clarify these remarks, we've developed a high-level model of the life cycle process that will be used throughout the remainder of the book. The model is constructed using SADT[8] -like notation (refer to Chapter Three's section on SADT), and presents first a management model, then a process model, and then a model to link the two previous models together.

Figure 2-7 depicts the management life cycle process model. The model is called an event driven model, state transition model or behavioral model. It depicts the states that the process can be in, and is used to depict sequential as well as concurrent dependencies, and at the lowest level, resource allocation and budgeting. The states are referred to as modes, because they represent only artificial groupings of states that seem to be related in some way. Observing the diagram, we see that the inputs and outputs are conditions or events that can cause state transitions. At the highest level diagram (B-0), the input condition is to "begin the project" and the output is the "software product is retired." The resources are time, money, people, equipment, etc.,— in other words, all things that can be "consumed."

As the diagram is decomposed to a lower level (B0) to show more detail, the more familiar phases appear. For this book, we have chosen six major phases or time boundaries of the life cycle: Requirements Analysis, Specifi-

Management Resources (Time, People, Funding, Facilities)

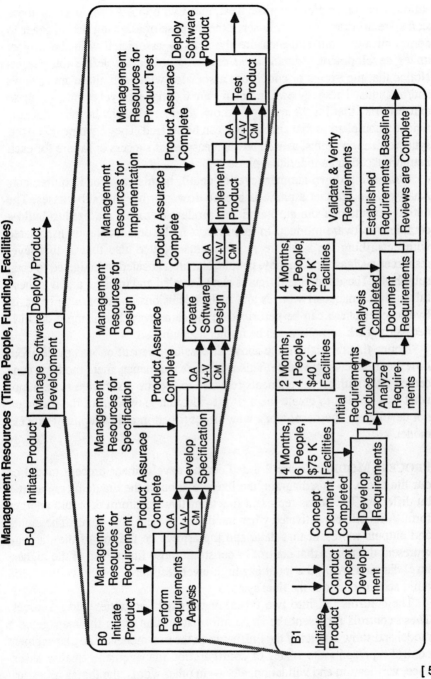

Figure 2 - 7   Simplified Management Process

cation, Design, Implementation, Test, and Evolution. Again, each of these states are arbitrary,[9] and only serve the purpose of allowing the manager to communicate about and measure the activity associated with the project under development. *Management* concerns ultimately define the phases. Notice that the events or conditions associated with each phase are reviews and/or audits. These reviews and audits are the highest level events (or phase exit criteria) that let the manager know whether a particular phase is sufficiently complete so that another one can be entered. They become, in effect, synchronization points, as well as the measures of success or failure for each item produced in an individual phase.

Proceeding down another level of detail, in this case for Requirements Analysis, we see that a phase is broken down further into sub-phases. The outputs events of them are individual product elements required to build a complete software product. In this case, it is the documentation associated with describing the software requirements. Notice also that at this level resources such as time, money, people, etc. are allocated or budgeted to each sub-phase. These individual figures can be totaled and tracked, and it is these things that a manager worries and makes decisions about on a daily basis. Every other phase can be described in the same way, and if more detail is necessary, each sub-phase can be further decomposed.

Notice that throughout the above discussion no mention was made about **how** the products were made. This is because the management model is concerned only with all the elements required to acquire a software system, not what was needed to create them. It provides the viewpoint of the manager, not developer. The developer's view is described in a development process model.

PROCESS MODEL. Figure 2-8 depicts the development process model of our life cycle. In this diagram, the interpretation of the diagrams are a little bit different. The boxes represent functions that transform data into another form. A function is activated when the data is present at its input. The inputs and outputs represent that data, and the arrows on the top of the diagram represent the things that control or constrain those functions. At the highest level diagram (A-0), the input is a high-level description of the system to be built, and the output is the final system.

The controls fall into two types, management activities and resources. These controls represent the same information that is on the management model and show implicitly the link between the two models. The management control represents the issues of configuration management, quality assurance, verification and validation, etc. — in other words, the things necessary to manage progress, rectify problems, and communicate the development plans to the organization. Management concerns span the entire life cycle model and are phase independent.

As with the management model, each level can be decomposed into lower levels of detail. Notice that at the A0 level the inputs and outputs are the documents themselves. The information contained in a requirements document is used and transformed into a specification, which is in turn used and transformed into a design. What this means is that if information isn't documented, it doesn't exist! As one decomposes these documents further, the information that makes up the documents is defined. One could theoretically continue to decompose these inputs and outputs until each information "packet" that is required in each individual sub-paragraph of every document produced could be identified. Similarly, each function that is required to produce the information could also be identified. At the lowest levels, these functions would be the software engineering methods or techniques themselves. Note that one can be in many functions simultaneously, with the only criteria being whether the information is present to activate a function. Also, information traceability as well as reuse is now available.

MANAGEMENT/DEVELOPMENT MODEL LINKAGE. Notice what we have accomplished so far. In the management model we have described the temporal nature of the life cycle model by identifying the events and conditions required to move from phase to phase from an acquisition point of view. The fact that these events and conditions may have nothing to do with the time actually necessary to do a development (assuming the development could be given as much time as needed, independent of material resources is a frequent source of problems.) One aspect to good management is to align the budgeted development time with the actual (but a priori unknown) development time.

In the development model, we have described the information and functions necessary to transform the information into a usable form by some other function. This model is data driven and is time independent. Each provides the proper perspective to the right user. However, what is still missing is the explicit linking of the two models. We show this linkage using a simple Entity-Relationship-Attribute (ERA) diagram in figure 2-9.

The ERA model depicts how the management model and development model are linked. At the highest levels of the models (B-0 and A-0), decisions, such as passing a review, are made by certain managers in accordance with exit criteria defined by quality assurance rules. For

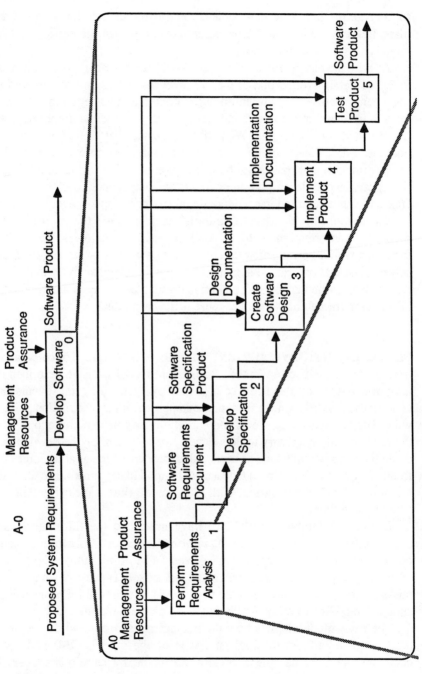

Figure 2 - 8 **Simplified Development Process**

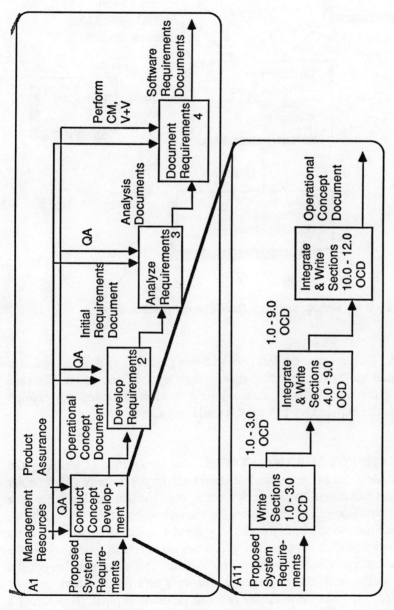

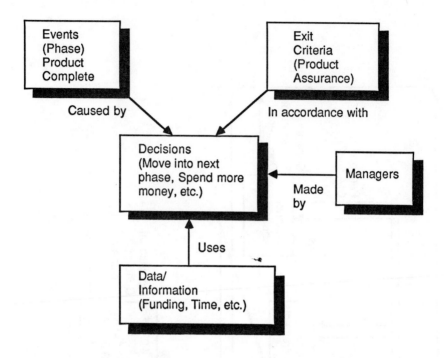

Figure 2 - 9   **Management and Development Relationships**

example, the particular product reviewed was produced by developers and is controlled by the configuration management system, and so on. For each level of the models, more detailed ERA models depicting the explicit relationships between the two models could be created.

THE NEED FOR MULTIPLE VIEWS. The importance of building the three models cannot be stressed enough. Each model describes a particular viewpoint that cannot be gained by creating one model alone. For instance, a distinct development model allows for the separation of the knowledge or functions needed to create the software for the particular application from the knowledge of the application. A distinct management model allows the control and visibility necessary to be in multiple phases simultaneously. Additionally, with the management process and development process separated, the links between the two can be made explicit. This forces a clearer definition of what is supposed to be built, why the decisions are made, and what the goals of the project are.

PROCESS REVIEW. Before moving on to discuss the method aspects of a software engineering environment, some general guidelines about process models brought out in this section should be reviewed. First, determine what it is that is going to be built. In other words, what are the products of the software development. The specific software system being built will determine these.

Second, the process model should be repeatable to help understanding, and usable on a wide range of systems.[10] This indicates a need to standardize on a process model that can be tailored to an individual project's need and provides measurement about how well the model works.

Third, realize that every model must be tailored to the specific circumstances encountered. Although the development model can be expected to be fairly stable, the management model may change dramatically with each project. An underlying assumption about the management model is that it is assumed to be perfect. Iteration caused by imperfect development practices is assumed, but those caused by bad management have never been explored.

In addition, what is happening in one part of the development process is never carried out in isolation. As Wasserman points out, one may envision any time in the development as a moving window covering more than one phase of the life cycle [WASSERMAN79].

And finally, the process model eventually used is the foundation for everything else that follows in a software engineering environment, and ultimately affects the cost of the system, and the productivity, effectiveness and practice of the users. If it is ill-defined, the environment and all systems built using it will probably be ill-defined also.

2.2.3 Methods

The second element constituting a software engineering environment are the software engineering methods that are to be applied in the creation of the software product. Chapters Three through Seven provide discussions on many methods so there is no need to do the same here, but a general foundation will help clarify issues which may come up later.

The term "method" has many definitions, ranging from "principles of practice" [RIDDLE80] to "tricks of the trade" [REDWINE84]. For the purposes of this book, we will define methods as:

> **"Explicit prescriptions for achieving an activity or set of activities required by the life cycle model used to develop a software product."**

Thus, the requirement to implement the life cycle process as defined by the development and management models define the range and domain of methods to be used. Note the dual nature of software engineering methods: to create a product and to implement part of the life cycle process. This becomes clearer by examining figure 2-10 which illustrates the life cycle development process model decomposed to another level. As the model is decomposed into finer levels of granularity, notice that the lower levels are represented by specific methods that are used to implement or create the software product. It is this difficultly in separating the individual processes defined by development model from the methods used to implement them that makes progress slow on developing new life cycle paradigms. Paradigms like the Operational model blur the distinction even more. Another way to look at this is to consider the boundary between the process model and methods as "wavy" rather than straight in figure 2-1.

Do not confuse the term methodology with method. A methodology, in software engineering terminology, is the combination and integration of some or all of a number of methods into a comprehensive whole for some particular purpose. A good way to think of methodologies are that they coerce a person to use a group of methods.[11] In a software engineering environment, one would like to have all the methods integrated together in some way to fully support the life cycle process model. As we will see, a method that can't be integrated with another is of little practical use. This does not mean that all the methods will necessarily be automated. For instance, reviews of documents and code are two methods that may never be automated, but the information provided should come from documented and repeatable methods. This issue will be discussed in more detail in the next section.

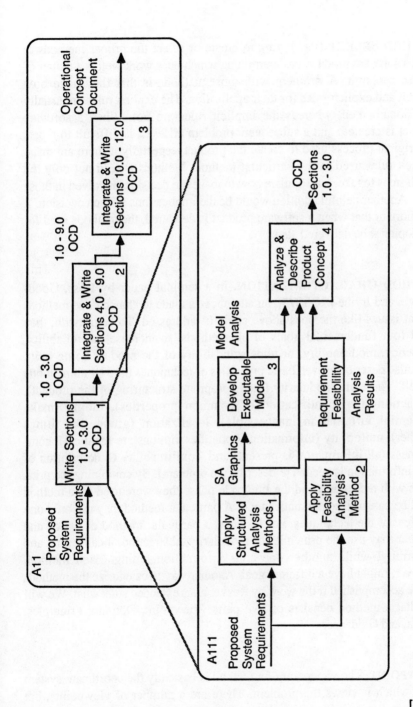

Figure 2 - 10   **Decomposition to Methods**

METHOD SELECTION. Trying to create or select the proper methods to build a software product, or determining which ones work well is a matter of intense research. A problem with most methods is that they have both implicit and explicit rules for their application. The explicit rules are usually well documented, whereas the implicit rules are not. When a software product is created, and a subsequent problem arises, it is difficult to repeat the original process used to create the product, especially if there are many implicit rules used in the particular method. Methods should not only tell which steps to take, but stipulate how to make the decisions involved in those steps. Another helpful addition would be the implications of each decision. It is important that when a software product is delivered, the methods used for developing it be delivered also.

METHOD CHARACTERIZATION. In a seminal paper by Ross, Good-enough, and Irvine [ROSS75], an attempt was made to characterize methods so that issues like the ones above could be addressed. To begin with, they listed four fundamental goals of all methods: to increase the reliability, efficiency, modifiability, or understandability of the product being built. They also described seven basic principles or techniques used by all methods as well. These are modularity (the appropriate structuring of the product), abstraction (the identification of common properties), hiding (make inessential information inaccessible), localization (group like things together), uniformity (information format descriptions are identical), completeness (all information is present) and confirmability (a description of what information is needed to describe the problem). By combining the principles with their goals and the life cycle phase they were used in, a method could be categorized and understood. A particular method may use only one or a few of the techniques. For instance, a particular method of divide and conquer may use the principles of modularity, abstraction, localization, and uniformity, while another one adds information hiding. Each method, however, might have a different goal. Another way to categorize the methods can be accomplished if the work by Ross et al. is extended somewhat. We will say that a method consists of five parts: Viewpoint, Domain, Principles, Media, and Guidance.

VIEWPOINT. The viewpoint of a method is basically the coordinate system from which it views the problem. There are a number of viewpoints, but three are basic: informational, functional, and behavioral. Informational views relationships between data. Functional means viewing data flow and transformations of data. Behavioral views concern the sequencing and concurrency of the data transformations.

As in mathematics, the above viewpoints can be transformed into one another to provide a different perspective on the problem. Each problem being solved with a method has a viewpoint that is more useful than another, and if the view is not supported by the method, it will not work well.

DOMAIN. The next aspect is that of the method's domain. The domain consists of two elements, one defined by the software product itself [BLUM85], and one defined by the phase of the life cycle the product currently resides in. By the first element we mean that a product being created has certain attributes associated with it, such as: possesses time critical interfaces, requires numeric computations, has human interface interactions, etc. By associating values with each attribute, a product can also be placed into certain classes. It can be shown that there exist orthogonol software product classes where not all methods may be appropriate [BLUM85]. A method, to be useful, must be able to be applied to a suitable class of problems.

The other element that makes up a method's domain is the phase of the life cycle the product is currently in. The information required to be transformed in one phase is different than that found in another. Figure 2-11 illustrates that in general, the types of information found and manipulated in each phase form a type of sinusoid alternating between "semantic-information" and "syntactic-information" transformations. The use of these terms may be a little misleading, so we will diverge here for a while.[12]

What we mean by semantic-information is the "mental activity or knowledge "that is necessary to be captured and manipulated by the methods used in a phase. The syntactic-information transformations are how this information can be described. For example, in requirements analysis, we are faced with an "unbounded" or, at best, fuzzy idea of what the software product will be like in the end. We try to bound the context of our ideas, giving them meaning that others can understand by using methods that can shape, define and document them. A common way to do this is to draw a box, circle or a cloud on a piece of paper and labelling it as representing something, like a processing algorithm, for instance. The methods used in this phase generally are applicable to almost any problem domain.

In contrast, during specification, we have a fairly well-defined and bounded problem with which to work; i.e., the requirements which have been documented in some form. We use these and change their representation, maybe by taking our box that represents the algorithm and listing its inputs and outputs in a table or matrix, such as a decision table. Moreover, as we will see, the knowledge or meaning needed to describe the software product (e.g., "processors," "module," "interface," etc.) is often embedded in the specification syntactic representations themselves.

In design, we shift focus again to how the requirements will be implemented, and once again the problem space becomes "unbounded." An infinite number of possible (but not necessarily correct) design choices are available to choose from, and again the methods used don't embed much knowledge of the application in them. In other words, we represent the design using boxes or circles which we label. (In specification the labels are usually given.)

Once a design is fixed, it is transformed once again, but this time into a physical realization by way of a syntactic description(i.e., code) of its execution. This syntactic representation is what is required to be transformed by a compiler into the form used to eventually control the pattern of a computer's execution.

Probably an easier way to think about it is that the amount of magic required to define requirements and design is greater than that of specifications and implementations.

Notice that as the level of abstraction becomes more detailed, the quantity in each transformation category increases. Interestingly, it will be shown in the next section that the majority of automated methods that exist occur in the phases with syntactic information transformations, and that the hardest methods to automate are those that attempt semantic information transformations.[13] Again, a method that is not appropriate for the transformation required will not be very useful.

PRINCIPLES. The third aspect that characterizes a method is the software engineering principles it uses. The principles of a method are the fundamental "laws" or concepts that are used to define its actions. Software engineering principles are immutable in the sense that they are technology independent by definition. Similar to software engineering principles are the three basic structures, sequencing, selection, and repetition, that are the minimum number required to do any programming. However, these are used in different combinations to form other, more powerful control structures to make programming easier.

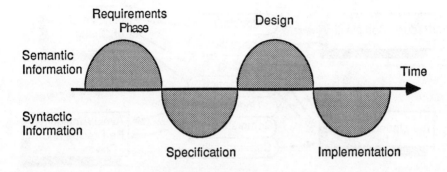

Figure 2 - 11   **Dominant Types of Information**
                 Manipulated Throughout Life Cycle

Instead of creating control structures, software enginering principles are used to form methods that either synthesize information, analyze information or, more commonly, do both. Synthesis creates new ideas to decompose, and analysis creates new ideas to synthesize. The seven principles listed by Ross et al. are probably the minimum required to define most methods, and it would be guesswork on our part to add any others.

Software engineering principles, in addition to the providing for synthesis or analysis of information have other properties such as limiting the impacts of change, reducing complexity, etc. These are illustrated in figure 2-12. Selecting the types and kinds of principles used by a method either restricts or enhances its usefulness.

MEDIUM. Another aspect that method is characterized by is the graphical medium used to implement the principles above. Figure 2-13 illustrates the spectrum of different media representations that can be used to describe a method, each differing in the level of interpretation required and information conveyed. Less formal representations are to the left, more formal to the right. Which representation is selected is important to the ability of the method to capture and convey information to the person or computer (if it is automated) using it. It also defines how usable the method is for a particular application. For example, an electrical engineering circuit diagram is useful

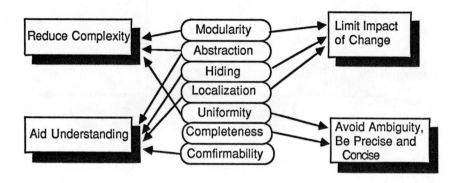

Figure 2 - 12   **Properties of Software Principles**

for conveying information in a precise and concise way to a specific audience. Text is not as formal or precise, but is usable by a wider audience. New representations like those found in Iconic languages [BURR84] may challenge conventional thinking about using traditional method representations in particular phases of the life cycle.

GUIDANCE. The final aspect of a method is the guidance provided for its use [WALLACE86]. This is somewhat intangible, but goes back to the problem of implicit and explicit rules for its use. Methods should provide guidance in what decisions are to be made, how to make them and in what order they should be made [FREEMAN77]. In other words, they should describe how to get started, how to stop (i.e., when it has accomplished its goal), and what happens in between (i.e., what comes next). If this is not possible, a method can't be automated, nor when it is applied to a single problem repeatedly, will the same solution likely appear.

This is not to advocate that a method should restrict an individual's creativity in its use. Methods don't replace the thought processes required to create a software product. However, they do help to guide them. For example, guidance can be in the form of directions similar to a road map. How two individuals get from Point A to Point B is (somewhat) irrelevant as long as by following the directions they both can arrive. If they don't, the path can be retraced to find out why not.

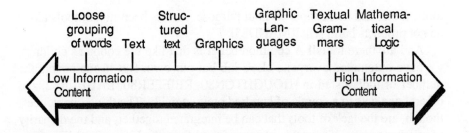

Figure 2 - 13   **Spectrum of Media Types**

OTHER CHARACTERISTICS. The integration of methods into practical methodologies to cover greater parts of the life cycle is only now being addressed [CHARETTE85, 85a, CHARETTE86], but is a vital problem to be solved if one is to have a comprehensive software engineering environment. A way to accomplish this aim will be discussed in Chapter Eight.

An item deliberately not listed as a characteristic of a method is whether or not it's automated. A method may be used if it is automated or not, but it is not a basic characteristic of a method. However, it is a significant characteristic of a software engineering environment, and the automation of methods is most important here. This is the subject of the next section.

2.2.4 Automation

The final aspect of a software engineering environment is the automation of its methods. The term automation is preferred to the one more commonly used: "software tool." The term software tool implies a focus on a singularity of purpose; i.e., the automation only of a single method without a context of which it is part. Automation, on the other hand, means to support a method which is an integral part of the total process of a software product development. The automation of a single method that cannot interact with the other methods used is not very useful. This has typically been the case with software tools, which also tend to fail to support a development process, or are too narrowly focused [WASSERMAN82].

But remember, the solution to the problem lies with integrating the methods into a comprehensive methodology, not in their automation. Automation is the final step, not the first. Too often, the focus has been on providing tools, tools, and more tools without purpose. As has been noted, tools alone do not products build [GARMAND85].

And are there tools!! A common belief is that like the cobbler's children, we have automated everyone else's job but our own. But if one counts the number of tools listed in [HOUGHTON80, REIFFER80, LAUBER82, and others] one gets to a couple of hundred pretty quickly. The thing one notices, though, are the lack of tools that can be integrated together, and the disparity of relative numbers in certain phases of the life cycle. Figure 2-14 illustrates the types and relative proportion of tools currently available across each phase. Notice that it also has the same cyclic pattern as was shown in figure 2-11. One reason is that it is hard to automate methods that manipulate highly semantic information. Another is that most of the methods used in the beginning of the life cycle are highly graphic in nature and only recently has the graphic hardware been economical.

Automation has a number of obvious benefits. The most important is that it reduces the labor needed to use the methods, and in some ways is the only realistic manner for applying some methods. The clerical aspect of most methods requires the keeping of large amounts of information and it is mentally and physically impossible to do so by hand on any system of size. Because the clerical aspect of using methods is reduced through automation, there is a corresponding rise in productivity and a decrease in development cost and schedule. Less quantitative but just as important, automation results in an increase in creativity because the developer or manager can concentrate on the task rather than on the shuffling of information. Moreover, automation facilitates learning and communication among project participants.

TYPES OF AUTOMATION. There are basically two types of automation: automation that creates new information and that which does not.[14] The former type we will term "reference-type" automation (RTA), and the latter "value-type" automation (VTA). Each type of automation serves much the same purpose as a call by reference or call by value procedure call. RTA creates new information that will be retained and used to develop the software product baseline. Each individual method determines the nature and the use of reference information. All methods have access to this information. VTA uses reference-type information that is extracted and analyzed, or only temporarily created, but these actions do not change the value of the reference information. This information may be saved, but as non-baselined data. The reason for defining two types of automation is to allow the proper resolution of the question "What should be automated?"

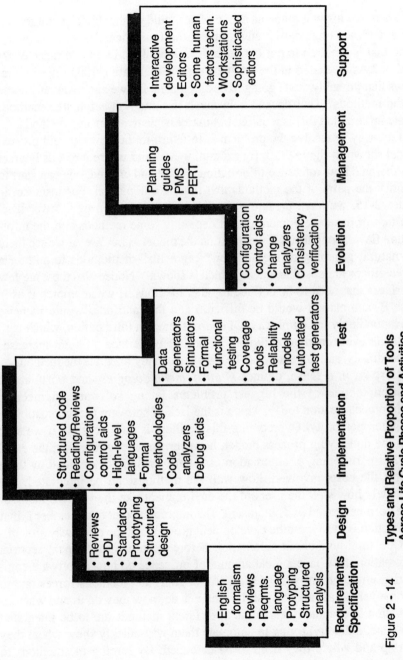

Figure 2 - 14   **Types and Relative Proportion of Tools
Across Life Cycle Phases and Activities**

[73]

There are many arguments about what should or shouldn't be automated. For a software engineering environment the fundamental answer is everything that is required to put out the software product. Does that mean every method? As we stated in the previous section there are certain ones like reviews that probably aren't going to be automated. Do we automate only some of the methods? That doesn't help much if some non-automated methods create information that is required but inaccessible to automated methods.

One way to resolve the problem is to return to the development process model shown in figure 2-10. By examining how and where methods interact together and how reference information is used and created, one can start to identify the parts of the methods that require automation. For instance, in figure 2-15, we have created a symbolic representation of a lower-level partition of our development model depicting some methods and the information flow among them. If we partition the model as in Case A, we see there are natural grouping of methods or "fragments" of methods to automate (three groups are possible, one of which is shown.) Notice also there are few interfaces that need to be defined to other methods. If we attempted it as in Case B, automation would be difficult, and the interfaces would increase correspondingly in complexity. Of course there is a third option, which is to automate every method individually, but then interface problem increases tremendously, and there may not be a way to cleanly integrate the methods.

Case A, in a sense, defines *natural methodologies,* and postulates a solution to one of the biggest problems facing software engineering environment creation today, which is the lack of software tool compatibility and interoperability. Overcoming this problem is only possible if we start with the underlying process model, however. In an environment, the exact level of partitioning or automation granularity will be determined by three things: the costs involved, how well the methods can be integrated, and ultimately how well the users of the environment like the way the methods have been integrated *and* automated. The important point to remember is that automation is to support the development process, not the other way around.

One final note about automation before we move to the next section. Automation does have a great amount of influence on how a software engineering environment will be built. Automating the methods forces one to become very exact about what the methods do, how they do it, and what information is eventually captured. If different methods are to be integrated into a methodology, trying to automate them will quickly show where they overlap and where they need to be extended. By forcing the methods to support the development and management processes, we force these processes to become more exact as well. The building of an environment should

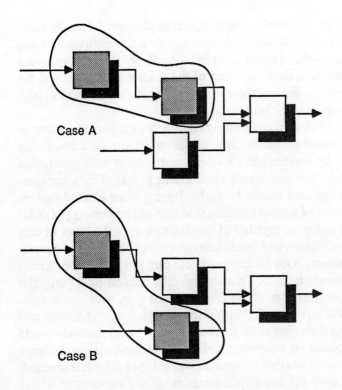

Case A

Case B

Figure 2 - 15   Automation of Method Strategies

proceed in a sense "top-down," with the primary requirement being its total automation. We will return to these ideas in Chapter Eleven.

Now that all three basic concepts of a software engineering environment have been explored, how are these concepts integrated into a unified whole?

2.2.4 Unifying Concepts

So far, we've discussed a conceptual model of a software engineering environment, which consists of a development and management process model supported by software engineering methods, and implemented through computer automation. In order to successfully implement the environment and use it properly, three other factors must be considered: the capture of the environment information, the structuring of the environment itself and the users of the environment. Each of these issues will be studied in detail in later chapters, but an overview is helpful here.

A key factor in a software engineering environment is how the information created by a method should be captured. Its retention must allow for its integration and use by various other methods and support their automation wherever possible.[15] The underlying requirement is that of data transparency; i.e., all data captured should be usable by any other method that requires it. Development of a global schema using the object models [COX84] as a basis; i.e., the grouping together of the description of the types of data required and their attributes and interrelationships, is one means of providing this data transparency. Objects comprise both data and the set of functions that can be performed on them. Thus information created by a particular method would be considered an object of a particular type, with certain attributes describing that type, its relationship to other objects, and having certain allowable operations able to be performed on it. Other methods would have access to the object via a database, and be able to manipulate and change the values depending on whether the method was value or reference oriented. This technique allows for the implementation of the concept of active integration of information.

Another major question is what should be in this database, and how should it be tracked? The database of the environment logically should consist of all the information required to create, replicate or modify the software product. The granularity of the data objects captured will depend on each method. For instance, a specification document might be considered a single object. A problem arises when not all the methods are automated and the information resides outside the database. Care must be taken to retain this information as well.

A factor affecting the successful implementation of a software engineering environment is its structure. In this chapter a conceptual model consisting of process, methods, and automation was presented with interfaces defined between each section. However, there also exists another logical structuring that defines the environment interfaces from an implementation view. Figure 2-16 illustrates the conceptual environment interfaces that must be supported for the environment to be supported on multiple host architectures [CHARETTE85b]. The model resembles the ISO communication

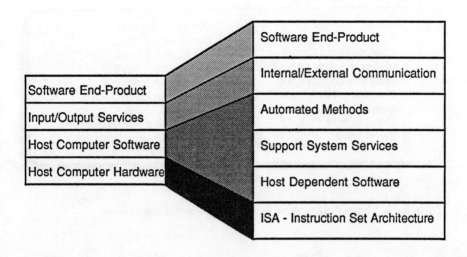

| Software End-Product |
| Input/Output Services |
| Host Computer Software |
| Host Computer Hardware |

| Software End-Product |
| Internal/External Communication |
| Automated Methods |
| Support System Services |
| Host Dependent Software |
| ISA - Instruction Set Architecture |

Figure 2 - 16   **Software Engineering Environment Information Model**

model and describes the mappings required from a host architecture to the user interface.

The final factors requiring consideration are the users of a software engineering environment and the organization required to support it. Many different types of users must be supported by the environment and each has slightly different needs. Table 2-3 lists just some of the potential users of the environment. Moreover, an environment can greatly influence the business practices of a company. It is, after all, a sophisticated way of "crowd control." However, if the environment does not match well to the company organizational structure then it will probably not be used to its full potential as it "doesn't support the way we do business." It may also impede the creation of a quality software product by just "getting in the way." Therefore, it's critical that the underlying process model that the environment was built to support be the same, or close to the same, as that the organization uses currently. These two issues will be discussed more fully in Chapters Eleven and Twelve. In the next section we will describe what makes an "ideal" environment.

System Analyst	Configuration Manager
Software Architect	Knowledge Engineer
Requirements Engineer	Application Expert
Human Factors Engineer	Management Staff
Software Logistician	Automation Engineer
Program Librarian	Application User
Security Specialist	Technical Writer
Office Supply Staff	Environment Administrator
Programmer	Test Engineer

Table 2 - 3   **Potential Software Engineering Environment Users**

2.3 An "Ideal" Software Engineering Environment

The spectrum of software engineering environments range from those with lots of software tools which support no particular process model, to those which are completely "unionized" [RIDDLE80]. It was only half-jokingly observed that there might be over $2^{1,000,000}$ possible types of environments [OSTERWEIL82]. Remember too, everyone has their own opinion of what a software engineering environment is. Today they come in all sorts of flavors: programming support environment, programming development environment, computer-aided programming support environment, ad infinitum.[16] Each has different capabilities, and may help an organization build a particular software product. Right now, because building environments is still in its infancy, it is hard to tell whether a specific environment is very useful.[17] It's not unlike being in a flower garden in spring where the flowers and weeds all look alike. How can we distinguish between the two?

Earlier in the chapter, we depicted an environment as being somewhat pyramid shaped, with the foundation being the life cycle process model, with methods supporting the process model, and automation being used to support the methods. If one were to examine most environments today, one would see this same shape: a fairly complete life cycle model supported by some methods supported by even less automation. On the other hand, an "ideal"

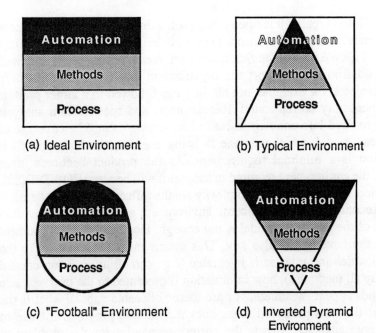

Figure 2 - 17   **Different Types of Software Engineering Environments**

software engineering environment would look more like a box: a complete process model fully supported by methods which are in turn fully automated as illustrated in figure 2-17a. The "gap" between the two indicated by the white areas in figure 2-17b is what has to be added to get to an "ideal" environment. In other words, in the environment shown in 2-17b there isn't a completely described process model, nor is the process completely supported by methods, nor are all the methods automated. Other environments may appear football-shaped (many methods, little support for any specific process-model and little automation) or inverted pyramid shaped (many tools, few defined methods, no particular life cycle model supported), as illustrated in figures 2-17c and 2-17d. The next question is how does one determine the extent of this gap?

This question is not so easy to answer. The solution lies in whether the environment drives the product, or the product drives the environment

DLE86]. Since in reality it is often both, a software engineering environment has to be measured in both dimensions: i. e., in breadth of scope and applicability [OSTERWEIL82]. The first dimension, breadth of scope, is how well does an environment support the organization creating the product. In smaller projects, for example, not all the steps followed in a larger product development may be replicated. Requirements and specification analysis might be merged into one step instead of separating them. The coverage of the process model, whichever one is being used, by methods and their automation is a minimal requirement. As the product becomes more complex, the environment required to support it will be also [HOWDEN82]. Thus project size and product complexity are the influencing factors here.

The second dimension concerns environment applicability. Providing coverage of the life cycle model is not enough. How well the environment provides the coverage is also key. This means measuring items like the degree to which information is integrated (e.g., can all information created be used by all methods?), how information is presented to the user (e.g., do the methods appear "seamless," or are there noticeable gaps?), what is the quality of the data produced (e.g., does the method provided for use in requirements analysis provide the correct viewpoint for the problem at hand?), etc. These metrics are very subjective, and a complete list is impossible to compile. We will return to this issue in later chapters.

As we stated earlier, this book is concerned with the development of mid to "Probably Won't Work Today" sized projects, so the software engineering environment that is required to support these are, by necessity, towards the "ideal" side of the spectrum. By ideal, we don't mean "nirvana" either. An ideal environment does not imply it has everything one could possibly wish for regardless of cost, but means instead the minimum required to do the job. Just as in airline travel, the first goal is to arrive safely, the second on time, the third with your luggage, and somewhere way down the list, to have ice in your drink. The extras are nice, but not required. In Chapter Nine we will outline an ideal software engineering environment that hopefully meets the above criteria. The environment described will be one which satisfies the minimum requirements each phase, and each activity, imposes on an environment. Since these requirements are derived from our current paradigms of software development, the environment won't represent a revolutionary approach, but an evolutionary one.

The goals of our ideal software engineering environment are three-fold. First, to try to make the software development process as we currently know it better than it is today, and second achieve that goal in a short period of time. Thus the ideal environment envisioned should be able to be built by the early 1990's.

The last goal is to use as much current technology as possible. This means we will stay within the state-of-the-practice most of the time, and only occasionally stray into the state-of-the-art when necessary.

There may be revolutionary approaches that promise bigger gains, but these are only now being explored [MYERS85] and are beyond the scope of this book.

2.4 Summary

In this chapter, we have outlined how a software engineering environment can be created to successfully attack the three problems confronting the production of software systems: the high cost of software; the variation in practice, and the lack of productivity. The provision of integrated methods that are automated help to reduce the variation of practice and increase productivity. Over a period of time, software costs will decrease.

It is important to note, however, that software engineering environments are not a panacea for the software problem either. Environments don't replace thinking, don't guarantee good management, don't eliminate human error, don't guarantee we know what we are doing, don't stop changes in the scope of work, don't stop the Congress or corporate management from cutting the budget, nor stop a crummy system from still being created despite the best of intensions. An environment attempts to reduce these problems by improving the quality of the process with the assumption that improved product quality will result. Unfortunately, the ultimate validation of whether an environment is successful at attaining these goals comes only after the product is delivered. And since no one has built anything resembling an ideal environment yet, we are still years away from seeing how successful they will be.

However, we do know that large software systems can't be built without software engineering environments either. When one is confronted with the problem of specifying the construction of an environment, though, sometimes one does start to feel like the a member of the British Admiralty in World War II at the height of the U-Boat menace. A prominent British scientist wrote to say that to solve the submarine problem, all one had to do would be drain the North Sea, the submarines would therefore be stuck in the mud, and then British Commandos could parachute in and capture the crews. When the Admiralty wrote back and asked just how they were to accomplish the task of draining the North Sea, the scientist said it was an engineering problem, and since he was a scientist, it wasn't his problem.

APPROACH TO THE REMAINDER OF THE BOOK. To aid the understanding of the material that follows, and to relate it to the introductory material already presented, the next five chapters will follow the same basic format of this chapter. This means:

> A review of the development and management processes which occur in that particular phase;

- A discussion of a representative set of methods that are available to implement the above processes;

- An examination of some automation that has taken place to support each phase;

- A compilation of the general requirements the phase imposes on a software engineering environment.

We then examine each of the life cycle phase processes, methods, and automation support; we will examine them from a "realistic" viewpoint, not an ideal one. This means that we will not necessarily present what the ideal development process should look like, but how it exists today and how it can be improved by an environment. Thus, a somewhat negative or cynical tone might (mistakenly) be conveyed, and one might be left with the feeling that the process of developing software that works is hopeless.

The reason for this approach is that a software engineering environment must support the way software is developed today, and how it should be developed tomorrow. Only by taking an unvarnished view of what actually happens can one truly start understanding the dynamics of the problem. Too often, it is forgotten that the development of software on large projects is a sociological activity, fraught with confusion and human error. For any software engineering environment, or technology for that matter, to be successful, it must work in the real world, and not be created for a pristine model of one.

Let's now look at how all these can be integrated together to create an environment. The first phase of the life cycle we will examine is the Requirements Analysis phase.

FOOTNOTES:

1. Excluding the commenting of code, of course.

2. This is not to imply smaller-sized projects wouldn't benefit from an environment, it's just the cost/benefit ratio might not be in its favor to use one.

3. One shouldn't take this as dogma. Prototypes are not *required* to be built. Sometimes building a prototype will not reveal anything worthwhile [BOEHM84].

4. The first life cycle models were imposed to help manage the software development, not to help develop the software. Most managers think they are one and the same, with normally detrimental effect.

5. We will explain the term "Ideal" in more detail later in the chapter.

6. For example, the standards used to describe the life cycle model for the Department of Defense run two volumes and close to 300 pages. Appendix A provides a brief description of DoD STD 2167, Defense System Software Development.

7. The first life cycle model was based upon an arbitrary scaled time-axis to help management control the development of a product. See [ROYCE70].

8. SADT is a registered trademark of SofTech, Inc.

9. They are arbitrary in the sense that where one phase boundary ends and another begins is irrelevant as long as all the phases occur in the development. The natural occurrence of related activities will most likely define phase boundaries.

10. Unique process models might be appropriate for certain products, however.

11. Notice also that a methodology not only coerces a person, but a method does also. A method forces a person to get very detailed, and somewhat exact, very quickly.

12. All syntactical representations possess some meaning.

13. In a sense, each type represents an entropy level of a phase, with phases dominated by semantic information having a higher entropy level than those that are syntactically dominated.

14. Remember once again, a specific method creates new information. Automation only implements the method. We speak here of automation performing this task because the information that is created must be captured somewhere, and this is an automation problem, not a method problem. This will become clearer as we go on.

15. We will assume for the remainder of this discussion that all the methods are being automated.

16. Notice that most concentrate on supporting the implementation phase, not the full life cycle.

17. Some have remarked that where software engineering environments are today, the Fortran Compiler was in 1955. See [OSTERWEIL82].

3. REQUIREMENTS ANALYSIS

"When I use a word," Humpty Dumpty said, in a rather scornful tone, "it means just what I choose it to mean - nothing more nor less"
Lewis Carroll: Through the Looking Glass

3.0 Introduction

The first aspect of our life cycle model to be studied is what we are calling "the front-end" of the life cycle development process for a software product. It consists of the requirements analysis, specification, and design phases of the life cycle — in other words, those life cycle phases that occur before implementation.

Errors in the the front-end phases account for 35 to 75 percent of the errors that will occur in a common software development. Recall that the studies cited in the previous chapters have shown that these errors also contribute the greatest negative impact on a software product's cost and completion schedule. Cancellation of multimillion dollar projects, such as in the cases of the Univac/United Airline reservation system ($56M) or the Advanced Logistic System ($217M), are not uncommon as a result of performing poorly in these phases [BOEHM81].

The software requirements phase is actually a continuation of the refinement of the system's requirements phase. The definition of software requirements is usually accomplished separately from the system (hardware) requirements.[1] The reason is each is usually created separately and then merged into a system at integration time. Software requirements are a description of what (and why) functionality was accorded to the software in a system. Moreover, the description of the requirements are independent of

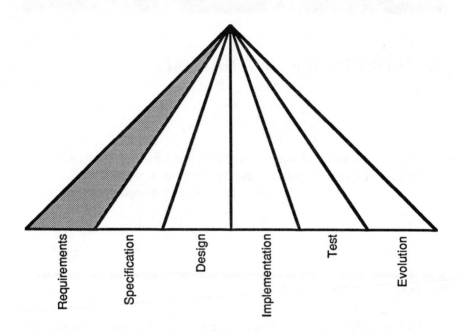

Figure 3 - 1   **Model of a Typical Software Engineering Environment**

the means by which they are to be accomplished. This will be described in the actual implementation.

For the purposes of this text we have chosen to consider the requirements phase as separate from the specification phase. Usually, requirements analysis and specification are considered as a single step, not two. Some argue that a step between requirements specification and implementation doesn't exist since the two are so intimately intertwined and constantly iterate as one [SWARTOUT82]. This is in large part true, and ours is an arbritrary decision, but the same can be said of any of the phases. We do believe, however, that too close an integration of these life cycle phases may mean that neither the requirements nor the specification receive the attention they properly require.

For example, it is extremely important to decide what is required of the software to meet the overall system's needs. These requirements impact everything that follows in the software product's development, and it is vital that their importance be recognized and not hidden nor glossed over. As Ross [ROSS85] so aptly puts it, overspecifying too early only builds in your own ignorance. The software specifications, which we will discuss in Chapter

Four will bind the *software requirements* to the *software implementation.*
The *software requirements,* on the other hand, bind or obligate the *software
implementation* to meeting certain of the *system requirements.*

In this chapter we will examine the processes, methods, and automation
that make up the requirements portion of the software engineering environment shown in figure 3-1. With these few words of introduction, let's examine the requirements phase in detail.

3.1 The Requirements Phase

What exactly are requirements? A working definition is that they are a
binding condition which states a mandatory characteristic of an abstract or
physical object. Requirements may appear in many different forms, such as a
description, or a constraint, or as an evaluation criteria for judging quality.
They also may be implicitly defined, implied by the context in which they
occur. The basic notion is that a requirement is a condition that must be met
for a software product to be acceptable to its uses. Since we are concerned
mostly in this book with mid-to-large size software projects, to adequately
develop requirements for them, we need to understand a little about their
nature.

A NEW PROJECT BEGINNING. Most of us like to have this fantasy every
time we start off in a new project. First, we are going to begin with a fresh,
clean sheet with nobody's preconceived notions or prior commitments in the
way to constrain how we will develop the product. Next, there will be no
tight schedule, no lack of funding, and all the resources one would ever want.
Then, we are going to use all the best software engineering techniques available to develop a software system that will be, in our modest opinion, the best
of all time. Well, it will be at least better than that *last* disaster we worked on.

Reality begins to crowd out our fantasy, however. We begin to
experience premonitions of the frustrations and disappointments that will
surely come, as night follows day, in the development we are about to
embark upon. We know the schedule will start to slip, that the product we are
trying to build will still be as clear to us as mud on a spring day three quarters
of the way through, and that the costs and quality problems will begin to
sprout like weeds. And if we listen closely, we can also begin to hear the new
legions of visionaries (aka critics) marching forth to attack these problems

with more and more rigor, knowing their coming only marks the time when things will get worse.

We can also see the system requirements being changed by "the powers that be" to meet what they think we have built, knowing all the while these won't come any closer either, because *we* still haven't figured out which monster, Godzilla or Frankenstein, we have ended up creating. But sometime in the future the money or time will then (mercifully) run out, and we can then proclaim the wondrous marvel of software we have wrought, all the while looking for someone to blame for the mess. And we can once again see ourselves swearing never to be part of a project like that again.

But we will let all these dark thoughts slide quickly by for now, since it is the beginning of a new project, we have enthusiasm, and everything always looks possible at the beginning.

INCREMENTAL DEVELOPMENT. Are all the developments of mid-to-large projects plagued by this confusion? Although there hasn't been a survey on the depth of hopelessness vs. hopefulness developers feel during software developments, based on personal experience and on books such as *The Mythical Man-Month* [BROOKS75], one can be reasonably confident that the ratio is something like 9:1 against feeling hopeful that one will ever totally succeed. What keeps most of us going is that sometimes projects do succeed, and the major reasons seem that the system and software requirements are well thought out and documented. However, these tasks are not particularly easy, nor for most developers, interesting to do.

The reason is that large systems usually are created by what is termed "incremental developments." Because of their size, the system development is broken down into a set of "pieces," called increments, each providing some basic level of functionality that will form the basis for the next increment of the system. Each successive increment reuses the one previously built to add more functionality, usually by integrating the new functions with the old ones. Eventually a complete system is created. Incremental development is different from maintaining or evolving the software since the increments are preplanned.

As discussed in Chapter Two, incremental development seems to have a number of advantages. The most significant are the easier project management required, the "build a little, test a little" approach that allows a user an early look at the product, and the (postulated) better quality of the final system. But it also has a number of drawbacks. The enhanced management aspects can be mostly illusory, since typically many increments of the "system" are being worked on simultaneously. This means a system will be in many phases of the life cycle at once, where any slip occurring will affect each following increment. Keeping small problems from becoming big ones requires very tight management control over the process. Moreover, each increment (ideally) should have its functionality defined based upon the equal partitioning of the total system requirements [PARNAS76]. In reality, increments are usually based instead upon funding available, schedule, etc. This also produces a negative effect on product manageability.

Additionally, since each increment has requirements that are only a partial reflection of the complete system, they need to reflect the modifications which will occur in each of the future increments [MUNSON81]. In other words, the set of requirements that define a particular increment must be complete but at the same time not unduly constrain the development of the increments that follow. This usually doesn't happen, either, because: a) the total system requirements aren't known, and; b) the same group doesn't create the requirements for each of the individual increments. Aggravating the problem is that new projects don't start with the proverbial clean sheet, but have many requirements pre-imposed, such as which computer will be used, which further constrains the developer's options.

CONSEQUENCES OF POOR REQUIREMENTS. Remember the goal of a development effort is to build a system that performs its intended functions, with adequate performance at reasonable cost (either explicitly or implicitly defined). This really means building a system that meets the user's needs, that can accommodate change after the system is "complete," and that uses only the resources that have been allocated to the project. What is done during the requirements phase definition will determine how well we can accomplish these goals, and manage the tradeoffs among efficiency, maintainability, reliability, etc. What is interesting is that the requirements disproportionally impact project schedule and cost, yet receive the the least attention, if they are done at all! Only 5 to 10 percent of a typical project's time is spent on requirements analysis.

The consequences of wrong requirements include system rejection, system fixing or retrofit, the installation of a dangerous system, failure of the project, and/or the loss of future business. Wrong requirements are requirements that may be those perceived or stated by the user, but aren't the "real requirements." It is not uncommon for the user to not know what he or she wants. Thus, a major task of requirements analysis is to ferret out the real requirements. The final requirements that are defined or not defined will impact every aspect of the resultant system, so performing this phase correctly is of primary importance to the future success or failure of the system development.

A graphic example of what can happen because of poor requirements definition occurred in the 1960s during the joint U.S. Air Force/Navy effort to build a common aircraft. It was meant to save money by providing a common airframe that could be tailored to meet each service's individual mission requirements. The TFX's (Tactical Fighter, Experimental) airframe was required to support the minimum aerodynamic properties necessary for it to be tailored for use as a tactical fighter, interdiction strike aircraft, low-altitude supersonic penetrating nuclear bomber, or fleet air-defense aircraft.

As it turned out, these requirements were incompatible. When the aircraft which was finally produced landed aboard a carrier for the first time, the deck buckled. The requirements to support all the other missions had increased the weight to such an amount that the plane was too heavy to land on aircraft carriers. Needless to say, the Navy never got its plane, and had to start over.[2]

3.1.1 General Goals of Defining Requirements

The idea of defining requirements correctly is one that must be constantly re-emphasized. Two key questions must be asked continually throughout the system development process: "Are we building the right system?" and "Are we building it right?" If the answer is forever "maybe," then a hard look at what has been defined is necessary.

There are a number of reasons for requirements definition that go beyond the mere necessity of defining which product will eventually be built, however. Requirements definition is an important aspect of achieving consensus among all the participants involved in the development: the developers, the managers, the sponsors of the project and most importantly, the users of the resultant product. If consensus cannot be reached very early in a project, then someone, and most likely everyone, will be dissatisfied in the end. This will eventually lead to great pressure to change the product requirements as the project progresses. And that can be lived without.

A HUMAN ENDEAVOR. Requirement changes will happen often enough as it is just because being human, people forget, miscommunicate and change their minds. Remember, no single person knows all the answers [HENIN-GER80], and different people will give different answers depending on the person's point of view in the organization [BOEHM84b]. Mistakes occur naturally without any extra assistance being necessary. However, if consensus can be reached — and this may happen only after intense negotiation — then all the stakeholders will tend to work together to make the product work, and keep changes to a minimum. So first, requirements definition is a human endeavor.

AN INFORMAL CONTRACT. The results of requirements definition also form a "contract" between the users of the product and its developers. Remember, a requirement is an expression of need, an imposed demand, or something someone will pay for, thus it takes on a form similar to a legal document. In fact, if the output of requirement definition were taken as legal contracts, we would be sure much more care would go into their creation, and much less changing of them later on would occur, especially if the penalties for doing so were spelled out. So second, as a contract, requirements form the standard against which the product will be judged by the user and sponsor.

OBTAIN FEEDBACK. Like all good contracts, requirements need to be heavily documented. However, from our viewpoint of what requirements should be, these documents are used as more informative than formal legal documents. The reason is that a requirements document must first fulfill the role of providing understanding of what it is to be built in a way understood by all parties involved. It is difficult enough to get the software developers and users to understand each other's view without requiring the document to be readable only to a lawyer. Each party may be an expert in his own domain, but is a novice in the other's [YEH84]. The documents are also needed to show progress and provides the required information to make decisions about the project status. Thus third, requirements provide the basis for obtaining feedback about the software product.

In summary, the requirements form the contract of what the software will provide to the system to meet its needs, whereas the software specification (which we will examine in the next chapter) binds the resultant product to the software requirements. These ideas will become clearer as we proceed.

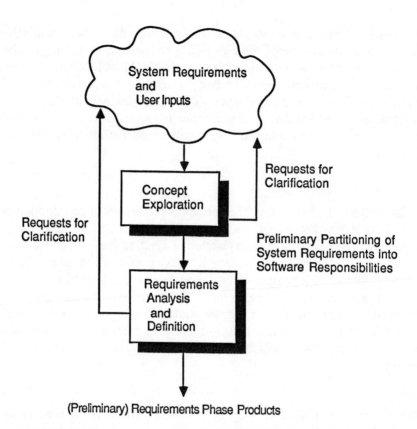

Figure 3 - 2   **General Requirements Phase Process Model**

3.1.2 A General Requirements Process Description

It helps to think of requirements definition as being composed of two sub-processes: concept exploration, and requirements definition and analysis, as shown in figure 3-2. We will discuss them separately, but realize they are tightly coupled.

3.1.2.1 CONCEPT EXPLORATION. Concept exploration is the time when the over-all technical, strategic, and economic foundations for the software

Efficiency	vs.	Maintainability
Testability	vs.	Efficiency
Efficiency	vs.	Productivity
Productivity	vs.	Reliability
Efficiency	vs.	Understandability
Efficiency	vs.	Effectiveness

Table 3 - 1   **Tradeoffs of Software Product Goals**

product are laid out. Thus, at the start of concept exploration, it is important to establish the relative importance of the system's objectives and how the software product relates to these objectives. For example, is it more important to have a system that is modifiable, or is the system needed very quickly? If it is the latter, it might be preferable to make the system simple to build initially (and maybe harder to change later). The establishment of the relative importance of objectives allows the tradeoffs of the individual goals. Some are in conflict, such as system efficiency vs. understandability. Fortunately, many goals are mutually compatible. Table 3-1 lists some of these tradeoffs. Typical questions to ask are which of the current limits and capacities may change? How is technology used likely to evolve? Which parameters are fixed, and which are flexible? [MUNSON81]

Concept exploration is really the process of needs fulfillment. It determines the needs or requirements that the software product must fulfill if the system is to work correctly, and proposes solutions to those needs. We say solution or solutions because it is during this process that one determines what is or isn't possible with respect to fulfilling the system requirements. For instance, software requirements may have been "pre-defined" by the system designers. Are these reasonable requests for the software to fulfill, or acts of fanciful thinking, given the technical, economic, and political considerations? Or the system designers may not yet have decided what will be in hardware or software, so what is or isn't reasonable? Also, there may be multiple levels of requirements that have been defined, say first for the system, then the hardware, and finally the software. How are conflicts resolved?

During concept exploration, the developers should strive to understand the real requirements. Questions like "why is the system being built?", "what is the system trying to accomplish?" and "what design constraints must be observed?" require answering [RAMAMOORTHY84]. Many systems have been built, tested and made operational, only never to be used because they didn't meet the "real" requirements, although they met the stated ones.

FUNCTIONAL AND NON-FUNCTIONAL REQUIREMENTS. There are two types of requirements that must be identified during concept exploration: functional and non-functional. Functional requirements are those that are absolutely necessary to the functioning of the system, describe the input/output behavior of the system [RAMAMOORTHY84] and are the "shalls" of the software that can (and must) be tested. Non-functional requirements are the desirable, but optional requirements that are subjective in nature, such as maintainability or ease of use, and therefore not conclusively testable [RALSTON83].[3] It is difficult to measure the success with which these non-functional requirements are met until after the product has been developed and delivered. In real systems, the non-functional requirements often are more important than functional requirements. For example, in two large development efforts, an average of 80 percent of the software had to be rewritten after delivery because of user/requirement mismatches [BOEHM73].

In summary, concept exploration means the thorough examination of the rationale for using software to solve a system requirement. It also means asking whether it helps the user get the job done. Techniques such as prototyping, simulation, and experimentation are used to help resolve other issues such as minimum performance requirements the software must reach to satisfy a levied system requirement. The output of concept exploration is a specified problem domain that the software will help solve, recommendations on how the software will solve it, and identified potential risk areas and tradeoffs. The primary focus of concept exploration is to create a body of knowledge about the system and how the software product relates to it. This information is to be used by the requirements definition and analysis process that comes next. The best solution isn't necessary, just a feasible one.

3.1.2.2 REQUIREMENTS DEFINITION AND ANALYSIS. Requirements definition and analysis is a more formal continuation of the concept exploration process. The outputs created by the concept exploration phase are analyzed for use in creating the requirements of the software product. A primary difference between this process and the previous one is that the outputs from concept exploration are not formally reviewed, and therefore are not binding. The definition process has products that are developed and reviewed, and therefore creates the baseline information for the rest of the development process.

The definitional process does exactly what its name implies: It defines the software product. To do this correctly, the developers should formally create the vocabulary, standards and conventions necessary to communicate among the project participants ideas and comments about the product. The methods described in the next section will demonstate how this can be accomplished. Each software requirement uncovered should have a description of its motivation and what system requirement it fulfills. Moreover, the focus should be from the user's viewpoint. Questions such as "what is going to happen with this?" or "how often must this be done?" or "what information is required to make this decision?" will go a long way toward finding the proper requirements. The focus should be on what is to be done by the software, not how it is to be done.

3.1.2.3 DOCUMENTS. The process model to be used to actually accomplish requirements definition will revolve around the documented products of this phase. The products fulfill a crucial role in determining what information is to be captured and used for the remainder of the project, and determine the form of the software engineering environment. Recall from Chapter Two that the focus of a process, methods and their automation is the creation of products. At the very least, a software engineering environment must create these products, i.e., the information required to produce them. Keep in mind this general rule: Anything not described in these documents does not exist! Great care must be taken in determining what should not be captured in a requirements document.

There are many products created during a requirements phase. Product selection and the packaging of information depends on the exact life cycle model that is used, but typically included are a preliminary software requirements specification (not to be confused with a software specification which will be discussed in the next chapter), a preliminary interface requirements specification (i.e., how will the software interface with the system it is part of), a preliminary operational concept document (i.e., how and why does the software meet the system's operational requirements), and a preliminary users guide (i.e., how is the software to be used by the users). Tables 3-2, 3-3,

1. Scope

Provides an identification and summarizes the
purpose of the software item.

2. Applicable documents

Identifies other documents which form part of
this specification.

3. Requirements

Specifies in the following subsections all physical,
interface, functional, performance, and quality
requirements for the software item.

4. Qualification requirements

Specifies the methods and levels of testing necessary
to satisfy the requirements in section 3.

5. Preparation for delivery

Format of tape, disk, floppy, etc.

Table 3 - 2 **Software Requirements Document.**   (Topical Outline)

3.1 Programming requirements - Identifies
programming languages and compiler/assembler
requirements

3.2 Sizing and Timing requirements - Specifies
memory and processing time allocated to
the software item

3.3 Interface requirements - typically refer to
the interface requirements specification

3.4 Detailed functional and performance requirements

      3.4.X Funtion X - Identifies an individual
         function indicating the states it is used in,
         inputs, outputs, and processing

            3.4.X.1 Inputs - Describes the input information
               required by function X. Identifies sources,
               formats, units of measure, limits, etc.

            3.4.X.2 Processing - Specifies the operations that
               make up function X. Identifies logical
               algorithm, sequencing, timing, parameters,
               restrictions, and allocation of requirements.

            3.4.X.3 Outputs - Describes the output information
               generated by function X. Identifies range of
               values, accuracy, precision, and frequency.

3.5 Adaptation requirements - Identifies data that can be centrally
modified to define the scope of operational functions within
prescribed limits. Identifies environmental data, system parameters,
and system capabilities

3.6 Database requirements - Describes the structure of any database
which is part of the software item

3.7 Quality factors - Specifies correctness, reliability, efficiency, integrity,
usability, maintainability, testability, flexibility, portability, reusability,
and interoperability requirements

3.8 Traceability Requirements - Provides a map from higher level
specifications to these specifications on a requirement by requirement basis

INTERFACE DOCUMENT

Purpose
- Provides an identification and summarizes the purpose of the interfaces to/from the software item.

Applicable documents

Requirements
- Interface block diagram - Identifies the relationship of the software item and other software and/or hardware items.

- Interface identification/documentation table— Identifies interfaces and where they are documented.

- Detailed interface requirements— Specifies for each interface datum source/destination, timing, transfer protocol, format, etc.

Qualification requirements

Preparation for delivery

Table 3 - 3

OPERATIONAL CONCEPT DOCUMENT

1.0 Purpose: To describe the mission of the system and its operational and support functions

2.0 Mission

3.0 General System Characteristics

4.0 System   Functions

5.0 Computer System Functions

6.0 Operator and User Interaction

7.0 General Computer System Characteristics

8.0 Computer Hardware

9.0 Computer Software

10.0 Appendix

Table 3 - 4

SOFTWARE USER'S MANUAL

1.0 Purpose: To provide the user with instructions
             sufficient to execute the software of one or more
             particular product components
2.0 Component Name
3.0 Function
4.0 Initialization
5.0 Execution Options
6.0 User Inputs
7.0 System Inputs
8.0 Execution Sequence
9.0 Termination
10.0 Restart
11.0 Outputs
12.0 Errors
13.0 Diagnostics
14.0 Appendix

Table 3 -5

3-4, and 3-5 identify typical contents of a software requirements specification, an interface specification, an operational concepts document, and a users manual, respectively.

Notice that the adjective "preliminary" is used before every document described above. The creation of these documents doesn't mean the requirements process is over. These documents are "living" documents in that they continually change as more is learned about the software product. Ideally everything is known before moving on, but this isn't a realistic expectation. Changing of the requirements is inevitable, and should be expected and planned for since it means a better software product in the end. One can only fully describe the requirements of a system after it has been retired from use. Thus, requirements reflect an understanding of a desired and achievable reality at a given point in time.

3.1.2.4 MANAGEMENT. The final aspect that needs to be discussed about the process of requirements definition before looking at specific requirement methods is that of managing the process. Management is really the process of making decisions. During concept exploration and requirements analysis, planning, coordination, and decision-review activities are also occurring. Software schedules, milestones, priorities, and budgets of money, people, time and equipment must be planned. So must the tailoring of the life cycle process model to meet the particular software product being developed. For example, if the product under development is well understood, the requirements time might be shortened to allow for more testing later.

Team conflicts, communication among project participants, and the results of decisions must be coordinated and documented. This is very important since the requirement documents, as do all documentation created later, serve as "corporate" memory. They are useful in resolving questions that are asked later like "why was it done that way?" especially if the person who originally made the decision has left the project.

And finally, reviews of the products produced, tradeoff and feasibility analyses, and audits of the project must be conducted. Products other than the requirements, interface specifications, etc. are also produced by management during the requirements phase. These include software development plans, preliminary software test plans, software quality evaluation plans, life cycle support plans, and software standards and procedures plans. These will be examined in later chapters.

Everyday management problems such as hiring, scheduling of meetings, personnel reviews, keeping morale high, etc. must also be taken care of if the project is to run smoothly. However, management's foremost concern is to determine when the requirements process has progressed far enough to begin the next phase in the life cycle. It is management's responsibility to make certain that the requirements are defined to at least the minimum acceptable level.

In the next section, we will examine some methods that can be used to help develop the software requirements.

3.2 Requirement Methods

Defining requirements is not an easy job. It is difficult to get started, since it requires the difficult task of trying to "freeze one's ideas" into a form that can be communicated to and understood by the wide range of participants involved in the project. In our minds these ideas may seem clear and simple enough, yet they mysteriously become ambiguous, contradictory, error fill-ed, and not very understandable to ourselves or to anyone else when written down. These ideas continually go through the cycle of synthesis and analysis until we are satisfied with the results. Thus the fundamental problem of requirements definition is the capturing of our "mind's view" and transpos-ing it to a medium that can be communicated.

Recall that the first step of requirements definition is concept formu-lation. The source of information used by the requirements analyst in this stage is usually the overall system specification which has at least the outline of what the responsibilities of the software are. A number of general methods are used to bound the software aspect of the system, to gain overall insight into the problem, and determine its feasibility. Feasibility analysis should include postulating several paper designs in an effort to find at least one that seems to meet overall system requirements. This means modeling its hypo-thesized performance, as well as the cost and time to build. Simulation models, either by analytic or mathematical models, can be used at this stage. After enough information is gathered so the analyst feels comfortable with the overall software requirements, and feels that they can be met within the time, cost, and technology constraints, the process of requirements definition and creating the baseline information that will drive the remainder of the development process can begin.

There are many specific methods that have been advocated for use in requirements definition, and a software engineering environment ideally should support many types (although the more that are supported, the more difficult it is to automate, as we will discuss later). Table 3-6 lists some of the methods currently advertised as useful in requirements definition. Each takes a slightly different approach to the requirement's problem. Some are very formal, using grammatical-based approaches while some others are more informal, such as structured textual descriptions that are later analyzed. No one method seems capable of allowing all the various viewpoints and media required to fully define requirements, however.

The larger the software project, the greater the need for effective communication. Each new person added to a software team increases the number of communication channels by {N (N-1)/2} [BROOKS75]. In large systems, twenty or more people might be involved in creating the software requirements for the system. This means miscommunication, or non-com-munication is more the rule than the exception. This should be expected and efforts made to overcome this problem.

Additionally, since the primary goals of requirements analysis are to create and document an understanding of the software requirements to all

Mnemonic	Full name of method
ACM/PCM	Active and Passive Component Modelling
DSSAD	Data Structured Systems Analysis and Design
DSSD	Data Structured System Development
EDM	Evolutionary Design Method
GEIS	Gradual Evolution of Information Systems
ISAC	Information Systems Work and Analysis of Changes
JSD	Jackson System Development
PRADOS	Projektabwicklungs- und Dokumentationssystem
SADT	Structured Analysis and Design Technique
SARA	System Architect's Apprentice
SA-SD	Structured Analysis and Structured Design
SDM	System Development Methodology
SEPN	Software Engineering Procedures Notebook
SREM	Software Requirements Engineering Methodology
STRADIS	Structured Analysis, Design, and Implementation of Information System

Table 3 - 6   Some Methods Claimed Useful for Requirements Analysis

participants in the development, not only among the analysts themselves, the communication medium used takes on added importance. Most requirement documents use textual descriptions which are prone to misinterpretation, are difficult to check for consistency, and are imprecise. Before a representation medium is chosen, issues such as, what kinds of questions are trying to be answered, who are going to be using it, how will it be used, and what is the background of the practioners should be addressed [HENINGER80]. Finally, any method used must be able to define, document, and manipulate the tremendous amount of conceptual knowledge (or information) involved, a hallmark of the domain of requirements definition.

Graphical methods seem to handle both the communication and domain problem very well. Logic or mathematical-based techniques are more formal and precise, but are not understood by as wide an audience. Two graphic-based methods that have proven to be very popular in requirements definition are Structured Analysis [DEMARCO78] and Structured Analysis and Design Technique [ROSS77].

3.2.1 Structured Analysis (SA)

Structured Analysis is a general method for analyzing systems to determine their requirements. Two very similar versions exist: one described by Gane and Sarson [GANE79], and the other by DeMarco [DEMARCO78]. We will discuss here the DeMarco version. To help structure our discussion, we will use four of the five characteristics of methods described in Chapter Two, namely: Viewpoint, Domain, Media, and Guidance.[4]

VIEWPOINT. SA views the world from a primarily functional perspective, i.e., data flow and its transformation. However, the system being analyzed is seen from the data's perspective, not from functions performed by the system. Processes are used to transform data. SA also allows a restricted informational view, i.e., relationships between data, by use of a data dictionary.

DOMAIN. In terms of its primary application, SA has most often been used in traditional business data processing where data flow is the dominant factor.

The other domain aspect, the area of the life cycle SA is most useful in, is requirements analysis. Since SA is primarily used in business applications where the processing requirements are well-understood and not of a time-critical nature, the distinction between requirements and specification is not as critical as in other types of software developments. Thus, SA tends to blur and merge the requirements and specification phases, with the output resulting from an application of SA to a problem being called a specification. If performance or timing were critical to a system, SA would only partially aid the understanding of the problem since performance issues are not addressed at all.

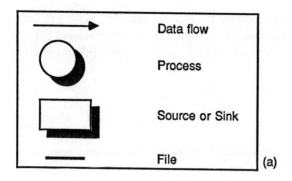

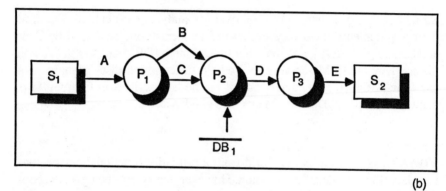

Figure 3 - 3   **SA Components and Diagram**

MEDIA. SA makes extensive use of graphics and text to capture information. Complete use of SA consists of applying five techniques:

- Data Flow Diagrams
- Data Dictionary
- Structured English
- Decision Tables
- Decision Trees

Each of the techniques uses different ways of representing data. For instance, Data Flow Diagrams (DFD) are graphics annotated by text. As illustrated in figure 3-3a, there are four elements that make up the graphic portion of DFD.

— The first is a named vector, or data flow, which shows a data path. The name represents a data packet of known composition and is unique. Data flows only show a set of possible paths, however, and not their initiation.

— Next comes the "bubble" or process, which transforms the data. Incoming data flows are transformed into outgoing data flows.

— A box, or source, or sink, depicts the originator or end receiver of the data. It usually represents something outside the system being analyzed.

— Finally, a straight line portrays a file or database. It represents a temporary repository of data.

Each of the graphics can be combined together to form a data flow diagram as shown in figure 3-3b. Source S1 creates data A that passes over the data path to process P1. Process P1 then transforms this data into two unique data packets B and C. Process P2, requiring access to database DB1, transforms the data into data packet D. D is then transformed by P3 into data packet E which arrives at sink S2.

Each process may be expanded in a heirarchical fashion to show increasing amounts of detail. A process may be used to represent a number of processes and their data flows, as shown in figure 3-4. This is called leveling, where one process is the parent of children processes. Along with this is the concept of balance, where the input and output data flows represented on the parent process are also represented on the child diagram. This is also shown in figure 3-4.

The data packets are kept in a data dictionary where they are further defined. The data dictionary rigorously documents the structure of the data flows (interface flows) and data stores in the DFD. Each data flow is uniquely defined by a textual description such as:

Personnel-Description =　Employee-Last-Name + ID-Number
　　　　　　　　　　　　+ Social-Security-Number + Data-of-Birth
　　　　　　　　　　　　+ Place-Of-Birth + Sex

The "=" symbol represents "comprises," whereas the "+" represents a concatenation of data, showing that a single data flow is composed of the specified subordinate data flows. Other possible symbols that can be used to further define the data are "[ ]" representing "selection" of one of the components,

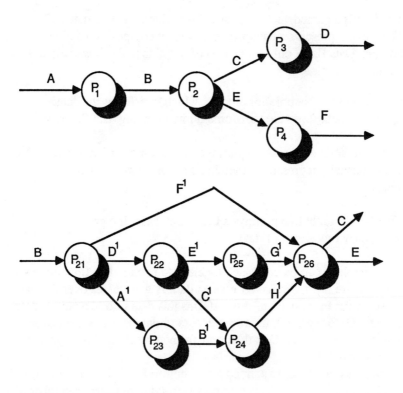

Figure 3 - 4   **Leveling and Balancing**

"{ }" which represents "iteration of" a component, and "( )", which represents an "optional" component

The other elements of SA, Structured English, Decision Tables, and Decision Trees are used to specify algorithmic processing details. Each uses a combination of text and graphics to represent data. For example, Structured English uses indentation, Decision Tables use templates, and Decision Trees use directed graphs to logically group information.

GUIDANCE. SA provides guidance from two sources: via the use of the graphics and their definitions, and through a number of component studies. The graphics describe the implicit rules on how to read the diagrams and how information will be represented. The component studies give explicit directions on how to start, what to do next, how to assess the information modeled, and how to package the result. Great emphasis is placed on analyzing the system from a data viewpoint. Each study depends heavily on the use of DFD and a data dictionary. The end result of the study is a Structured Specification consisting of DFD's, a data dictionary, and transform descriptions documenting the internals of the data flow processes via the use of Structured English, Decision Tables, and/or Decision Trees.

Overall, SA is a very useful method to quickly understand systems and document their requirements. It has the capability to capture the information prevalent in the requirements phase in a fairly disciplined manner. Another technique which is similar to SA is SADT.

3.2.2 Structured Analysis and Design Technique (SADT)

SADT is a method whose purpose is to aid the understanding of the functions of complicated structures. Understanding the functions aids in understanding what the system is suppose to accomplish. Developed by Doug Ross and colleagues at SofTech, Inc. [ROSS77], SADT consists of a graphic notation, a set of modeling principles, a set of review procedures, and a set of (proprietary) interviewing techniques.

SADT's goal is to produce models of the system that can be analyzed and reviewed by all parties in a development. These models are similar to blueprints, each showing a limited amount of detail in an easy-to-grasp unit. SADT analysis proceeds from a top-down fashion, first presenting an overview of the system, then exposing details one step at a time, where each detail is related to higher and lower levels. This is the same concept as the leveling and balancing principles used in SA.

SADT itself does not address the performance of a system, but by allowing some modifications to the basic graphics this aspect can also be addressed. Although not official extensions to SADT, these modifications will be discussed to provide another viewpoint on what is needed to perform adequate requirements definition. Called behavioral diagramming, a more detailed description can be found in [CHARETTE85].

Again, we will analyze SADT using the five characteristics of methods.

VIEWPOINT. SADT views the world, as did SA, from a functional perspective. Data flows through the system and is transformed by a function or activity that acts upon it. Creation of such graphs is called activity diagramming. SADT also has the capacity to construct an activity model's dual, where activities flow through the model and a datum takes the place of a function. This is called data diagramming. This allows for consistency and completeness checks, as well as highlighting all activities that might be affected by a data object. Activity diagramming is the more popular form used.

A behavioral viewpoint, i.e., viewing the sequencing and concurrency of the transformation of data, can also be expressed by modifying the SADT notation. In this case conditions or events are passed through the system which are triggered via activities. This use of SADT is called behavioral diagramming.

DOMAIN. SADT has been used on all types of problems, ranging from business applications to real-time embedded systems to AI systems. The largest sustained use of SADT is in the field of manufacturing technology, where the U.S. Air Force has adopted an SADT-based version (called IDEF-0) to help analyze the aerospace industry.

SADT is primarily used in the requirements phase of a product's life cycle. Its primary purpose is to gain understanding of the requirements, communicate this understanding, and reach concensus among all the parties involved in the product development. It is not rigorous enough by itself to yield a specification, although the techniques have been applied with some success in the design phase. The addition of behavioral modeling adds to the use in the requirements phase by allowing performance information to be modeled as well.

MEDIA. There are many different types of media that SADT uses, depending on what is trying to be accomplished. The primary one, used in developing the requirements, is annotated graphics. We will limit our discussion to activity and behavioral diagramming.

ACTIVITY DIAGRAMMING. An SADT activity diagram consists of boxes, arrows, and diagrams, as illustrated in figure 3-5.

—A box represents a function or activity which transforms data. Each of the four sides of the box has a meaning associated with it. The left side

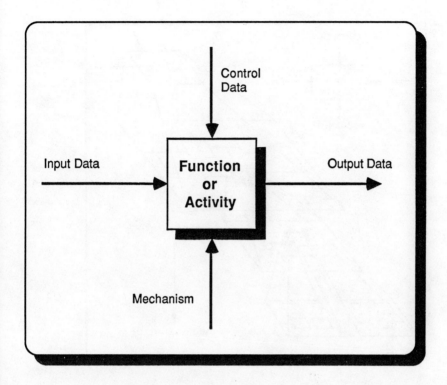

Figure 3 - 5   **SADT Diagram**

is where input data arrives from other activities. The right side is where output data leaves to be used by other activities. The top is where the controls or constraints on the activity are shown. These constrain how an input is modified to produce an output, or control how an activity can be used to produce an output. The bottom is where the mechanisms, i.e., the means, that are used by the function or activity to accomplish its task, are labeled. Mechanisms are not essential to an SADT model. A box is used to bound the problem space and is annotated with a label. The label is a verb or verb phrase which shows the data transformation action.

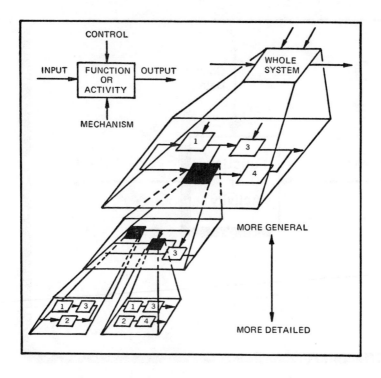

Figure 3-6 **SADT Decomposition**

— An arrow represents data and its flow. An arrow also relates and connects boxes. Each arrow takes on a different or even multiple meanings depending on which side of a box it originates or arrives at. Each arrow is labeled with a noun.

— A diagram consists of a set of boxes, arrows, labels, and any annotations which add information to improve understanding. Usually no more than six and no less than three connected boxes are shown on a diagram to maintain clarity.

A diagram shows all the possible activations of an activity. In other words, whenever certain data become available, boxes become "active." An activation is a way a box can operate using some of its inputs and controls to produce some of its outputs. A specific activation may not use all of its input

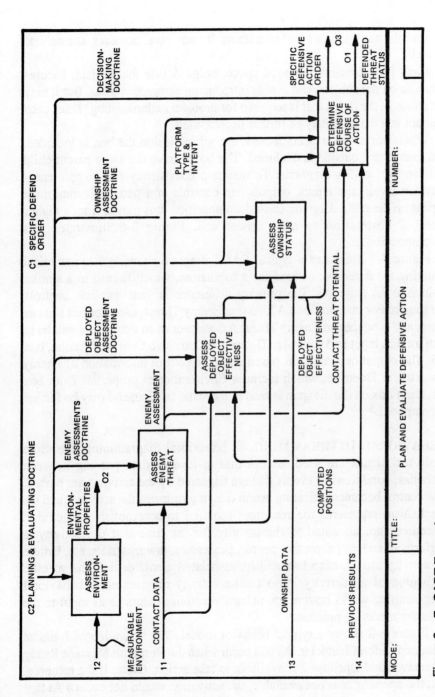

Figure 3 - 7 SADT Example

or controls, nor produce all of its outputs. It must have, however, at least one of each.

Each box, being a bounded space, helps define the subject, focuses attention on the subject, and avoids introducing extraneous ideas. But it may not show all the detail that is required for problem understanding. Thus, each element in a diagram may be further decomposed.

Whenever a box is decomposed, everything inside the box is included, and everything outside is excluded. The boxes have the same parent-child relationships as SA diagrams. To maintain consistency and completeness between levels, the inputs, outputs and controls of a parent diagram must appear on the child diagram. Each decomposition thus moves from a higher level of abstraction to some lower one. Figure 3-6 illustrates this decomposition.

Figure 3-7 illustrates a typical SADT diagram showing a hypothetical planning for defensive actions for a submarine, which is read in a similar fashion to SA diagrams. The primary difference is that explicit controls are shown. For instance, box A2, Assess Enemy Threat, uses Contact Data as input, and produces an Enemy Threat Assessment as an output that will be in turn used as input and control to Determine Defensive Course of Action, box A5. The output occurrence is based upon the control information of Enemy Assessment Doctrine, which includes Environmental properties from box A1. Each box on the diagram is read in the same fashion, and may be further decomposed.[5]

BEHAVIORAL DIAGRAMMING. In behavioral diagramming, the same basic techniques are used, except that instead of data passing between activities, conditions or events that are triggered by the activites are passed. The control becomes a clearing action (i.e., it terminates the activity), and the mechanism represents the resources required to accomplish the activity. Resources are allocated to the activity for the time that the activity is performed, and may represent people, processors, raw materials, etc. Unlike an activity model, each box and its associated arrow depicts the specific activation of an activity. Also unlike activity diagramming, behavioral diagramming works bottom up, using the activity diagrams as input to the behavior modeling process.

Figure 3-8 shows a typical behavior model. The activation of Intialize Communication Channel in B2 will occur when the Response Message Ready is received and Operator 2 is available to take action. (Note: If the resource, i.e., the operator, was not available, the activation would not occur.) At that

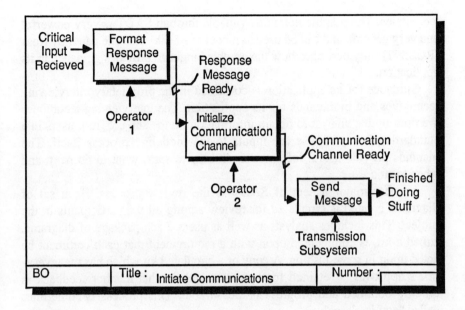

Figure 3 - 8   **Typical Behavior Model**

point, the Communication Channel Ready output is created and sent to B3, Send Message.

There exist over forty features that fully describe the graphic language that can be used to perform activity and behavior diagramming. Not all are necessary, but using the full complement ensures defining the requirements in a rigorous manner. Some aspects of the system that can be characterized are feedback, boundaries, interfaces, dominance, constraints, relevance, necessity, and exclusion. Along with a diagram is packaged a short textual description that may be used to provide additional information about the subject being modeled.

SADT also uses standard templates to draw the diagrams on, and to review and collect comments from participants on the diagrams as they are created.

GUIDANCE. SADT, like SA, provides guidance in its application both through the use of the graphics and by a list of standard application techniques. The graphic notation available through SADT is very powerful and very general, and can be used to model most subjects. The paper by Ross [ROSS77] fully describes how the graphic language provides guidance in its application.

Guidance for its application is contained in the proprietary interviewing techniques and in manuals for its application. The interviewing techniques are used by the analyst to obtain information on the subject from users in a standardized way. These are inputs to the modeling process itself. The manuals provide useful information on how to start, what to do next, and when to stop.

Another major aspect of SADT is the review process. Each set of diagrams created is circulated for review among all the participants in the project. This includes analysts as well as users. Each package of diagrams, called a kit, is commented upon with a requirement that each comment be acted upon in some fashion. A copy of a circulated kit which has met everyone's approval is retained for later retrieval. In this manner feedback is quickly obtained and progress is measurable. This process is sometimes called "ego-less" analysis.

3.2.3 Comparison of Methods

Both SA and SADT are very robust methods for doing requirements analysis. There exist many more similarities than differences between the two. The following is a brief, and subjective, appraisal of the two methods.

DOMAIN. In the domain of application, SADT has been used by a wider audience than SA. SA is used mostly for business applications, while the explicit modeling of controls in SADT allow it to be used in this and other application areas. Both cover basically the same area of the lifecycle.

VIEWPOINT. In expressing a viewpoint, both approach the subject from a functional perspective, although SA emphasizes the viewpoint of the data. SADT emphasizes the viewpoint of data and the functions that transform it.

However, SADT also forces each model of the subject to have its own "viewpoint;" i.e., the diagram may be a model from the perspective of the analyst, the user, the hardware, etc. Each model must be read with this viewpoint in mind. Having a viewpoint indicated allows the reader of the diagram to understand the context in which it was created. A complete model of a subject may have many kits showing different perspectives. This is a weakness of SA.

MEDIA. In the use of media, SADT is more robust and "disciplined" in its use of graphics. It can capture more types of semantic information on a diagram than can SA. SADT uses a graphic language, whereas SA uses graphics only to express a small variety of information. SA makes up for this by adding data dictionaries. SA also allows more of the capture of algorithmic information than SADT via decision tables etc., although behavioral diagrams can do something similar.

GUIDANCE. SA provides more explicit guidance than does SADT. SA provides a step-by-step approach to its use, whereas SADT is much less specific. SADT has a refined review process, where SA is more ad hoc. Both stress the need for user involvement.

SA's relative simplicity makes it easier to describe and use than SADT. SADT's guidance is embedded in the graphics language, and is not as readily understood as SA's. Courses are taught on both methods.

SUMMARY. Overall, both methods are good for requirements analysis. SADT is more powerful, and can capture more semantic information than SA can in its diagrams. It also has a very defined review process, but provides rather weak guidance on its application.

SADT's very power makes it difficult to automate, however. The graphics contain so much information that a change in a diagram may change the meaning of a whole model. But to use it on large projects also mandates it be automated. This has been the Catch-22 which faces all methods like SADT that capture highly semantic information. And that is also why very few have been automated to date.

3.3 Automation

In a software engineering environment, the third aspect that is needed is the automation of the methods, like SA and SADT, that will be used to create the products of requirements definition. Unfortunately, in this phase of the life cycle, there are relatively few methods that exist, and fewer still that are automated. This is one of the primary impediments to creating software engineering environments today: the "top" of the process and its automation are missing.

Automation of a method should be aimed at two goals: increasing its creative aspect by alleviating its clerical aspect, and capturing the reference information that will be used in the later phases of the system development. One of the reasons that methods such as SADT are not widely used is the notion (not totally incorrect) that one spends more time drawing and keeping track of the diagrams than thinking about the problem. One has to remember which diagrams relate to each other, where the inputs and outputs go, etc. And if a change is made to a diagram, the ripple effect causes much more drawing to occur. Even though the method is very exact in describing how things are to be accomplished, the shuffling of paper by an individual and among individuals during reviews tends to be overwhelming, especially in a large project. It is hard to be creative in this atmosphere.

Even if the clerical aspects of the problem are taken care of, there is still the matter of what information is to be kept. The major determinants of this are: first, what are the products (i.e., documentation) that need to be created at this stage, and; second, what methods are going to be used later in the development process. The answer to the first requires a careful understanding of the reasons why a particular product is necessary, what information it should contain, and how it relates to the overall system process. These are very dependent on the life cycle process model being used.

As for an answer to the second question, we would like to be able to reuse as much information as possible, not only for productivity's sake, but also to insure consistency and traceability between life cycle phases. For instance, we want the ability to work on only one set of information, and be able to trace every requirement to a unique specification, or trace any part of a design back to a unique requirement. This is important since any change that is made to a requirement may change everything that follows. The capability to input these changes and quickly investigate their impacts is an important advantage provided by automation. The methods ultimately automated must also be able to use the information created, however. A method like SA which creates much information that is graphical in nature must store it not only in this form but also in one which is usable by a method that is not, such as one that is more textual in nature. How these inconsistent formats, or changes in viewpoint, can be overcome, will be discussed later in Chapter Eight.

These automation issues present software engineering environment builders with a real problem. If the methods selected are not amenable to information integration or automation, should extensions to the methods be made? How will that affect the usability of the methods? Will it detract from their original purpose? If the methods don't provide mechanisms for traceability, the environment designer must build it in. Automation also raises the expectation of what a method should do over its paper-based cousin.

For example, it would be very useful to be able to draw our requirements diagrams using a graphic device that could keep track of the information on the screen, relate inputs on one level to inputs on another, automatically mark inconsistencies that occur, or inform the user of the correct way to use the method. As an example of what is available today for requirements analysis, we will examine one such product now available for the automation of SA diagrams.

TEAMWORK/SA® Cadre Technologies Inc. of Providence, Rhode Island, has developed a powerful workstation-base environment that integrates a number of software methods for use in the front-end of the development life cycle. Called Teamwork®, it has the capability to perform requirements analysis as well as design. The goal is to provide the requirements analysts with the capabilities necessary to increase their productivity by 200 to 300 percent, as well as allow the production of much higher quality systems.

Currently, three methods have been automated and integrated. The first product is called Teamwork/SA, which automates the construction of DeMarco SA diagrams and associated information. We will examine this in more detail in a moment. The second is called Teamwork/RT™, which allows for the addition of real-time modeling information to the SA diagrams. The third is Teamwork/SD™, which supports the structured design concepts of M. Page-Jones [JONES80].

Teamwork/SA supports a sophisticated interactive graphics system that is tailored for the construction of Data Flow Diagrams (DFD) diagrams, process specifications, and data dictionaries. It consists of a syntax-directed editing system, a project library, model configuration management functions, query and browsing functions, cross-referencing, an annotation facility, consistency checkers and a project data activity facility, all completely integrated together. This integration is a necessity if the stated goal of increasing productivity is to be met.

[118]

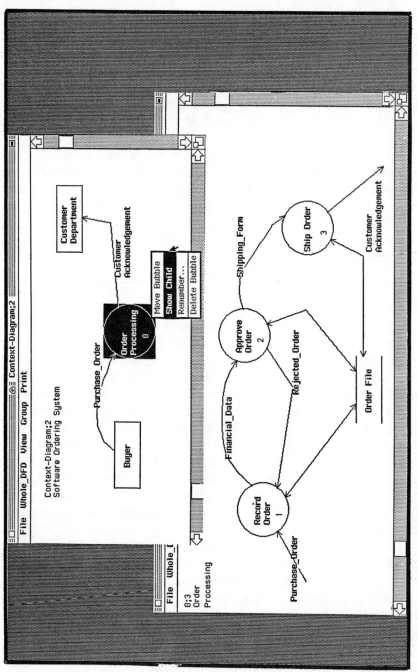

Figure 3 - 9 Data Flow Diagrams

An interesting aspect of the editing system is that it contains individually tailored editors that are used to create the DFD, the process specifications, and the data dictionary. For instance, the DFD editor has embedded in it the established rules for making DFDs and their relationship to other objects in the specification. Along with the consistency checker, this aids in the detection of problems in the specification as it is being created. Figure 3-9 illustrates a typical DFD diagram as it appears on the display.

A multi-windowing capability along with an extensive set of menus eases considerably the clerical aspect of drawing and redrawing diagrams. For example, the user can select from a wide range of graphic entities to easily build the DFD, or apply a function to repartition the DFDs without having to redraw the total diagram. Figures 3-10 a and b illustrate the latter capability.

Another clerical aspect that is taken care of is consistency analysis. When using a paper-based method consistency analysis is often overlooked or too difficult to do because of the volume of information required to be checked. Even if it is possible to perform, doing it by hand is subject to error. The automated consistency checker in Teamwork/SA is very powerful, detecting errors within and between data flow diagrams, data dictionary entries, or process specifications. Like the editing system, the consistency checker knows certain principles about structured system specifications, but at a deeper level. It uses this knowledge when assessing the accuracy of the specification and can be used to balance a system at a number of levels of complexity, including a complete check to the data element level to find undefined data elements. Figure 3-11 shows an example of the consistency checker output.

In the previous section, we mentioned that automation changes the viewpoint of the user of a method by raising his expectations above that which he or she would have if using the method in a non-automated fashion. The user requires a friendly interface, a means of keeping multiple copies of diagrams, reviewing work of associates, etc. Cadre recognized this fact by adding a number of features to Teamwork/SA that aren't directly related to the SA method per se, but are necessary to support the requirements of using SA in an automated fashion. For instance, up to 16 working copies of DFDs, process specifications, and data dictionaries are allowed. The user interface is consistent in all functions as well, reducing the "noise" encountered in performing user functions.

The project library is another example. It serves as the centralized database that includes the data dictionaries, DFDs, process specification, etc. The project library may be located a. a single workstation, in a central library processor, or distributed across an entire network of workstations.

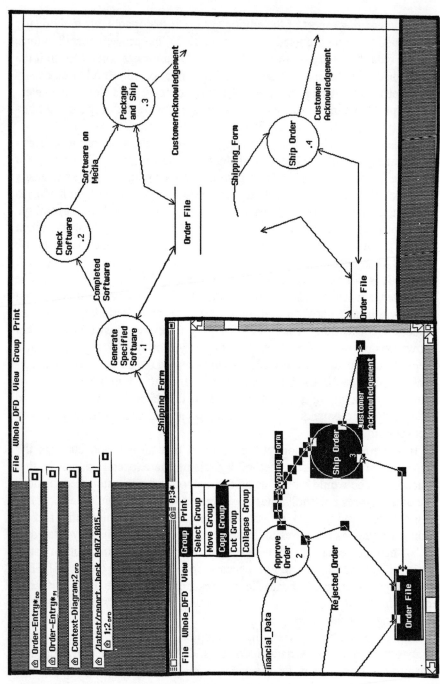

Figure 3 - 10 (a) DFD Creation

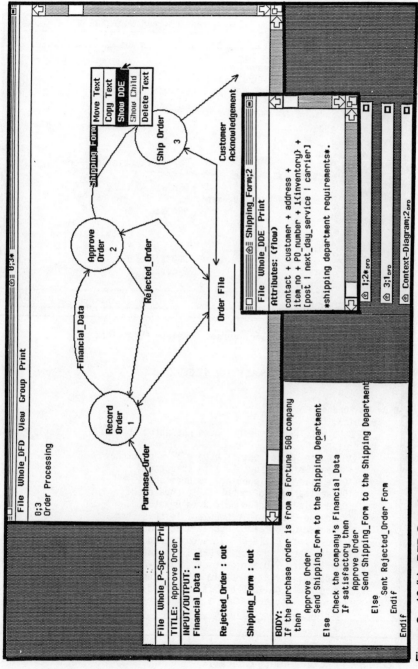

Figure 3 - 10 (b) DFD Creation

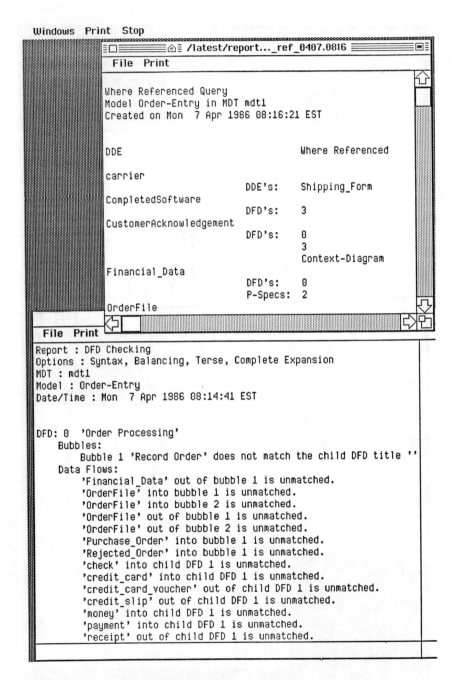

Figure 3 - 11 **Consistency Checker**

team*work*

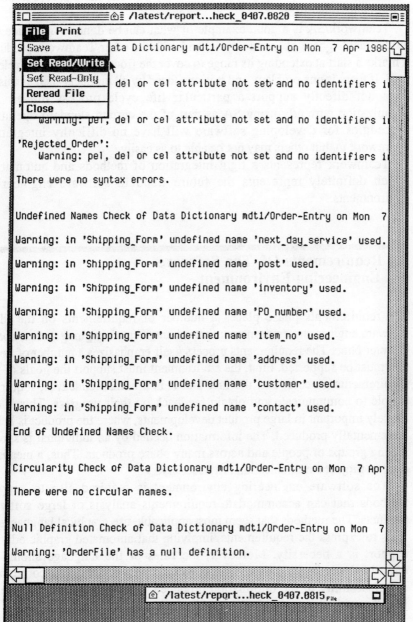

Access is entirely transparent to the user, who can share access to information with other users.

Teamwork/SA is a good example of what can be done to automate the requirements phase of the life cycle, and with the other Teamwork products it marks a start at extending its range to cover the front end of the life cycle as well. If there is one problem, and it is one faced by all products such as this, it does not directly support a particular life cycle process model. An organization currently using SA as part of the current standard operating procedures for developing software will have no difficulty integrating Teamwork in, but others may not be able to as easily.

Teamwork represents a tight integration of methods and automation which definitely represents the future trend in software engineering environments.

3.4 Requirements Of The Software Engineering Environment

The requirements phase places a number of requirements on the ideal software engineering environment that we are eventually going to describe in Chapter Nine. The requirements process itself emphasizes a number of items that must be supported. First, the environment must support the goals of the requirements process; i.e., the fact that it is a human endeavor, requiring people to communicate and obtain feedback on their progress. This is extremely important in large product developments, where the product is being incrementally produced. The information needed by an individual is spread among groups of people and across many phase products. Thus, a means to support project communication is a necessity.

The software engineering environment is required also to support methods that can accommodate requirements analysis of large software products. The methods that seem most applicable use graphical languages or rules to express the requirements, implying that automated graphic editting support is a necessity. Moreover, the rules of the language should be embedded within the graphic editors to help with consistency, correctness and traceability of the information produced. The addition of guidance on how the methods are used is also a requirement.

The software engineering environment also requires a means to keep track of the incremental requirements being created, and assure that based information keeps its integrity. This implies some type of configuration management must be provided, with errors noted and tracked within the baselined products.

Finally, since document production is expensive and not very timely, a means to easily obtain products produced in the required formats is required. They also should be able to reflect the latest approved changes in the baselined product, as well as in the currently worked version.

These are some of the major requirements the requirements phase of an ideal software engineering environment must satisfy. As we examine each following phase, we will see they require in general the same type of support as needed in the requirements phase.

3.5 Summary

During the requirements phase we are concerned primarily with trying to understand the requirements laid on the software by the system designers and the eventual users of the software product. The software requirements obligate or bind the software to meet certain system requirements. We also document our understanding in a variety of requirement documents that represent an informal contract among all parties as to what the software is generally supposed to do, not how it is supposed to do it.

The requirements developed during this phase of the life cycle are a critical element in determining the future success of the remainder of the software development. If the requirements identified in this phase are poor, incomplete, or inconsistent, it is also probable that the specifications and design that follow will be the same. Each following phase depends on reusing what is determined in the one before it. No matter how well a software engineering environment can provide traceability, analyze inputs, do consistency checks, etc., it can't perform these functions on something that is not there to begin with.

Therefore, it is important that the software engineering environment provides a wide range of capabilities to support the performance of requirements analysis. These include the ability of an environment use to:

- Assess the validity of the system requirements on software,

- Formulate, conceptualize and communicate the software requirements to all parties,

- Express the requirements in an unambiguous manner,

- Capture the requirements for automated storage, update and reuse by textual and graphic means in this phase and latter phases of the product life cycle,

- Evaluate the requirements for internal completeness and consistency and,

- Evaluate the feasibility of the requirements in terms of performance, resource utilization and cost.

The next phase we will investigate is the specification phase. Here is where we will bind the software requirements to the eventual software implementation.

FOOTNOTES:

1. Don't be confused by the multiple meanings of the term "system." It is common to use "system" to mean both the life cycle of the total system — i.e., a system consisting of both hardware and software — or just the hardware development, separate from the software development.

2. The airframe did later become the basis for the F-111 and its variants. For a fascinating story of how not to create requirements, read *Illusions of Choice,* by Robert F. Coulan [COULAN77].

3. Most of the elements listed in table 1-5 are non-functional requirements.

4. By definition, each method uses all the principles.

5. Activity and behavior diagrams have a notational scheme to help keep track of the decompositions and to identify what type of diagram it is. A capital "A" indicates it is an activity diagram, a "B" a behavioral diagram. The number after the letter indicates the box on the diagram, level and decomposition where it can be found.

4. SPECIFICATION

"Don't specify today what you can specify tomorrow, or better yet,
the day after tomorrow."

D. T. Ross[1]

4.0 Introduction

Specification forms the second aspect of our software engineering
environment as shown in figure 4-1. In some ways it can be considered the
most important phase of our software life cycle model. It is here that we must
begin to explicitly define and describe the tasks of the software itself. As with
requirements, if these are not described correctly, the cost of fixing them
later in the development is extremely high. But before we go on, let's try to
clear up some of the confusion with the term "specification phase" because it
is often confused with either the requirements or design phases [HASSE82,
MEYER85]. There are a number of reasons why this happens.

First, one often sees the term "requirements specification," which may or
may not be the same thing as a software specification, depending on the
context in which it is used. Some life cycle models don't describe an
independent requirements and specification phase, instead intermingling the
two. We believe that this is unfortunate because requirements and specifications serve complementary but different functions. The requirements
phase is meant to achieve consensus among all the participating groups as to
what responsibilities are given to the software aspect of the entire system.
The requirements bind or guarantee that the eventual software product will
meet certain **system** requirements. Agreement on these is necessary to
satisfy the customers' needs, and communication of these needs to the
developers is of paramount importance.

[127]

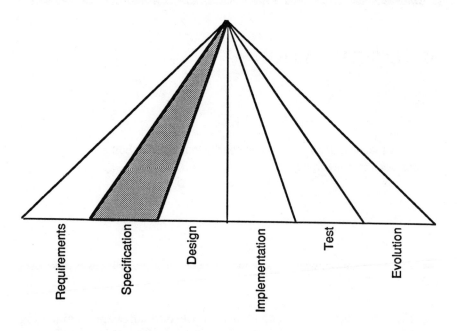

Requirements   Specification   Design   Implementation   Test   Evolution

Figure 4 - 1   **Model of a Typical
Software Engineering Environment**

Specification represents a shift in focus in that it binds the software requirements to a particular implementation. In other words, the products eventually produced must satisfy the **software** requirements. By making this step explicit, it can't be overlooked, as often happens. We will use the term software specification (instead of the awful-sounding, but more correct term "specification specification") to indicate the precise, concise, and unambiguous descriptions of the software tasks to be accomplished as outputs of this phase. How this can be successfully accomplished is the major focus of this chapter.

Specifications are often confused with the outputs of the design phase as well. The confusion lies in the use of the term "description of the software tasks." These descriptions are of what must be done, not how they are to be implemented. This is the key distinction. Designs, as we will see in the next chapter, describe the form of a particular implementation, while specifications are the inputs to this process, describing only the external behavior of the software. A design, then, describes the means by which this external behavior can actually be produced.

A good way to think of the difference between requirements and specification is that the requirements phase is the time to develop one's thoughts, and try to communicate them to others. It is the idea formulation and concept argumentation stage. Specification is the time to clarify those thoughts into crisp and concise descriptions, because these will be the items that will be referred to later in the project for answers when questions arise. The specifications are our ultimate reference documents and need to provide exact guidance on how to proceed.

In this chapter, we will once again investigate the process, methods, and automation that are the necessary foundation for supporting this phase in a software engineering environment.

4.1 The Specification Process

Specification is the process of describing what the software component of a system will do without describing the means by which it will be accomplished. The focus is primarily on the software's intended behavior as seen from an external viewpoint. The inputs to the specification process are the requirements documents and any associated data which were produced and baselined in the previous phase, as shown in figure 4-2. Remember though, these documents were only preliminary in nature. They form the best understanding of what the software system as a whole must do to perform the job the system developers have laid out for it *at this time*. Since it is rare to have omniscient users, sponsors, or developers, it is likely that something has been overlooked or is incorrect. Moreover, these documents are informal, in that they are created and written with the primary goals being to define, communicate, and reach agreement among the users, sponsors, and developers of the system as to what role software will play in the overall system. Thus the information contained in them may still be open to interpretation. An important aspect of the specification process is to review these requirements from the viewpoint of making them verifiable.

As was hinted at in the introduction, many software systems are built without specifications being formally written. The requirements documents are usually viewed as being good enough from which to specify the system design. Unfortunately, even good requirement "specifications" have a number of problems, especially as the size of the project undertaken grows.

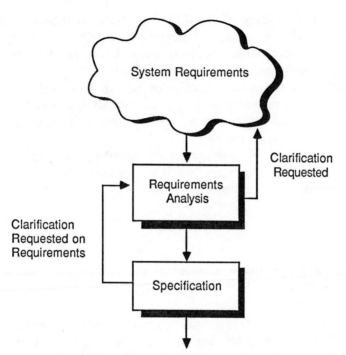

Final Requirement and Specification Phase Products

Figure 4 - 2   **General Specification Phase Model**

Typically requirements documents leave out information, such as performance information, the interfaces between the system and the software, the
types of data that go across those interfaces, and the general functions that
produce them. Usually these items are left until the design stage where a
specific design de facto defines them . An outcome of this approach is that it
is difficult to reuse parts of a software system in another one, or to accommodate change later if there is a mistake found, or if the system expands.
Since large systems tend to be built in an incremental manner, neglecting to
create specifications usually leads to very costly rewrites of large amounts of
software.

Another problem is in the way typical requirement specifications are
captured. Most are captured in textual form, i.e., natural language, which
makes it difficult to be precise. English is wonderfully useful to communicate
in, but is known for its susceptibility to misinterpretation. Just look at the

lawyers, all 750,000 of them in the United States alone, who exist to help us interpret what our "carefully prescribed" laws mean. Using graphical techniques helps, but even they have problems as they also depend heavily on natural language to describe what all the little circles, squares, lines, and arrows mean. One picture may be worth a thousand words, but the trick is to choose the picture that reflects the correct one thousand.

Third, not only do we have problems with what information is or is not captured and how it is described, but also with the sheer volume of it. In a large project, the textual description might run into the tens of thousands of pages. As way of illustration, let's take that system of ultimate high-tech, the tank. The technical documentation for the M-60 tank, a 1970s vintage vehicle, was 15,000 pages. Its 1980s successor, the M-1, has over 40,000 pages [AUGUSTINE83]. Granted, these figures may not be directly relatable to a software system,[2] but anyone who can keep in their head more than 50 pages of textual description of requirements coming from six different volumes, and can assure their consistency and correctness, is going to be very valuable to his or her company indeed.

There is one flaw in the above argument, though, namely that requirements or specifications are often not done at all. This is true even in large system developments where managers should know better. The number of horror stories about writing the requirement specifications after the fact are now folklore, and it is still common to hear those words, "I'm too busy coding to write down the requirements." The explicit specification step is meant to help fight this attitude, ensure that the requirements are correct, and keep the project manager from losing control of the development process.

4.1.1 General Goals of Specification

During the creation of software specifications we wish to keep two things in mind. First, specifications are necessary to completely describe the software requirements. During the requirements phase, preliminary documents were created. The system requirements on the software were explored, and defined. These were continuously reviewed by all the participants to make sure they were understood, and the major implications on cost, schedule, etc. agreed upon. However, they were developed to communicate only the higher levels of detail, and thus were incomplete in the sense that they were not extremely useful in developing a design of the system.

Towards this end, creating specifications makes it possible to learn and understand much more about the requirements placed on the software. They force the developers to ask many more detailed questions about how the system will work. Items that are overlooked or are incorrect, especially concerning the performance required of the software, tend to be found since these must be made explicit in the specification.

Second, the specifications created are used to describe the functions of the software system in a manner that can be used effectively in the design phase that follows. Because design is concerned with the management of scarce resources [YEH84], it is necessary that all the functions, interfaces, data, and performance required be identified as a minimum. This will allow trade-offs of the plurality of goals to be made with some assurance of correctness. If all the data is not present, then the design effort will likely fail. This also implies being able to properly communicate the specifications to the software designers in a form that is useful to them.

SPECIFICATION PROPERTIES. To be truly useful, the specifications must possess a number of properties [FAIRLEY84]. While these attributes were desirable at requirements time, they have added significance for specifications. In fact some believe that if these qualities are not present then the specifier has committed a terrible "sin" [MEYERS85]. Therefore, specifications *must* , as a minimum, be:

- Correct & Complete
- Consistent
- Unambiguous
- Verifiable
- Traceable
- Minimal
- Modifiable

Specifications are necessary to prescribe the binding or contractual agreements between the software requirements and the final implementation. This means they are going to be used as a standard for gauging the correctness of the implementation, and constitute the primary input to the design phase. Thus, the requirements, and the resulting software specifications, must be as *complete* and *correct* as possible at the completion of the specification phase.

The specifications also need to be *consistent*. Contradictory statements about what the software is supposed to do lead to confusion if not worse. If one group is working with a part of a specification that says one thing, and another uses the same specification but it says something different elsewhere, an incorrect implementation is guaranteed.

The specifications need to be *unambiguous*. Ambiguity makes it possible to interpret an item in at least two different ways. This not only makes it hard to build a correct product, it makes it difficult to verify the specifications.

Verification means that the specification must satisfy the system requirements, and that the resultant software product satisfies the specification. This implies that the specifications must be testable in some fashion. Not being able to realistically verify a specification means the specifier is guilty of the sin of wishful thinking.

Having specifications that are *traceable* aids in the verification process. Each requirement has a path defined to the specification, and vice versa. The paths to the designs must also be capable of being supported later.

The specification must also be *minimal*. Only the information that is needed to describe what is required to be done should be present. This implies that the specifier must not add in noise or overspecify [MEYER85]. Noise is when something is added that does not carry any information relevant to the problem. It may also be something that is redundant. Overspecification means adding information that is not a feature of the problem, but a feature of the solution.

Finally, the specification must be *modifiable*. Changes are going to occur either during the software product development, or later when it is enhanced. By separating and grouping together those things that change, the cost and impact of modification is reduced. This also helps reduce the problems of incremental development described in Chapter Three.

4.1.2 General Specification Process Description

If the project is going smoothly (no budget cuts, no change of venue, etc.) the specification phase should be a natural continuation of the requirements phase. Its purpose is to formalize the understanding of the requirements to a greater level of detail than was possible in the requirements phase. Much of the specification information was developed during the creation of requirements documents, of course. However, not all of it exists at the same level of granularity nor was it developed for the same purpose. For example, the behavior models in Chapter Three do define performance information. However, such information is not necessarily intended to be used to specify the timing the software must meet. Instead, it usually is used for the purpose of gaining a better understanding of the software and its limitations, and typically describes a range of values. One would want to make sure that the performance information placed into the specification is exactly what is desired, can be lived with, and can be tested for.

The process of specification also has another implied purpose that is important in large system development. It is to buy time for the developers. During the specification phase, the developers have one last chance to go over those requirements that everyone (especially the users and sponsor) has agreed to, and see if they should be changed. This protection mechanism, or self-preservation response, should not be underrated. Often, even after the requirements have been set down and everything looks under control, when the focus shifts to next level of detail, things don't seem as achievable as before. It is often like writing a paper where the first level outline looks wonderful, but as one develops it further there is no information to support some of the topic sentences.

THE FINAL QUESTIONS. The specification phase is also the time to ask all those final questions [VOSBURY84]. Is all the analysis that can be done, done? Is all the information that is required to implement the software defined? Is all input and output data specified? What are the validity criteria for the data? What should be done with bad data? What may change in the future? Can the correctness of the implementation be measured? What if....?

The question of testability is an important one for the specification phase. Specifications describe the "shalls" of the system. A requirement for a weapon system might read like the following: "The software subsystem shall provide the hostile target data over the datalink every ten milliseconds." This is something that can be tested. Either it comes every ten milliseconds or it doesn't. It doesn't say anything about quality of the data, however, and one expects that this piece of information would be specified someplace else. Something else that should be specified, but usually isn't, is what happens if the data doesn't appear every ten milliseconds. The exceptional events or converse conditions should also form part of a complete specification.

Another question that needs a definite answer is: Do I know exactly what I'm building? If this question can't be answered with a resounding Yes!, then the project better stop and start over. It will be too late, too costly, and too

---

SPECIFICATION DOCUMENT OUTLINE

1.0 Purpose: To describe the functional elements and the perfor-
    mance requirements of a particular computer product component

2.0 External Interfaces

3.0 Data Flow

4.0 Functions

5.0 Performance Constraints

6.0 Exceptions

7.0 Expected Changes

8.0 Testing Criteria

9.0 Appendix

Table 4 - 1

painful to go back and correct any errors later in the software development. As the old saying goes, you can pay me now, or pay me later. The cost is much cheaper now. We wouldn't harp on this theme so much if it weren't so important, and if managers would quit ignoring it.

The outputs of the specification phase are the finalized requirements document, the operational concepts document, the interface document, an updated users guide and the software specification. The format and content of the specification are shown in table 4-1. The primary differences between the requirements document and the software specification is that the former need not have testable items, nor precise performance information, described. The reason is that the software specification will be used to test and measure how well the software product meets the system requirements obligated on the software as reflected by the requirements document.

One can argue whether the specification really represents anything different from the requirements document, and in many ways they should, at the end of this phase, be *almost* identical. Both describe the "what" of the system, and both avoid the "how." But again, the requirements are meant to convey information to one set of participants, and the specification to another. As we will see in the next section on methods, the medium used again takes on added importance in accomplishing this goal.

All the normal management functions that occurred in the requirements phase also occur in this phase. The software development schedule is updated to see how well the schedule is being kept. The specification will be a primary aid to management to measure development progress as well as the success of the product. A check of which interfaces and functions have been designed at any particular moment gives a good indication to management on how the product is developing.

4.2 Specification Methods

When developing specifications, we are trying to develop a more thorough understanding of the software product we are going to be implementing from the requirements data we created in the previous phase. We want these specifications to be more precise and concise than were the requirements, and we want to really nail down the performance and accuracy required of the software. We also want the resulting specification to possess all the properties of being unambiguous, consistent, correct, etc., or in other words, to be without sin. This insures that when we start our design, we have all the necessary information at hand and in a form that makes it easy to use. And, finally, we don't want the specifications to imply any particular design. We want the maximum freedom to design in whatever manner is suitable.

SPECIFICATION METHOD PROPERTIES. If we take all the desires above, we can formulate a few properties [RAMAMOORTHY84] any of the methods used during the specification process should possess:

(1) A method should aid the understanding of the informal requirements that were previously developed in the requirements phase.

(2) It should simplify the process of developing formal specifications.

(3) It should permit the specification to be analyzed for consistency, correctness, etc.

(4) A method should facilitate the validation that the specifications (and implicitly the requirements) meet the users' needs.

(5) The method must not interfere in the decision domain of the design process.

The degree of success in meeting these properties may depend largely on other factors such as how well some of these functions can be automated, especially for property (3), which will be discussed more in the next section. However, most of the others should be inherent in the methods themselves.

For instance, almost any specification technique will help in understanding the requirements. The important point is that they use a different viewpoint than those used in the requirements phase in which to attack the problem. By varying the perspective, things that were hidden or not thought of become visible. If text was used in describing the requirements, then graphics are appropriate in specification, and vice versa. The capability to rotate the problem space is very important. A way of doing this is by using projection [YEH84], which enables the viewing of the system from multiple perspectives.

Simplifying the process of developing specifications is a more difficult property to meet, especially when coupled with the necessity to be precise, consistent, complete, etc. Most methods use the principle of formalism [DAVIS82]. Formalism comes in many flavors. In some methods, it means a strict mathematical approach, while in others a less rigorous approach consisting of tables and templates with rules specifying their organization, allowable operations, symbology and extensions are used. Other methods use formal languages, similar to programming languages, to express the specifications. Either way, formalism allows for detailed, precise and concise specifications to be developed that can be reviewed for completeness, consistency and correctness. This leads to easier automation of the specification for consistency and completeness, but not for correctness.

There are objections, though, to the use of formalism. Some argue that using formal techniques is difficult and interferes with the process of developing specifications. The arguments are developers don't have the necessary background, the end-users can't read them anyway, and they are an expense to use in time and money. Meyer makes a good case that formalism for the most part is no harder than basic calculus and set theory, and this level of understanding should be mandatory for those specifying systems [MEYER85]. Furthermore, although there is a need for the users to review and discuss the specifications, there also exists a need for the designers to have something they can use as well. Finally, formalism encourages the reuse of specifications, which is a way to increase productivity.

Validation of the requirements is an important aspect of the specification process and should be supported by the method used. Formalism helps, especially in determining correctness. Logical reasoning is still the primary technique to assure correctness, validation still being very much a human enter-prise. However, being able to execute the specification greatly aids validation of the requirements. Execution of a model is an excellent means to eliminate ambiguity and vagueness.

A SPECIFIER'S DILEMMA. The last property of not interfering with the design process is more difficult to accomplish. In requirements analysis, and in developing the specification, trial designs probably have been created to verify that a feasible software product that meets the performance criteria can be created. It becomes very difficult to avoid describing these resultant high-level designs in either the requirements or specification documents. Responsibility for avoiding this problem rests primarily with the specifier, but a particular specification method can either discourage or encourage it to happen.

For example, specifications are intended to describe the externally visible behavior of the software system without describing how it is accomplished. However, many methods use functional decomposition as the primary principle to specifying this behavior [HEITMEYER82]. In this case, as Heitmeyer explains it, a system is viewed as some function that generates output from input. This function is then reduced into subordinate functions whose composition performs the total system function. The resulting specification reflects the system via these compositions.

A problem is that this approach may exclude many acceptable implementations. For example, neither the function nor the functional decomposition documented may be unique. If the system has input-output relations that are not functions (i.e., more than one acceptable response to an input), any particular decomposition will exclude some acceptable responses. Furthermore, the decomposition is only one of many that can represent the required functions. Acceptable decompositions can differ with respect to level of decomposition, the order of invocation for subfunctions, and even the basic units of decomposition.[3]

These differences in decomposition become important because they imply a modularization of the way the software must perform its tasks; i.e., a decomposition may prematurely prejudice a designer. The way that the software is eventually decomposed into modules has serious ramifications. For instance, one decomposition can make certain parts of it easier to change as well as ease the reuse product components. The converse is also true. It has been shown, for instance, that using functional decomposition to achieve modularization is not the best method in all cases [PARNAS72].

SOLUTIONS. One approach to the specification is to acknowledge that using functional decomposition has these possible problems, and that one ought to be vigilant and avoid the consequences. This is an acceptable response, except it places the onus on the designer, not the specifier. The designer then must be aware of the fact that the decomposition doesn't imply a design, placing the burden on him or her to decide how far to stray from the specification. On the other hand, if the decomposition is taken as an acceptable cut at a design, it may discourage the designer from looking for designs that might be much better to implement.

Adherence to some of the basic software engineering principles can help overcome the above specifier's dilemma, and should be strongly supported in any method used to create the specifications. Three of the more important principles are the use of abstraction, the separation of concerns, and information hiding.

An abstraction represents some aspects of a system, but not all of them [PARNAS77]. For example, a road map is an abstraction of a particular road network showing directions, relative lengths, and possibly speed limits, but probably not whether the roads are banked or plowed in winter. By using abstraction, it is easier to investigate and study a system because irrelevent details are left out. Abstract interfaces are another example. An abstract interface represents more than one specific interface. Instead, it contains all the common assumptions of the interfaces it represents. It omits the details that would distinguish one specific interface from another. Remember, though, an appropriate abstraction is necessary if relevant details aren't going to be omitted.[4]

Another way to solve the dilemma is to use the separation of concerns [HESTER81]. Separation of concerns is the division of information about a system into clearly distinct and relatively independent parts. Separation of concerns has as its primary goal the minimization of the impact of change. For example, functionality is separated from behavior, representation is separated from logical meaning, input-output mapping is separated from functionality, and expected changes in the product from those things that aren't going to change. The latter is especially useful in systems undergoing incremental development. A byproduct of using this approach is that one always knows where to find an answer to a particular question.

Information hiding captures information likely to change into defined groupings or modules [HESTER81]. This grouping limits the amount of software that must be modified when a change is introduced. Notice information hiding and the separation of concerns describe the same principle, only from different perspectives.

By using abstraction, separation of concerns, and hiding, the designer is not constrained in any way. He is free to create whatever design can meet the specifications. For example, say we are creating a software product that we know will be evolving a great amount over time. We can use a modularity strategy based on the changes expected to occur as a guide to decomposing the requirements and specifications. The modules created will be separated into those that will likely change and those which will not, thus minimizing the effects of changes that do occur.

Furthermore, the decomposition is such that it does not imply any particular design either. This encourages the designer to explore many possible implementations, and the information contained in the trial designs is captured, so these are available, but not the designs themselves. Of course it would be useful if the specification information captured by such a method gave the developer hints in how to obtain feasible designs in that stage of the life cycle. Total freedom has its drawbacks, too.

4.2.1 The Software Cost Reduction (SCR) Project Specification Method

The Software Cost Reduction (SCR) Project is an experiment in applying a coordinated set of software engineering principles and techniques to the (re)development of a complex, memory-constrained, real-time embedded software product. The effort was started in 1978 and is being conducted at the U. S. Naval Research Laboratory (NRL), Washington, D.C., and the U.S. Naval Weapons Center (NWC) in China Lake, California. It was started in response to the recognition that many promising software engineering techniques were not being applied to any "real" problems. The project, which is still continuing, is an attempt to find out how well software engineering practices work, and whether, indeed, the assumption that they save money is true. So far, the results are positive.

One major aspect of the SCR project was to foster the improvement of the documentation which is required to be produced during a software development, with goals of lowering its cost and facilitating its automation. An outcome of this was a specification technique, which we will call the Software Cost Reduction Specification (SCRS) method.[5] The use of the method in one case claimed a 5,000 percent reduction in the amount of documentation necessary to specify a change to a system [REDWINE84].

The following is a description of the SCRS method using the aspects comprising a method, based upon the papers and documents by [HENINGER80, 81] and [HESTER81].

VIEWPOINT. The SCRS method is very robust in that it uses all three viewpoints to document a specification. It uses the functional view to trace how data flows throughout a system and what functions cause it to be transformed. It also uses the behavioral view to explicitly describe the sequencing of actions, and which events trigger the actions. Performance and accuracy information are explicitly described. Finally, it makes the relationships between data very explicit, so the influences that acted upon an individual data item can be traced.

DOMAIN. The SCRS method is primarily aimed at supporting real-time embedded systems for military applications. However, it also has been used in commercial applications as well.

The SCRS method is aimed at the specification phase of the life cycle (although see note 5). Some practitioners claim it can be used at the requirements phase, but it does not seem well suited for this domain, even if the document produced with it is called a requirements specification. There still is a need for requirements information, and work has been done on integrating requirement methods with the SCRS method [CHARETTE85].

MEDIA. The SCRS method uses a standard textual notation, templates and tables to capture information, augmented by minimal amounts of English prose to create the specification document. Much effort went into defining the document and its structure, and the document played an important role in the definition of the specification method itself. The focus of the document is

0.	Introduction
1.	Distinguishing characteristics of the computer environment
2.	Input and output data items
3.	Modes of operation
4.	Time - independent description of functions
5.	Timing requirements
6.	Accuracy constraints on functions
7.	Undesired event responses
8.	Required subsets
9.	Expected types of changes
10.	Glossary of abbreviations, acronyms, technical terms, indices, dictionary
11.	Sources of further information
Optional	Communication Protocols - specifies external protocol requirements

Table 4 - 2   **SCRS Specification Document Content**

twofold: to avoid redundancy by being as brief, precise, and concise as possible, and to force the answering of questions that should be asked.

The format of the document is shown in table 4-2. Notice the use of the separation of concerns to group similar information together, and the use of information hiding to capture information that is likely to change (e.g., required subsets, or expected types of changes). Notice, too, that the different types of viewpoint are expressed by its structure.

The standard notation is at a level of formalism that is a compromise between a rigid, non-intuitive mathematical or programming languages and possibly ambiguous English text. For example, all input items are surround-

Naming Conventions

/INPUT/	A system level input (typically hardware)
//OUTPUT//	A system level hardware output
/(OUTPUT)/	A shared display device output
$VALUE$	A mnemonic name for a non-numeric value
!TERM!	A complex or often used expression or term that is fully defined in a dictionary (text marco dictionary)
+DATA TYPE+	A data type
MODE	An operational mode or state of the system

Operators

<, ≤, >, ≥, =	Relational operators
ABS, MAX, MIN, SIGN	Arithmetic functions
AND, OR, NOT	Logical operator
+, -, *, *, /, etc.	Normal arithmetic operators

Table 4 - 3   **SCRS Notation Description**

ed by a single back-slash, outputs by double back-slashes. However, it is not all that intuitive a choice of symbology. Some of the notation used is shown in table 4-3. Notice this notation, once understood, allows for easy, effective review of the information, forces one to be precise, and is suitable for machine scanning.

There are a number of standard templates and tables in which to capture information. These include input and output data item templates, demand and periodic function templates, mode condition tables, and mode transition tables. A few are examined here.

Before we describe a template, it is useful to understand some of the reasons why it was created in a particular way. In the case of data item descriptions, the templates reflect two aspects of the principle of the separation of concerns. At a high level, all input/output processing or mapping is separated

Input Data Item:	Mode Rotary Switch
Acronym:	/MODEROT/
Hardware:	TC-2 Panel
Description:	/MEDEROT/ indicates the setting of the mode rotary switch, a six position rotary switch on the TC-2 panel. Switch nomenclature : PRES, POS, DEST, MARK, RNG/BRG, D-BHT, ALT-MSLP.
Data Type:	+ENUMERATION+
Characteristics Of Values:	

Value Encoding:		
	$None$	(000000),
	$PRESPOS$	(100000),
	$DEST$	(010000),
	$MARK$	(001000),
	RNG/BRG	(000100),
	$DBHT$	(000010),
	$ALTMSLP$	(000001)

Instruction Sequence:	READ 196 (CHANNEL 6)
Data Representation:	TC - 2 Panel input word 3 bit 0-5
Timing Characteristics:	/MODEROT/ = $None$ indicates that the switch is in transition between two positions.
Comments:	The Mode Rotary Switch has growth capability to eight positions.

Table 4 - 4 **Typical SCRS Input Data Item Template**

from the use of these data items. Within each description the essential characteristics — those elements that are unlikely to change even if a hardware component is changed — are distinguished from the arbitrary details, such as a bit mapping or value resolution.

An output is never set, modified, etc., by more than one function. No such relationship exists for inputs. They are treated as resources and any function can use any or all available resources.

There are a number of questions a data item template is meant to answer, such as "what are the acceptable range of values?" "is there a way to tell if the value is valid or not?" etc. Symbolic names are used for data types, data items and values. All data items must be of a defined data type, and are defined in a separate table. All acronyms are used in a consistent manner throughout the document, and descriptions of the more complex ones are contained in text macros which are kept in a dictionary. The dictionary serves to provide further information on the macro and what it means. The description is usually in common English prose.

An example of an input data item template is shown in table 4-4, while an output data item template is shown in table 4-5. Notice in the input data item template how essential and detailed information is separated.

Along with templates are tables. Tables are used to show decisions, events or actions that will occur.[6] One such table is a mode table. A mode is a view of the system from an operational, or user, perspective. It maps closely to the SADT idea of viewpoint. It is used to increase the understanding of the system being specified by creating abstractions of the common elements that need to be shared within the system. Table 4-6 shows a mode condition table. For each mode on the left, the values that will be present for the various inputs and text macros that can cause mode changes are shown on the right.

As was stated earlier, there are numerous other templates and tables that can be used for gathering and exposition of information.

GUIDANCE. The SCRS method provides a tremendous amount of guidance in its use. Not only does each template and table provide its own set of questions to be answered, but the relationships among the information gathered is made very explicit. Figure 4-3 shows how a typical specification document is packaged. Notice that for each function described there also must exist a data item description, a timing description, a list of undesired events, and a mode condition table. It is very easy to see if something is missing, thus making completeness checks easier to perform. The specification also provides a reader's guide and tutorial in the introduction.

The method, in providing guidance, asks what one might consider embarrassing questions that must be answered. It is obvious if a table or template is not filled in, someone will have to justify that fact. But it also does not inhibit one from moving on either, because unanswerable questions can also be grouped together for later resolution. When used in conjunction with the outputs of a requirements method such as SA or SADT, the two together provide thorough coverage of the first two life cycle phases.

Output Data Item :	Steering Error
Acronym :	//STERROR//
Hardware :	Attitude Direction Indicator
Description :	//STERROR// controls the position of the vertical needle on the ADI. A positive vale moves the pointer to the right when looking at the ADI. A value of zero centers the needle.
Data Type:	+ANGULAR MEASURE+

Characteristics Of Values:

UNIT : Degrees
RANGE :- 2.5 to + 2.5
ACCURACY±.1
RESOLUTION : 00122

Intruction Sequence:

WRITE 229 (CHANNEL 7)
TEST CARRY BIT = 0 FOR REQUEST
 ACKNOWLEDGED
 IF NOT, RESTART

Data Representation:

11-BIT TWO'S COMPLEMENT NUMBER,
BIT 0 AND
BITS 3 - 12
SCALE = 512/1.25 = 409.6
OFFSET = 0

( ) (INDICATED VALUE   )0 0 0
  Not Used
 0 1 2 3 4 5 6 7 8 9 10 11 12 13 14 15
BIT

Timing Characteristics: Digital to DC voltage conversion.

Comments: The pointer hits a mechanical stop at 2.5 degrees

Table 4 - 5   **Typical SCRS Output Data Item Template**

Condition / Mode	/IMSMODE/	/ACAIRB/=	Alignment stage completed	!latitude!	Other
DIG	$NORM$ OR $Gndal$	Yes	!CA stage!	1s 70o	!Doppler up! AND !IMS up!
DI	$Iner$ OR $Norm$ OR $Gndal$	Yes	!CL stage!	1s 80o	!Doppler used! AND !IMS up!
I	$Iner$ OR $Norm$ OR $Gndal$	X	!CL stage!	1s 80o	NOT !Doppler used! AND !IMS up!
Mag sl	$Magsl$	X	X	1s 80o	!IMS up!
Grid	$Grid$	X	X	X	!IMS up!
UDI	$Iner$	Yes	NOT !CL stage!	1s 80o	!IMS up! AND !Doppler used! AND !pitch small! AND !roll small!
OLB	$Iner$ OR $Norm$ OR $Gndal$ OR	X	NOT !CL stage!	1s 80o	X
IMS fail	X	X	X	X	!IMS down!
PolarDI	$Iner$ OR $Norm$ OR $Gndal$	Yes	!CL stage!	X	!Doppler used! AND !IMS up!
PolarI	$Iner$ OR $Norm$ OR $Gndal$	X	!CL stage!	X	NOT !Doppler used! AND !IMS up!

Table 4 - 6   **Typical SCRS Mode Condition Table**

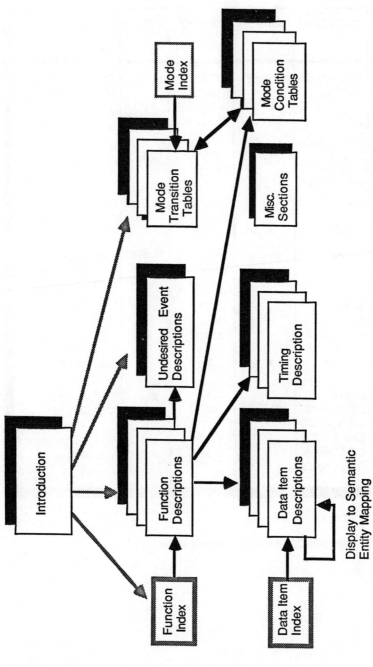

Figure 4 - 3   SCRP Specification Packaging

The SCRS method is an excellent method for creating formal specifications. It forces the documentation of the specifications in a very straight forward manner, and creates specifications that are very precise and concise. Unfortunately, the method has not been fully automated yet, but work is proceeding at SofTech, Inc. to automate parts of it [CHARETTE85a].

4.2.2 Software Requirements Engineering Methodology (SREM)

The Software Requirements Engineering Methodology (SREM) was an outgrowth of research conducted in the requirements area in the late 1960s. At that time, requirement documents produced were consistently poor. The systems implemented using them nearly always had problems. The cause was discovered to be the hierarchy-of-function models that were being used to specify the requirements [ALFORD85]. These models, and the methods used to create them, did not explicitly represent the conditions, events, or sequencing necessary to describe the requirements in total. The end results were ambiguous requirements.

SREM was developed by the TRW Corporation under contract to the U.S. Army Ballistic Missile Defense Technology Center (now the Advanced Research Center) in 1976 to try to overcome this deficiency in requirements definition. The results were: a language for specifying requirements, the Requirements Specification Language (RSL); a set of automated techniques called the Requirements Evaluation Validation System (REVS) to interpret the language, perform consistency, completeness and traceability analyses, create simulators to execute the requirements, generate graphics and produce the requirements documentation; and SREM itself, which is the methodology for the generation of requirements through use of the language and the provided automation.

Before we look at SREM in more detail, two issues need discussion. First, although SREM is often viewed as a requirements method, we still consider it more useful as a specification method. The studies referred to in the SREM introduction were correct in their determination that hierarchy-of-function models, like SA and SADT, suffer from not being able to model performance adequately. That is why behavioral models are very important. It is also why we advocate using SA and SADT in the requirements phase and not in the specification phase. Their greatest value is in increasing understanding and communication among users and developers. Neither SCRS nor SREM are well suited for this. Although requirements can be developed from "scratch" by either method, they usually require or are used with textual descriptions of the requirements as inputs to be analyzed [SCHEFFER85].

Second, SREM, although highly automated, is first a methodology. For this reason we chose to examine SREM here instead of after automation. We will examine another automation aid to creating specifications called PSL/PSA later. The primary sources for this discussion are [ALFORD80, 85], [LOSHBOUGH80] and [SCHEFFER85].

VIEWPOINT. SREM is a little different from any of the previous methods examined so far in that it uses an underlying model to describe the specifications. It uses a highly structured finite state machine model to define the processing requirements of the system under study. It specifies a set of inputs, a set of outputs, a set of states, and a function that maps the inputs plus the current state onto outputs plus the next state. Thus SREM applies all three viewpoints in creation of its specifications.

DOMAIN. SREM is for use on real-time embedded systems that can be characterized by stimulus-response networks. It is also designed for use in creating specifications of projects of large size.

Developed to be used in the requirements phase, SREM is more useful in the specification phase after a requirements document has been created. Some also claim it to be useful in the design phase.

MEDIA. The primary media used by SREM is the RSL language. The RSL is "English-like" in its structure, is restricted in its vocabulary and grammar, and is fairly readable. It is machine readable. It consists of four primitive language concepts: elements, attributes, relationships, and structures.

The elements (RSL nouns) identify classes of things with names. They form the foundation of the specification. Each element has a unique name and belongs to one of a number of classes called element types. Some of the types are ALPHA (the class of functional processing steps), DATA (the class of conceptual pieces of data necessary in the system), and R-NET (the class of

21 Elements	23 Relationships	21 Attributes	3 Structures
Alpha	Associates	Alternatives	R_Nets
Data	Composes	Artificially	Subnets
Decision	Connects to	Beta	Validation_Path
Entity_Class	Constrains	Choice	
Entity_Type	Contains	Completeness	
Event	Creates	Description	
File	Delays	Entered by	
Input_Interface	Destroys	Gamma	
Message	Documents	Initial_Value	
Originating_Requirement	Enables	Locality	
Output_Interface	Equates to	Maximum_Time	
Performance_Requirement	Forms	Maximum_Value	
R_Net	Implements	Minimum_Time	
Source	Includes	Minimum_Value	
Subnet	Incorporates	Problem	
Subsystem	Inputs	Range	
Synonym	Makes	Resolution	
Unstructured_Requirement	Orders	Test	
Validation_Path	Outputs	Type	
Validation_Point	Passes	Units	
Version	Records	Use	
	Sets		
	Traces to		
	(Plus their complements)		

Table 4 - 7   **SREM Keywords**

processing flow specifications). Table 4-7 shows the possible types for elements and the other language concepts.

Relationships (RSL verbs) correspond to the mathematical definition of a binary relation; i.e., a statement of an association of some type between two elements. An RSL relationship is non-commutative, in that a relationship is expressed as follows: subject element, relationship name, and object element. It does allow the complementary relationship to exist however.

Attributes (RSL adjectives) are the modifiers of elements which formalize properties of the elements. Each attribute has an associated set of values. Each element may have only one value for any attribute.

```
┌─────────────────────────────────────────────────────────┐
│                      RSL FORMAT                          │
├─────────────────────────────────────────────────────────┤
│  OUTPUT INTERFACE: RADAR_ORDERS_BUFFER.                  │
│  ABBBREVIATED BY:  ROB.                                  │
│  CONNECTS TO:  RADAR                                     │
│  RECEIVES FROM:  OPS                                     │
│  PASSES:  RADAR ORDER                                    │
│  ENTERED BY:  "SHAWN WALLACE"                            │
└─────────────────────────────────────────────────────────┘
```

Figure 4 - 4

Structures are the final primitive. They are the RSL representation of the flow graph. Two distinct types of structures have been identified. The first is the R-Net (or subnet) structure. It identifies the flow through functional processing steps and is used to specify the system response to various stimuli. The second type is the Validation-Path, which is used to specify the performance of the system.

By using the RSL, the system requirements can be used to describe the system specifications. A small sample of RSL is shown in figure 4-4.

REVS is used to translate the RSL into a database. It then analyzes the data for consistency and completeness against certain criteria. REVS can be used to generate graphic descriptions of the R-Nets and subnets as well as extend the RSL if it needs to be tailored to a specific project.

GUIDANCE. SREM provides a tremendous amount of guidance in its application. Obviously, the language provides some, but SREM describes a 7 phase or step process a specification will pass through before being considered finished. The sequence of steps is used to define the requirements, express them in RSL, and apply REVS in performing analysis upon the RSL. Each phase has a focus and criteria that should be met before moving onto the next phase. Each phase is also broken down into sub-phases to provide more detail as to what to do next. Table 4-8 shows the seven phases and some milestone criteria.

Basically, the process starts with some input, a system specification for example, which is translated and interpreted to determine the interfaces, the

SREM PHASES		
	FOCUS	**EXIT CRITERIA**
Phase 1	Define Kernel	All messages processed/generated
Phase 2	Establish Baseline	All naming consistent
Phase 2	Define Data	All data/value precence correct
Phase 4	Establish Traceability	All requirements satisfied
Phase 5	Simulate Functionality	All functions processed correctly
Phase 6	Identify Performance Requirements	Paths constraints set
Phase 7	Demonstrate Feasibility	Accuracy requirement satisfied

Table 4 - 8

messages across these interfaces, and the required processing relationships and flows. Any errors, ambiguities, or inconsistancies found are corrected. Next, the functional requirements, including all the input/output data relationships, processing steps, attributes, maximum and minimum values and allowable ranges are completed. These are input into REVS via RSL to test for completeness and consistency.

When all information has been inputted and errors corrected, the result is a functional specification. A simulator is then used to validate the functional specification.

After validation, performance requirements are developed. The paths of the defined processing are mapped and any constraints on the paths caused by the performance requirements are identified. Another simulator may be built to assist in analyzing the impact of the performance requirements, and to do trade off analyses where performance is unsatisfactory.

Once all paths are identified, and timing and accuracy requirements are specified, a software specification is created.

The last step is to verify that the system is feasible by creating another simulation using real algorithms rather than functional models. Although not necessarily executed at real-time rates, the simulation running with the algorithms should provide enough information to determine whether the system as specified can be built.

Overall, SREM is a very well thought out methodology that tightly integrates the methods used with its automation. The next section does a brief comparison between the SCRS method and SREM.

4.2.3 Method Comparison

Both SREM and the SCRS method are very well suited to creating specifications. A major difference is the support provided SREM via automation to perform consistency and completeness checks which the SCRS method has the same potential for, but does not currently possess. The automation also integrates much information which can be used by the various methods in each of the phases. To review:

VIEWPOINT. Both methods use all three perspectives to create and document the specification. Relationships are explicitly defined in SREM's RSL, whereas they are inherent in the structure of the SCRS templates, tables, and the specification itself.

DOMAIN. Both methods are meant to be used for real-time embedded systems. SREM has been applied more and on larger systems.

Both imply that they should be used in the requirements phase, but seem better suited to the specification phase. Both have ways of reusing their outputs for design phase efforts.

MEDIA. Neither use graphics in the sense of pictures, at least in the sense of inputs. However, both methods use formal notations to describe the specification. SREM uses a formal language which is translated and analyzed, and which can be used to create graphs of the processing flow. The SCRS method uses templates and tables which are used in a "fill in the blank" manner. Textual descriptions are added where necessary for added clarity.

GUIDANCE. The SCRS method provides built-in guidance by the structuring of its specification, and the questions that must be answered in creating the templates and tables. It does not provide a step by step method for its application, however.

SREM, being an automated methodology, provides very detailed steps on how to apply it. If it was not automated, these steps probably would not be as explicit. Courses are also taught on both SREM and SCRS method, although in the latter case not by its developers.

Both SREM and the SCRS method are being extended. In SREM's case, two extensions have been made called SYSREM (Systems Requirements Engineering Methodology) and DCDS (Distributed Computing Design System) [ALFORD85]. The SCRS method, on the other hand, is being tied to IDEF, behavioral models and Burr's Ada Iconic design language for the Software Technology for Adaptable and Reliable Systems (STARS) program [CHARETTE86]. For large systems, SREM, by virtue of its automation, is probably more useful than the SCRS method, although the latter seems easier to use.

4.3 Automation

The automation that is provided in the specification area is more extensive than that which was seen in the requirements phase. This is not a trend that we will continue to see as we move down to the next life cycle phase towards implementation, however. Many of the developers of the methods that are automated in this phase also claim they are requirements methods as well, but our criteria for specification methods compared to requirement methods don't support the claims. The reason is that almost all of them require, as a minimum, some preliminary requirements information as input from which to start. PSL/PSA [TIECHROW74] is a good example. Requirements methods should help one think and get started, while specification methods should help clarify those thoughts. This doesn't mean that the requirements could not be created from scratch using these methods, it's just that the methods are not as useful for starting the requirements process as they are for checking to see that the requirements are complete.

As usual, any method that is to be automated should be amenable to automation, and specification methods generally are. The use of formal methods aids automation tremendously since the rules for manipulation of data are already determined. Moreover, since little complex semantic information is involved (e.g., the syntactic elements of tables are manipulated, not the meaning of these elements) and since the volume of information is reduced due to the conciseness of encoding, automating specifications is much easier than automating requirements. This makes the clerical aspects of specification such as checking for consistency and completeness relatively straightforward.

However, checking for correctness is not yet possible in an automated fashion because this requires also manipulating the semantic information contained in the specifications, checking them against the requirements, and also probably some concise dictionary of terms and their meaning, as a minimum. Some advocate using strict mathematical logic to formulate proofs as a start, except they don't help determine whether the basic assumptions are correct. No one has determined how to check specifications for correctness to anyones satisfaction yet.

Automation in the specification area has aided in the provision of better specifications and requirements. As was shown in the previous chapter, the execution of requirements helps tremendously the understanding of the product being produced. Likewise, the capability to execute the specifications increases their quality, and hopefully the quality of the product as a whole.

EXECUTABLE SPECIFICATIONS. There has been much research in the executability of specifications, and this is often termed the "Operational Approach" [ZAVE84a]. This is the foundation for the operational life cycle model discussed in Chapter Two. The basis for the operational approach is that the specification represents a clear and simple procedure that can transform input stimulus to output responses. This procedure is then executed and demonstrated to the user who can verify whether they satisfy his or her needs. More sophisticated procedures include system states, synchronization, and the system's environment [YEH84]. The idea of executable specifications is not new, and has been applied in a number of different areas of computer science including language descriptions using grammars in compilers, query and schema languages in databases, and logic programming in artificial intelligence [RAMAMOORTHY84].

The advantages of executable specifications are significant. Always having to execute the specification discourages ambiguity. Some result has to be developed and checked for suitability by the user. This forces the specifier to look for information that might otherwise be left out. This is especially true of the performance and accuracy information that the software product must meet. Another advantage is that resource information may be included. Both the quantity and specific resources used can be included in the execution. This can help tremendously in design. This brings us to the disadvantages of executable specifications.

Foremost is the tendency of designing instead of specifying the software product when an executable specification is used. The capability to include resource information can lead to dissolving the boundary between design and specification, and concious efforts must be made to avoid it. However, in most large projects, many of the resources are already determined a priori, either due to financial or political reasons (rarely technical) so including them is probably not a bad idea. As long as the methods themselves, rather than the capability to automate, don't force the specifier to make design decisions, then little is lost. The ability to automate, and the new capabilities it spawns, for good use or abuse, will always be a problem.

There are also some other disadvantages with using executable specifications. The very fact that an executable model must be created may encourage the specifier to make something, anything, work, to the detriment of trying to better understand the software requirements. The amount of time it takes to develop an executable specification may also be significant, if the time it takes to create a program is any indication. And in very large projects, it may not be possible to execute the total product at once, thus making it difficult to verify the results. Moreover, the execution of the specifications might take up tremendous amounts of time, not to mention computer resources. As usual, project management must decide how worthwhile it is to create executable specifications.

Another automated technique that can help create specifications, but which is not method-based is PSL/PSA.

PSL/PSA. PSL/PSA (Problem Statement Language/Problem Statement Analyzer) was developed in the 1970s by Daniel Tiechrow of the University of Michigan [TIECHROW74,77]. It is concerned primarily with the automation of high quality documentation. It is based upon an entity-relationship model which can be used to describe a wide set of general system models.

PSL is used to describe the requirements of the system using a formal language, similar to that used in SREM.[7] It is a non-procedural language that can describe a system from several viewpoints. Aspects of the system that can be covered are its input/output flow (interaction between a system and its environment); structure (hierarchies among system objects); data structures (relationships among data); data derivations (data objects used by certain processes); size and volume (system size and processing volume); dynamics (system behavior); properties (attributes), and project management (project

Objects	Relationships
Input	Part of
Output	Contained
Interface	Use
Process	Derive
Set	Update
Element	Receive
Group	Generate
Relation	Consist
Entity	Consumes
System-Parameter	Performed by
Interval	Makes...
Condition	Termination
Event	Inception Happens Triggers

Table 4 - 9   **PSL Objects and Attributes**

related information). These system aspects are described in terms of a set of object types and the relationships among them.

An object is anything given a PSL name by the PSL user. There are over 20 objects predefined in the language. Relationships between objects can be described using one of the 50 relationships that also exist. Table 4-9 shows some of the objects and relationships available. Attributes can also be attached to the objects that describe values or properties about the objects. Figure 4-5 shows an example of PSL.

```
DEFINE PROCESS              Can_tgt_actions_be_predicted/A;

    /* DATE OF LAST CHANGE       - Jan 24, 1984, 15:32:24 */

    PART OF :       Tactical_Sit_Asmt_Func_Req;
    EMPLOYS :       Tgt_Bearing{M},
                    Tgt_Bearing_Rate{C},
                    TgT_Range_Bracket{C},
                    SNR{M},
                    OS_Posture,
                    OS_Position,
                    Time,
                    Tgt_Tonals,
                    Tgt_BB,
                    Bottom_Bounce,
                    Sensor_D/E,
                    Tgt_Course,

    TRIGGERED BY:   CLASSIFICATION;
```

Figure 4 - 5   **An Example of PSL**

The PSL description of the requirements is used as input to the Problem
Statement Analyzer (PSA) automated database manipulation/report generation tool. PSA is a sophisticated analyzer that checks the PSL description for
various information. There are over fifty types of analyses, called reports,
that are available. The reports are broken down into four major categories:
database modification reports, reference reports, summary reports, and analysis reports. Database modification reports record changes that have been
made, and provide diagnostics and warnings of possible data inconsistencies.

The reference reports can be used to do things like: identify all objects,
their type and date of last change (Name List Report); list all properties and
relationships for a particular object (Formatted Problem Statement Report);
or provide information about data within the system in a data dictionary
format (Dictionary Report).

Summary reports can provide project management information (Database Summary Report); show system hierarchy (Structure Report); or show
graphically data flow (Extended Picture Report), among other things.

Finally the analysis reports can analyze similarity of inputs and outputs (Contents Comparison Report); detect gaps in information flow or unused data objects (Data Process Interaction Report); or show the dynamic behavior of the system (Process Chain Report), as well.

PSL/PSA help tremendously with verifying completeness and consistency of a PSL description. However, it does not help determine the original requirements from which the descriptions are developed nor verify the accuracy of the original problem statement. It is a technique for documenting and communicating information.

PSL/PSA fits in the category of value-type automation. It is method independent and does not specify any document format that should be used. It provides only cursory guidance, leaving it up to the user to figure how best to apply it. For use in creating specifications it can help analyze the requirements for missing information forcing more questions to be asked.

By itself, PSL/PSA is weak and demonstrates the problems inherent with not automating a method tied to a process model. If it is used in conjunction with or integrated into a specification method, its power and usefulness would greatly increase.[8]

4.4 Requirements of the Software Engineering Environment

The following paragraphs review the specification phase and indicate the requirements it imposes on the software engineering environment.

The process of specification emphasizes the asking of specific questions concerning the requirements created in the previous phase, especially about the performance criteria the software must meet. It is important that the specifications developed by the process be correct, consistent, unambiguous, verifiable, traceable, minimal, and modifiable. Thus, the methods provided within the environment are required to support the creation and documentation of specifications with those characteristics.

The methods, to produce specifications with the above characteristics, must be able to simplify the process of producing the specifications. A complex method may mean a similar, but possibly poor, specification. Guidance on how to apply a method is required to limit this possibility.

Additionally, the methods provided within the environment are required to provide the ability to trace the specifications to the requirements, increase the ability to check for consistency and completeness, and be amenable to automation. Furthermore, the methods included in the environment are required to provide for the maximal amount of reuse of information.

The automation provided within the environment must support the capturing of information in both textual and graphic forms. Also required is the capability of baselined and non-baselined information to be passed among the various specification and requirement methods, as well as a capability to store and keep track of any changes to it.

The capability to perform automatic traceability, completeness, consistency and impact analysis on changes either to the specification or requirements is also required to be supported by the software engineering environment. And finally, the environment must support a document generation capability.

In summary, the specification phase imposes much the same requirements on the software engineering environment as did the requirements phase. The major addition is in the requirement to share information among the various methods, and for the methods to reuse the information. Chapter Nine will illustrate how these requirements can be met by our ideal software engineering environment.

4.5 Summary

In this chapter we have shown how specifications are different from requirements. Requirements are used to communicate and reach an informed consensus among all the parties involved, while the specifications are used to develop the formal contracts that will be used to evaluate the product when it is complete. The specifications will also be the documents referred to during maintenance, when questions arise as to what the product is supposed to do when working properly.

We've also examined some methods that allow us to describe those things the requirements left unstated (such as the performance information) in formal ways. These methods also continued to allow us to describe "what" the product will do rather than how the product will do it. We've also examined how automated methods can aid the specification process, and how the degree of help is related to whether or not the automation supports a method.

In summary, it is important that the software engineering environment provide the following capabilities to support the specification of a software product. The environment should allow its users to:

- Assess the validity of each specification defined;

- Trace each specification to its originating requirement;

- Evaluate consistency and completeness with respect to the specification documents themselves, and the requirement documents;

- Capture the specifications for automated storage, update, and reuse by textual and graphic means in this phase and latter phases of the product's life cycle.

The next phase that we will discuss is the design phase. Its function is to create a software architecture that will describe how the product is going to accomplish what was specified in this phase.

FOOTNOTES:

1. D.T.Ross, "Douglas Ross Talks About Structured Analysis," IEEE Computer, Vol. 18, No. 7, May 1985

2. Experience would say that the documentation of a new software system would increase by a magnitude, rather than only by a factor of three, over its predecessor.

3. Here we cross the fuzzy boundary into design

4. Not everyone agrees on the usefulness of abstract specifications. One author has labeled them "utopian dreams." See [LUDEWIG82].

5. The SCR Project covers the whole life cycle which resulted in a number of other methods being developed, especially in the design area. We won't, however, cover those in this text.

6. There is no implication here that templates and tables are mutually exclusive. A template is meant to gather information, and therefore may have a table associated with it, as in the case of a function template.

7. SREM's RSL was based upon PSL [FAIRLEY84].

8. PSL/PSA has been integrated with SA and is marketed by ISDOS, Inc. under the name Structured Architect.

5. DESIGN

"The leg bone is connected to the shin bone, the shin bone connected to the ankle bone, the ankle bone. . . "

Medical Student Rhyme

5.0 Introduction

The next phase requiring support within our software engineering environment is the design phase, as shown in figure 5-1. Here, an abstraction, commonly called the software architecture, is created that will closely map to the physical implementation of the product which we will create in the next phase. When implemented according to this architectural design, the product should meet the software specifications and satisfy the evaluation criteria necessary for it to be considered a success. The design process uses as input the specifications created in the last phase and produces as an output a blueprint to be used by the developers to implement the product, without the constant necessity of referring back to the specifications or making assumptions about how the software product is to operate, as shown in figure 5-2.

Design and specification are sometimes intertwined, especially in smaller projects. For large systems, which our software engineering environment is to support, the design process is an explicit phase required to separate problem understanding and definition from the attempt to define problem structure [WASSERMAN79]. The intellectual boundary is a bit fuzzy, but the focus is shifted from the activities of requirements and specifications which

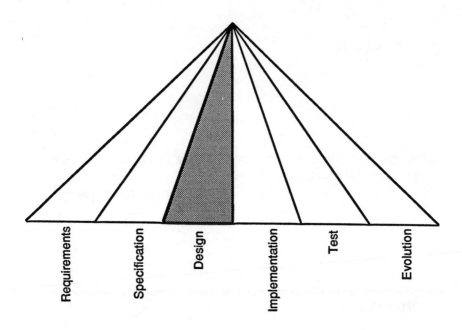

Figure 5-1   **Model of a Typical
Software Engineering Environment**

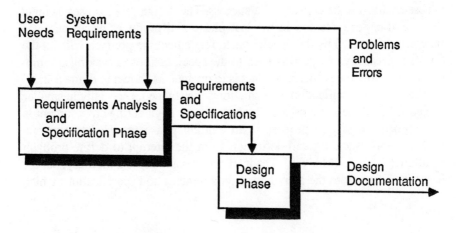

Figure 5 -2   **The Design Phase**

were meant to detail what the product will do, to how the product will do it. The process of design is predicated on the goal of making this transition happen.

Design also differs from implementation in that it presents a formal, coherent and well-organized representation of how a program is supposed to accomplish, while an implementation turns this representation into executable programs written in a particular programming language [ENOS81]. As we will see, there has been increasingly an emphasis to reduce the separation between a design and an implementation by the use of programming design languages, which can be used to describe both.

Design is usually defined as having two activities: external design and internal design [FAIRLEY84]. External design is the definition of the externally observable characteristics of the software product. Taken very loosely, it defines the product's "being" or "essence," i.e., "I compute, therefore I am." [1] Much of this externally defined behavior has been captured in the specifications that were created in the previous phase, which is one of the reasons why these two phases are so often confused. In practice it is nearly impossible to completely separate the two phases at this level. Internal design, on the other hand, defines the internal processing details and the structure of the software product.

Internal design is itself made up of two sub-activities: architectural and detailed. Architectural design is concerned with recognizing the overall system structure, the interfaces and interconnections among program pieces (or modules), and their precise definition. Detailed design is more concerned with the definition and/or selection of the algorithms and data structures that are necessary to fulfill specific software functions.

There have been arguments about where architectural design ends and detailed design begins, but for the most part the question is irrelevant. Design is such an iterative process that it is impossible to completely separate these two. The best way to view detailed design is that it is the bridge used to effect the transition from the high-level architectural design to the programming language used. Detailed design should produce specifications sufficient to code programs from. The actual detail necessary to fully describe the design depends on the complexity of the functions to be performed, the language used to code the program, and how much time is left at this point in the development.

In this chapter we will review the process of design, a few of the methods that are available to accomplish design, and the automation necessary for it to be used in a software engineering environment.

5.1 The Design Phase

The activities that occur in the design phase center around the themes of renewal and expansion. The design phase is a very interesting, and to most software developers, the most exciting. It is, in many ways, like starting the life cycle anew. In the previous two phases, we were concerned with what the system did. We needed to bound the software requirements and give them a context in which to be further expanded. Methods like SA and SADT were used to reduce the entropy level of the system requirements and capture all the semantic information they contained concerning the software requirements. The specification methods, like SCRS and SREM, having bound the context and the semantics of the information defined, could then concentrate on refining the software requirements by refining and detailing the boundaries of the context we had defined. After spending a great deal of time and effort, we were able to excise the extraneous and yield something that sounds precise and crisp, and is minimal.

At the design phase, we have as input a logical abstraction of the system that has a particular viewpoint. We must change from a focus on what the product will do to a focus on how it is going to do it. Thus, we have a perceptual gap to cross. The information is there, but it must be transformed (some pessimists would say transmuted) into a new form. In so doing we will create a large amount of new semantic information (and some noise). Thus our entropy level will rise again!

We are required to rebound the problem, describe it anew, and capture all the new semantic information we will create as well. Because of the "perceptual canyon" that separates the first two phases from design (and implementation), there may have been efforts to narrow the gap by incorporating design into earlier life-cycle phase.[2] Whether this is good or bad is debatable.

Another aspect of the themes of renewal and expansion concerns the organization that is building the product itself. Up until this time, we have viewed the product development as a monolithic process. The number of people involved in creating the requirements and specifications has been limited, and everyone has been busily working together as a team because they all can talk to each other. Ten or so people can work together rather nicely. Above that, it becomes difficult.

Ideally, the designers are the same ones that have created the software requirements and specifications. However, when the design phase begins, these people are usually not available anymore. They usually have new assignments working on requirements and specifications of the next increment of the product.

Therefore, the result is new people, many probably not involved at all in the previous work (except for the managers), are brought in to develop the design. Moreover, the numbers of people involved increases rapidly as the specification is divided among the design teams that are forming. If one is not careful during this time of expansion, the product will map to the organization, rather than vice versa.[3]

The end result is that the specifications had better be very good, because there isn't liable to be much communication between the specifiers and designers, nor possibly among the designers themselves. The number of communication lines will be just too large (remember Brooks N^2 law). In addition, the people doing the design tend to be less experienced than the requirement writers and specifiers, with the trend continuing throughout the development as each of the following phases are encountered. If incompleteness marks the specifications, one rightly can expect an incomplete mess to result.

5.1.1 General Goals of Design

The major reason why the design phase can be troublesome is that the process of design is extremely difficult to describe precisely. Many research efforts have tried to formulate a scientific foundation for it, but to date no single philosophy of design exists [FREEMAN77]. To illustrate what happens in design requires us to paint the scene in even larger brush strokes than in either the requirements or specification phases. Thus we will provide a very general description of the process that occurs.

Design is an information creating process [PETERS81]. It is characterized by an intensive creative aspect, which is the primary reason it is difficult to understand or categorize. The designer of a software product does not create this information at random, but instead tries to apply previously obtained knowledge and experience gained from other projects. What can be gleaned from the products of the previous phases is important in developing a line of thought based upon logical reasoning [KOOMAN85]. Occasionally, the results are unexpected, which restarts the process.

In most other branches of engineering, there is a tremendous amount of well-documented previous experience from which a person can draw in estimating what is needed to attack and solve a particular problem. In software engineering, and design in particular, this experience is almost always lacking [RALSTON83, FREEMAN77]. The quality, then, of the ensuing product depends substantially on the capability of the individual designer.

Brooks has made some interesting observations about the relationship of designs to designer's experience [BROOKS75]. He indicates that using a completely inexperienced designer is not entirely bad, for it is a designer's **second** design which causes the problem. The first is clean and sparse since the designer doesn't know what he's doing, so he's careful. New "bells and whistles" occur to him during this period to be saved and used on the next design project he participates in. Thus, second system then, as Brooks notes, becomes the most dangerous system a person ever designs. It is only after the third one that the designer realizes that he or she doesn't know everything and can begin to generalize about the problem.

Designers have a large number of degrees of freedom available from which to work with in the creation of the software product. The problem with this is that while it is easier for the designer to do an outstanding job, it is just as easy to do a terrible one. Software design is mostly a human and, therefore, manual job [RALSTON83]. This only reinforces the idea of design as an intensely creative process.

WICKED PROBLEMS. The ultimate goal in software design is to produce something that the implementers can use to code the software product. Thus, given a set of specifications, the designer must formulate an efficient search through the design space in order to select an appropriate set of components [DASGUPTA84]. To accomplish this successfully, the designer must solve two basic problems: identify the issues critical to the success of the design effort, and identify the design elements necessary to adequately meet these critical issues [PETERS81]. This means selecting a design approach, and then applying it to the specifications to obtain a design.

Selecting a design approach is not a particularly easy thing to do. It requires an in-depth understanding of the problem, which hopefully the requirements and specifications provide, and also of some things these documents may not provide. Information like: What dominates, data or functions? What hardware is required to be supported? Is the hardware appropriate when the software is partitioned into executable modules? (Note that we have, for the most part, avoided the issue of hardware selection in our previous discussions. We believe that theoretically hardware should not be selected until after the specifications are complete, but this is almost never true in practice. This consideration should be rolled into the requirements and specification phases, with the designer providing key data on suitability for meeting performance criteria. This brings out the larger issue of systems engineering, of which software engineering and hardware engineering are components. More on this will be discussed in Chapter Twelve.)

To better understand the challenges a designer is faced with, it is helpful to understand the nature of the problem to be faced. Peters, in his excellent text on software design, describes design problems as "wicked" [PETERS81]. A wicked problem is one that is particularly elusive, and the solving of one aspect of it may uncover others that present even more difficult solutions. He goes on to list various properties of wicked problems:

- Wicked problems cannot be definitively stated. Every formulation causes more information to be required, and necessitates a new formulation.

- There are no rules or guidelines for determining when a wicked problem is solved. Every "solution" provokes a proposal for a more refined solution, ad infinitum. The end is never apparent. Only when time runs out on the project schedule or the designer tires out does the design effort end.

- Wicked problems have only good or bad solutions, not right or wrong ones. These problems don't have closed form solutions like mathematical formulas, but instead depend on the feedback received after the design is implemented and in use to determine if the design was successful. The satisfaction of the non-functional requirements, such as reliability, modifiability, user friendliness, etc., comes into play here.

- Wicked problems can't be definitively tested, and the solutions are too significant to be experimented with. It probably is too dangerous (as well as probably politically unfeasible, not to say disturbing to the local residents) to test live the capability of a Pershing missile's nuclear warhead to stop an armor attack in the Fulda Gap. A designer normally gets one lick at solving a wicked problem.

- Neither the number of solutions to a wicked problem nor means to obtaining them is limited. Any approach that solves the problem is acceptable. As important, any solution is also potentially acceptable.

- Every wicked problem is unique, as is every solution. The process of design is meant to eliminate all but one eventual solution. This solution never existed before, meaning that it was non-existent prior to this time. No knowledge existed from which to gather previously detailed information or past history about the solution. This solution may thus change or affect the requirements in unexpected ways.

- Wicked problems may be symptoms of higher-level problems.If the requirements, or the schedule, or budget are unreasonable, or technology is unavailable, the problem may be unable to be solved by any way, shape, or form.

The above properties have been encountered by anyone who has had to deal with design, no matter what particular field of endeavor. One shouldn't despair about these problems though. It is natural that the search for a design approach take on the iterative (and creative) nature of the process itself. Many different approaches are going to be tried, each attempting to control the flow and ebb that is happening between creating more detail and structuring or abstracting it into less detail [KOOMAN85]. Although we will examine various specific approaches in the next section, it is useful to discuss the general activities of the design process next.

5.1.2 General Design Process Description

As we stated in the introduction, there are two primary activities occurring during the design process, external and internal design. We are going to concentrate on the internal design, because the external design should have been defined during the specification stage.

INTERNAL DESIGN. Internal design activities include architectural design and detailed design. Architectural design is aimed at trying to refine the conceptual view of the software product [FAIRLEY84]. This means performing a number of tasks such as: decomposing the specification into software modules; identifying internal processing functions; decomposing of these into sub-functions; identifying the interfaces and interconnections among the functions and sub-functions; identifying the data used and passed among the functions; and finally, identifying where the data is stored. An overall physical product structure can then be identified. This structure is the high-level physical mapping of what will be eventually executed, as opposed to the structure identified in the specification which was the virtual product structuring.

A number of documents are produced during the architectural design activity. A refined user manual, top-level design document, and preliminary test plans are created in this step. The refined user manual details the actual operation of the product on the target hardware. The top-level design document contains information on the software structure, its logical data structures and processing algorithms. The test plans describe the objectives of the tests, what constitutes successful test completion, the methods to be used for testing, the actual test cases and expected results. Tables 5-1 and 5-2 illustrate some typical outlines for the top-level design and test plan documents. The user manual was shown in table 3-5.

Before moving to detailed design, reviews are usually conducted by project management. The purpose of the reviews is to examine the high-level design proposed for feasibility and reasonableness, as well as to ensure that the design will meet the specifications. The design must be shown to be traceable back to the specifications before detailed design is usually allowed to proceed formally.

Reviews are very important in the design phase. In theory, reviews should be catching errors only in the documents being created during this phase, but actually will often catch errors that occurred in earlier phases as well. The more that are caught before implementation occurs, the higher the quality of the resulting product. Reviews are meant to catch errors, not to prove the product is correct.

A number of different kinds of errors can be made, and design reviewers must be aware of them. Parnas [PARNAS85a] has classified them into four categories. The first can be classified as inconsistencies. This is where the design probably won't work correctly in all cases. An example of this kind is if two design statements make different assumptions about an angle used for

```
┌─────────────────────────────────────────────────┐
│           TOP-LEVEL DESIGN DOCUMENT             │
├─────────────────────────────────────────────────┤
│ 1.0 Purpose : To describe the structure and organization of a
│               software product component
│ 2.0 Static software architecture
│ 3.0 Functional allocation
│ 4.0 Memory and processing time allocation
│ 5.0 Functional control and data flow
│ 6.0 Global data
│ 7.0 Specific function description
│         7.1 Inputs
│         7.2 Local data
│         7.3 Interrupts
│         7.4 Timing and sequencing
│         7.5 Processing
│               7.5.1 Algorithms
│               7.5.2 Special control
│               7.5.3 Error handling
│         7.6 Outputs
│ 8.0 Adaptation data
│ 9.0 Appendix
└─────────────────────────────────────────────────┘
```

Table 5 - 1

navigation. Whether it should be relative or true makes a very important difference.

Another kind is inefficiencies. These are places where the design imposes barriers to efficient implementation or use. An example might be where requests for shared data will result not only in the data requested, but unnecessary information as well. This will result in a waste of time and space.

A third kind are ambiguities. Here the design may be interpreted several different ways by the implementers.[4]

The last kind are inflexibilities. These are places where the design does not accommodate changes very well. These may happen when the specification is vague about what will or will not change later in the product.

These categories offer multiple perspectives to guide the review and help make the detailed design activity proceed smoothly.

SOFTWARE TEST PLAN

1.0 Purpose : Define the scope of testing for a software product component

2.0 Plans for informal testing

3.0 Unit Test Plans

      3.1.1 Unit test requirements
      3.1.2 Unit test responsibilities
      3.1.3 Unit test schedule

4.0 Integration and test plans

5.0 Resources required for informal testing

      5.1.1 Facilities
      5.1.2 Personnel
      5.1.3 Hardware
      5.1.4 Interfacing/support hardware
      5.1.5 Resource souce
      5.1.6 Test configuration

6.0 Plans for formal test plans

7.0 Formal test requirements

8.0 Formal test summary

9.0 Formal test schedule

10.0 Test data analysis

11.0 Test assumptions and constraints

12.0 Appendix

Table 5 - 2

DETAILED DESIGN. Detailed design is aimed at refining the architectural design even further. Its goal is to produce a design that the implementers can eventually code from. How detailed one must go depends on many factors, including the complexity of the system, how much testing is to occur, what language is going to be used, etc. During detailed design, algorithms and their data structures are specified that can implement all the functions, the protocols for handling the interfaces are described, and how the software product will be packaged for execution will be identified.

DATABASE DESIGN DOCUMENT

1.0 Purpose : To describe the architecture and design of one
     or more databases in a particular product component

2.0 Database management overview
    2.1 Database manager
    2.2 Database definition language
    2.3 Database query language

3.0 Database structure
    3.1 Item
    3.2 Field
    3.3 Record
    3.4 File

4.0 Database file interrelationships
5.0 Database file design
6.0 Database references
7.0 Appendix

Table 5 - 3

Detailed design yields its own set of documents, including the detailed design document, the database design document, the interface design document, and the final test plans. The test plans created here are a refinement of the ones created during architectural design. Table 5-3 and 5-4 shows the outlines of the database and interface documents.

Management (in this case, normally lead designers or team leaders) also reviews the information produced during the detailed design activity using similar checks as before. Checks are made for consistency and completeness with respect to the documents produced during the architectural activity, and for the level of detail produced. The final design documents must be sufficient to implement the software product.

ASPECTS OF A GOOD DESIGN. What makes a good design? Although highly dependent on a product's charateristics, Parnas has listed some

INTERFACE DESIGN DOCUMENT

1.0 Purpose: To describe the detailed design for one or more
        interfaces between particular product components

2.0 Interface name

3.0 Interface summary

    3.1 Data
    3.2 Messages
    3.3 Control functioons

4.0 Interface formats

    4.1 Data
    4.2 Messages
    4.3 Control functioons

5.0 Appendix

Table 5 - 4

properties that all designs should be able to meet [PARNAS85a]. A good
design is:

- Well structured. It should be consistent with whatever   principles
  were used in creating it.

- Simple. It should be as simple as possible, but no simpler.

- Efficient. Each function should be computable with the available
  resources, and not waste time and space.

- Adequate. The design should meet the specifications.

- Flexible. The design should make it possible to respond to the
  inevitable requirement changes that will occur.

- Practical. Cleverness and unneeded capability should be left out.

- Implementable. The functions should be computable from the information provided, and by the implementation method to be used.

As we said in the beginning, the process of design is difficult to describe. There are many concerns that must be balanced if the design, and ultimately the product, is to work successfully. The following is a short, certainly non-inclusive, list of thoughts about design.

DESIGN HINTS. Plan to throw the first one away, because you will any-how. This is a piece of advice by Brooks [BROOKS75] that has helped a generation of designers. Don't be afraid to take it.

Remember that design is a process of making tradeoffs, especially among efficiency, understandability and modifiability. The toughest tradeoff is often with efficiency. A design that is very efficient may not be understandable or modifiable. And when it is modified (and it surely will be if it's a large system) it probably won't be efficient any longer.

Don't do the implementer's job. Design the product. Don't worry about the exact language representations. If they can understand what is required, and your design has met the properties listed above, then you're done. One of the problems designers have is that they were probably once implementers and can't seem to set aside that perspective.

Don't go to the implementation phase if the design isn't good. A good design should strive for architectural unity, cohesiveness among its parts, and regularity in its structure [DASGUPTA84]. Once coding begins, the investment in the product is normally too high to go back. The user is going to have to live with the design for the rest of the product's existence.

Design is the last stage before physical software product creation, and the last chance to correct mistakes. If the properties of a good design don't exist at the end of detailed design, they will always be unobtainable, no matter how much time and money are spent later on. "Slow is beautiful," is a useful slogan [KRUTCHTEN84], and should be in the minds of all software managers in a hurry to put out a product.

Finally, remember the old saying, "Allow me to change what I can, accept what I cannot, and the wisdom to know the difference."

In the next section we will explore some of the ways to obtain that wisdom.

5.2 Design Methods

In this section we will examine some of the primary techniques that are used in most design methods, and then discuss two methods in general and their use of these techniques in particular. More exhaustive treatments are found in texts like [PETERS81] which cover the field fairly comprehensively.

No single design method is right for all types of problems that a designer may encounter, thus increasing the importance of matching the right method to the particular problem. As was mentioned earlier, the creation of several trial designs before an approach is selected is a common occurrence.

Design methods in general are meant to define the structure and construction of the software product [BERGLAND81]. Design methods are very similar to requirement methods in their emphasis on disciplining the creativity of the designer. The designer has great freedom in creating a design, but only a disciplined approach will keep this freedom from turning into chaos. Moreover, most methods can be used in both architectural and detailed design, thus presenting the designer with the paradoxical problem of keeping extraneous detail out of the early design.[5] As in specification, details that can be postponed should be.

5.2.1 Design Principles

Some of the basic principles and techniques used in design are abstraction, structuring, coupling and cohesion, and information hiding. Notice that each is used in some way to help define the structure of a software product design.

ABSTRACTION. We've seen how abstraction was used in both the requirements and specification methods we examined, and it is applied in design in much the same way, except with a different domain and viewpoint. Abstraction is used in two ways. First, it is used as a means to concentrate on one set of problems at a time to reduce the amount of complexity required to be understood at once. This has also been termed "parsimony" [ENOS81], meaning never do more than you have too. Second, it is used as a means to separate similarities from differences in the software design. These are expressed through some type of abstract interface [PARNAS77].

For instance, in architectural design, the specifications are needed to construct the functional and structural attributes of the software product, whereas in detailed design, this structure is refined into implementation details. Thus complexity is controlled. These similarities and differences are defined by using functional, data, and control abstractions [FAIRLEY84].

Functional abstraction is the grouping of functions of the product into discrete collections of entities based upon particular properties that all the entities share. The properties inherent in these entities, sometimes called subprograms, packages, or groupings, implicitly define the relationships between entities. These relationships may change on invocation or during execution of the program which will eventually define the product.

Data abstraction is the specification of a data type or object through the definition of particular operations that are legal to be applied upon the data type or object. All other details such as underlying representation and manipulation are suppressed.

Control abstraction is the specification of control actions, such as the sequencing and selection used in parallel or concurrent execution, without defining the actual mechanisms to be used.

STRUCTURING. Another technique used in software design is that of structuring. Structuring is the linking of a system that has been decomposed into smaller units through the use of well-defined relationships with other units. These units may or may not be packages, depending on whether abstraction was used or not. The number of ways the units may be linked is generally infinite, with the designer trying to establish the minimal number of links necessary to perform the tasks specified. Some aspects of structuring are connectivity and modularity.

Connectivity [BERGLAND81] is the specification of how the packages that were created are logically linked. These linkages define (from one specific viewpoint) the number of interfaces and dependencies among the various packages in the product. The connections can be modeled graphically through the use of directed graphs as illustrated in figure 5-3. The number and types of dependencies may have a great impact on the product's potential reliability.

For example, if the packages have a serial set of dependencies, such as Package A is dependent on the information created in Package B which is dependent on C, etc., as shown in figure 5-3 then an error in any causes errors in the one above. By rearranging the processing and changing the connectivity, as shown in figure 5-4, a reduced dependency occurs. Packages

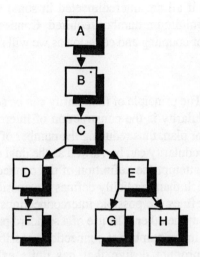

Figure 5 - 3   **Module Interconnection Graph (Poor Connectivity)**

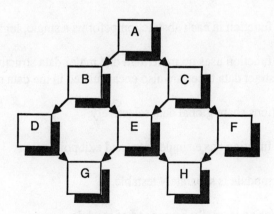

Figure 5 - 4   **Module Interconnections Exhibiting
Good Connectivity**

with fewer dependents seem to have fewer errors than those with more [CARD86]. Note that "N" number of packages may have as many as N(N-1)/2 interconnections if all are interconnected in some way, and N-1 interconnections are the minimum number required. Connectivity is closely related to the principles of coupling and cohesion as we will see a bit later.

MODULARITY. The principle of modularity can be seen as another aspect of structuring. Modularity is the construction of interconnections using some standard pattern or plan, thus reducing the number of linkages that a designer need consider. Modularity can be viewed as the dual of connectivity. In other words, one may attempt the definition of the connections required between system units, which then implicitly defines the possible units. Defining units first implicitly defines the possible interconnections between them. Neither truly exists without the other. The use of a standard pattern of linkages causes a prior reduction in the number of connections possible.

A software product design that has units exhibiting the following properties [FAIRLEY84, BERGLAND81] is said to be modular. Note also that abstraction is used to implicitly define the connectivity pattern. Properties of modular designs are:

- Each processing abstraction defined is a well-defined, independent sub-system that is potentially useful in other applications.

- Each function in each abstraction peforms a single, logical task.

- Each function uses no more than one major data structure. Instances of abstract data types are also encapsulated in the data structure.

- Functions share global data selectively.

- Each function has a single entry and exit point.

- Each module is separately testable.

- The design is totally comprised of modules.

The units that are defined in the above manner are called modules, rather than packages.[6] Modular designs seem to enhance reliability, and ease

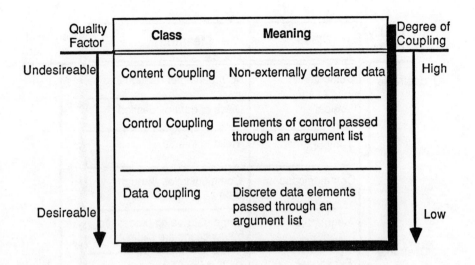

Figure 5 - 5   **Classes of Coupling**

implementation, documentation, and the evolution of the software product [FAIRLEY84].

COUPLING AND COHESION. Other principles used in design of the software product are those of coupling and cohesion [STEVENS74]. Coupling is aimed at reducing the number and types of interconnections that exist between modules. These interconnections are defined by the type of information communicated in the interconnection, whether it be data, control, or modification of internal module information. Figure 5-5 depicts the various levels of coupling that exist, ranked from a scale of strong coupling to weak coupling. Content coupling is when one module modifies data or instructions in another module. Control coupling occurs when one module passes information to another that can control its processing sequence. Data coupling occurs when data items are passed as parameters between modules.

Some type of coupling has to occur between modules, since all attempts to eliminate them would seem to be counter to the principles of abstraction and structuring. However, coupling based on content is the least desirable, whereas data coupling is most desirable. Data coupling also seems to lower the later cost of the implementation [CARD86]. Low coupling and minimal interconnections are a desirable property of a design.

Quality Factor	Class	Meaning	Degree of Cohesion
Undesirable	Coincidental	No meaningful relationship	Low
	Logical	Class of data processed	
	Temporal	Related in time	
	Communicational	Communication through data	
	Sequential	Some data being processed, but functions are distinct	
Desirable	Functional	Simple discrete functions	High

Figure 5 - 6   **Different Types of Cohesion**

Cohesion is aimed at increasing the relationship among elements within a single module. The stronger the binding, the better the module can be viewed as a single entity. Figure 5-6 depicts the different types of cohesion [YOURDON75] and the relative strength of each. Coincidental cohesion is when elements within a module have no obvious relationship to one another. Logical cohesion is when some relationship occurs, but the relationship is complex and/or superficial. Temporal cohesion occurs when the elements are bound by time, i.e., all elements execute simultaneously. Communicational cohesion means that the elements within a module use the same set of input or output data. Sequential cohesion is when the output of an element is the input to another. Finally, functional cohesion occurs when all the elements are related to the performance of a single function.

A designer should attempt to use the principles of coupling and cohesion in his design. The goals that should be strived for are low coupling, i.e., data coupling, and high cohesion, i.e., functional cohesion, as shown in figure 5-7.

INFORMATION HIDING. The last principle we want to review is information hiding. We discussed information hiding in the last chapter in relation to

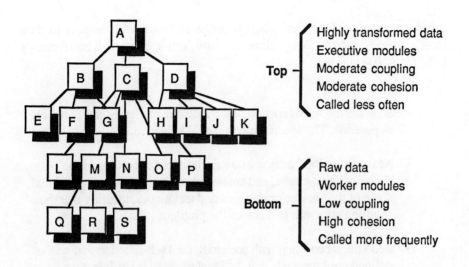

**Figure 5 - 7 A Good Control Structure with Low Coupling
                 and High Cohesion**

specifications. It is used in a similar way in design. Each module that is defined hides information about its internal processing from other modules, and only presents well-defined interfaces through which to communicate to other modules. This enhances the effectiveness of the principle of low-coupling. Moreover, information that is likely to change is also grouped together, enhancing cohesion within an element.

5.2.2 Design Approaches

Next we are going to discuss some of the generic approaches that use the above principles in various forms based upon a particular design viewpoint. There are basically four design methods: functional decomposition, data-flow design, data-structure design, and procedural design.

FUNCTIONAL DECOMPOSITION. Functional decomposition is simply the old divide and conquer technique or "step-wise refinement" [WIRTH76]. It usually involves the step by step division of functions into subfunctions, in a top-down manner. One can decompose the software with respect to data flow, time, control flow, time or any other criteria. The strategy [BERGLAND81] is to:

- State the intended function of the software as clearly and concisely as possible. The specifications should help here.

- Next, divide the function into sub-functions according to the decomposition citeria, and connect them in a way keeping in mind some of the previous principles and techniques, insuring that the resulting structure still solves the problem.

- Redo the second step with each indivdual sub-function that was defined until one feels that the level of detail is sufficient.

The generality of this approach is both an advantage and disadvantage. The advantage is that it promotes general applicability to numerous problems, and by doing so, it is probably the most used approach. The disadvantage is that there can be innumerable decompositions of the same problem. No two designers will decompose the product in the same way, and in large systems this often leads to confusion as one group will use one set of decomposition criteria while another will use something else. Functional decomposition also has a disadvantage in that it usually works best with specifications that are well understood and stable. If this isn't true, the decomposition may need constant and "infinite" re-iteration.

DATA FLOW. Another general method is the data-flow design approach. In its simplest form, it is the same as functional decomposition but with the decomposition limited to data-flow [BERGLAND81]. The specification is decomposed into input modules, transformation modules and output modules [RAMAMOORTHY84]. A series of "black boxes" (i.e., functions) are created that transform an input data stream into an output data stream. Each blackbox is refined successively, and then all are linked together to form a complete system. The principles of coupling and cohesion are extensively used.

An advantage of this approach is that it works well in data-driven systems, and most of the modules created exhibit very high cohesion. A disadvantage is that not all systems are data driven, thus leading to artificial partitioning because transformations on the data may be difficult to identify.

The data-structure design approach is based on the hierarchical decomposition of data structures that perform input and output functions. The relationship between different levels tends to resemble a "is composed of" relation. A basic premise of this approach is that the data structures created closely map to the problem space (i.e., the actual implementation) thereby ensuring that whatever decomposition is attempted will be consistent between designers. A problem with the approach is that it is too difficult to apply to processes that are highly concurrent [RAMAMOORTHY84].

PROCEDURAL. The last approach is procedural. Here the focus is on specifying the set of algorithms and their control flow. The design is described as a set of procedures using some type of language. The language may range from an informal textual description such as a psuedo-programming language called Programming Design Languages (PDL), to something very precise like axiomatic mathematics using predicate calculus. The idea is to be able to describe precisely the software implementation, yet still be expressive enough to design with. A major push has been made, as in the data structure approach, to closely map to the problem space. An advantage is that in the case of using axiomatic mathematics the implementation can be proven to be correct as it is designed, while in the case of PDLs the design closely matches the implementation. The disadvantages are that it is hard to build large systems this way, designers will tend to concentrate on the implementation rather than the design, and the expressive power of the language used may severely limit the design capability.

To give a flavor of some of the design methods in use today, we will examine a method that can be used at the architectural level, Jackson's Structured Programming Method [JACKSON75] and one at detailed design level, PDL. Again, when examining the methods, try to think how an environment might need to support these methods, and how they might tie into the methods previously reviewed.

5.2.3 Jackson Structured Programming (JSP) Method

The Jackson Structured Programming (JSP) method is a design method that was developed in the 1970s by M. Jackson of England. Very similar to the Warnier method [WARNIER76], JSP views the world through its data

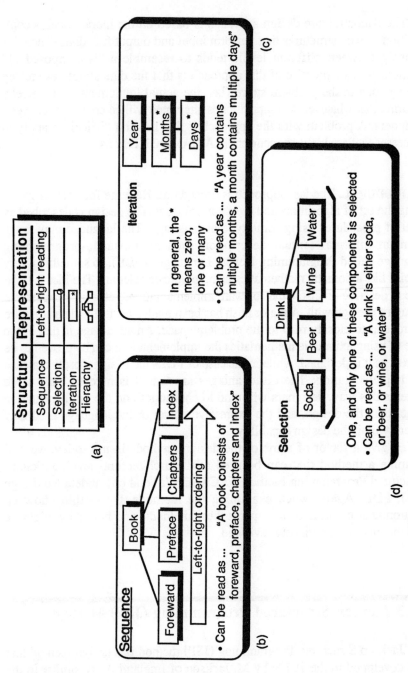

Figure 5 - 8   JSP Notation and Example Usage

structures. It is based upon the notion that implementation structures mirror data structures which mirror problem structures. In other words, the implementation should reflect the structure of the data which the implementation will ultimately process. Thus, the JSP method sees the designers problem as matching the structures of the input data, the output data, and the implementation.

With these few words of introduction, let's use the characteristics of methods to examine JSP. Our primary sources used in the discussion are [JACKSON75], [PETERS81], and [BERGLAND81].

VIEWPOINT. The JSP method uses primarily an informational viewpoint in its application. The functional viewpoint is implicitly supported.

DOMAIN. The domain of JSP has been primarily the business application area where Cobol is the main implementation language. The products developed are the small to medium size given our categorizations in Chapter Two.

JSP is primarily used in the design (and implementation) phase.[7] Although considered an architectural design method, it has elements of detailed design as well.

MEDIA. JSP makes use of both graphics and text. The designs use the graphics to show sequence, selection, or iteration. Figures 5-8 a, b and c illustrate the basic notation and its use. Hierarchies are also shown in figure 5-9. Hierarchies are structures having elementary components, i.e., those that cannot be further decomposed, and component functions; i.e., those that bring together in correct relationship, the parts which they comprise.

GUIDANCE. JSP is basically a three step method, as illustrated in figure 5-10. First, find the data relationships through your understanding of the problem. This means defining the input and output data structures. Draw the resulting data structures using the graphic notation. Second, convert these to a skeleton implementation structure using the same graphics that match the structure of the input and output. Third, fill in the skeleton by listing the elementary operations of the implementation and assign each to a component of the design. It may happen, and often does, that no match occurs between and input and output data structure. This is called a structure clash. Since this

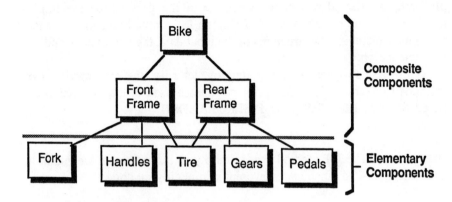

• Hierarchies are structures having :

Elementary Components — Those that cannot be further decomposed

Composite Components — Those that bring together, in *correct*

relationship the parts which they compose

Figure 5 - 9   **Example of JSP Hierarchy Usage**

violates the requirement that a common program structure must exist throughout all data structures, it must be made to conform. This is done by creating intermediate data structures that reorganize the data until a match is achieved. For full details on how to apply the method refer to [JACKSON75].

The JSP method is very straightforward and repeatable. It is claimed that two designers using the method will end up with the same design. There is one caveat, however. There is no method to tell the designers how to structure the data initially.

JSP seems to work well for the design of large data driven systems where the data is relatively well known and stable. In other arenas, where the data being manipulated is not well understood, where the data structures change dynamically, or where the implementation is composed of many programs communicating with each other, the method may not be the one of choice.

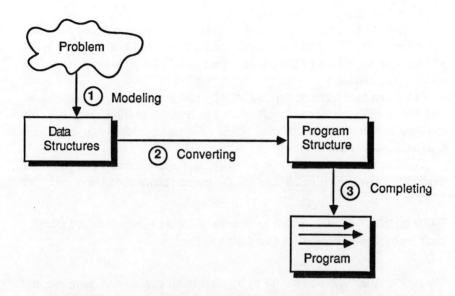

(1) **Modeling:**   Define input and output data structure using Jackson's graphic notation

(2) **Converting:**   Create a general program structure (same graphics) that matches the structures of both input and output

(3) **Completing:**   List elementary operations and assign these to modules

Figure 5 - 10 **Jackson Structured Programming Method**

5.2.4 Program Design Language (PDL)

A Program Design Language (PDL) is a textual language, precise enough to describe a software implementation, yet expressive enough to design with. PDLs grew out of the need for a better way to express a detailed design than through a flowchart, and that could overcome the problems inherent in changing and redrawing them as well. A basic assumption in using a PDL is that an architectural design exists.[8]

PDLs are meant to enhance the quality of the design by enhancing the communication between the designers (they all use the same language) and by increasing the capability for doing completeness and consistency checks, especially if the PDL can be run through an automated analyzer. As in the JSP method, the idea is to reduce the conceptual distance between the design and implementation.

PDLs can also increase productivity by making the design visible early, and if the PDL matches closely with the implementation language, the implementation can proceed rather quickly.[9] A side benefit is that it will also reduce personnel training.

To illustrate what a PDL is, we will use the draft Ada PDL guideline description given in [IEEE85] and use the method characteristics.

VIEWPOINT. Ada PDL is able to describe all three viewpoints. A PDL that can't probably will not suffice as a design method.

DOMAIN. Ada PDL was meant to be used in all application domains, and especially for large real-time embedded software products. The larger the product, the more useful a PDL becomes.

Ada PDL is for use in the detailed design phase. It is not for use as an implementation method. The temptation is to use a PDL to implement the product, instead of as a means to further refine the design. Executable PDLs compound the problem unless they are expressly aimed at checking for consistency and completeness.

MEDIA. Ada PDL uses structured text. A standard style of indentation is indicated to help with readability and understandability. Comments are added to the text for explanatory purposes. Ada syntax is extended by the use of structured comments to help express information not easily expressible in Ada. An example of Ada PDL is shown in figure 5-11.

A question in PDLs is: when using one that closely matches an implementation language like in the case of Ada PDL, whether the full syntax of the language should be allowed. The arguments basically revolve around whether the language is expressive enough without the full syntax and whether the full syntax provides more temptation for a designer to implement instead of design.

GUIDANCE. Ada PDL can support all the design approaches. The only guidance provided is implicit in the language itself. PDLs are a good way to

```
package body translation is
  --...
  -- [  (  polish := polish_notation(infix(-)||infix(+) ). @,
  --   infix(-)||infix(+).@) ]
procedure convert_infix_to_polish
    (infix : in out sequence; polish : out sequence) is
tok : token;
  package tok_stk is new stack_facility (token);
use tok_stk;
  deffered : stack;
  --...
begin
  -- reset pointer position of the infix and polish sequences,
  -- and make the deffered stack empty;
while
    condition -- more tokens in the infix sequences
loop
  get_next (infix, tok) ;
    -- (tok is operator -> put_next (polish, tok) ;
    -- | tok is operand ->
    --   move any operators of higher precedence than tok from
    --      top of the deffered stack to end of the polish sequence;
    --   put_top (deffered, tok);                                ..
    -- |...);
  end loop;
  -- move any remaining operators from top of the deffered stack
  -- to end of the polish sequence;
  -- make polish sequence empty beyond current pointer position;
end infix_to_polish;
```

Figure 5 - 11   **Ada PDL Sample**

express the details of the design, if they are used for design. And if they are, the implementers must not try to take them too literally because: a) they may not to execute in the same fashion as the language would, and b) they may be implementation inefficient [SUTTON81]. Overall, PDLs are a very useful method to help bridge the gap to the implementation phase.

5.2.5 Comparison of Methods

Comparing JSP and Ada PDL is something like comparing oranges and grapefruits. They are related, but the results of the comparison are interesting, though not really useful. Given this disclaimer, we will do one anyway for completeness.

VIEWPOINT. JSP takes an informational viewpoint from which to design. Ada PDL can support all three.

DOMAIN. JSP is primarily aimed at business applications where much is known about the data. Ada PDL can support all types of applications.

MEDIA. JSP uses a small set of graphics and annotated text to represent a design. Ada PDL uses structured text alone.

GUIDANCE. JSP provides a step by step method for its application. Its repeatable and complete. Ada PDL provides none. It is up to the individual user to apply it.

Each method is useful for its own purpose. It is up to the designer to decide which is the best one for a given situation. Remember, methods by themselves don't build products, people do.

5.3 Automation

The automation provided the design process is relatively low, just as was the case in requirements analysis. One reason, if one recalls Chapters Two and Three, is that both of these phases try to capture semantic information, which is an extremely difficult task. Automation in this area is also stymied because it is difficult to automate the support necessary to stimulate and capture creativity, which is unique to each individual designer. There are so many

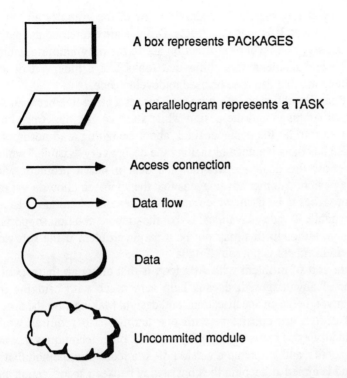

A box represents PACKAGES

A parallelogram represents a TASK

Access connection

Data flow

Data

Uncommited module

Figure 5-12   **Ada Iconic Language Graphics**   *Source : [BURR84]*

generic approaches and design heuristics that exist, rather than individual methods, that this phase is probably the one which will be automated last, at least in any standard way.

We can see some of the difficulty by noticing how the requirements phase methods captured information. SA and especially SADT used a extensive a-mount of graphics to accomplish this goal. However, most of the approaches, like Structured Design and Jackson's method use graphics to a minimum.[10] For automation to be useful in design, some type of graphics have to be supported by the methods. One that does is Burr's Ada Iconic language, or Ada Icon for short [BURR84].

ADA ICON. Ada Icon is meant to support the learning of the Ada program-ming language through the use of a graphical notation. The notation provides a specific one-to-one mapping between the graphics and key features of the programming language. Figure 5-12 shows a few of the graphics and their correspondence to Ada language constructs. Designs are expressed using the graphics, which stay at a level of abstraction above the programming language itself. The end result is something that looks like a blueprint of the software architecture that can then be used to develop code.

The nice thing about this approach is that it makes a clean link between the implementation language and the design while still keeping the conceptual distance necessary to let the designer think about designing, and not implementing. It also has the advantage of making the design very "visible," which can rapidly show the designer whether the design has a problem with coupling or cohesion. Another advantage is that the approach allows a variety of design approaches to be used, which makes it a general technique. Also, it is very automatable. The disadavantage is that the graphic notation supports a single language, although this may not be a major problem if the software engineering environment is not multilingual.

A different sort of problem with Ada Icon is that although there exist a great number of advantages, it doesn't help very much with bridging the conceptual canyon between specifications and design. Making sure the specification and design are consistent with one another still requires work. Efforts are underway to reduce the gap by utilizing other techniques that act as transition agents, and automate a version of Ada Icon. One method that is automated and is aimed at keeping the consistency between specification and design is Higher Order Software [HAMILTON76, MARTIN85].

HIGH ORDER SOFTWARE. Higher Order Software (HOS) is a method that is somewhat graphical in nature that emphasizes the generation of provably correct software. Since its birth in the mid-1960s HOS has been used as both a specification and design method. It is based on a set of mathematical axioms that describe how to functionally decompose a system in a hierarchical manner, a set of representations that can be used to graphically show the decomposition, and an automated language called AXES for describing processing transforms and data.

The axioms control the decomposition of the functions used to describe the design. A function can be a mathematical formula, a processing algorithm, a database query, or a set of specifications. The axioms allow a parent function to invoke only its offspring, control the order of their invocation, and control their inputs and outputs (i.e., access rights). The results of the design are treelike structures that represent the flow of control of the application.

When applying HOS, the designer uses an interactive graphics editor (Interactive AXES) to build and manipulate the HOS control maps. A text version of the tree is also created via Textual AXES that can be checked by an analyzer. The analyzer checks that the axioms have not been violated, thus guaranteeing that the application is logically correct (within the set of axioms). This output can also be sent to a generator that can produce executable program code in Fortran, Cobol, Pascal, or C.

Automation in design still has a long way to go, and software engineering environments must be able to support a wide range of methods in this phase Accomplishing this is a difficult task.

5.4 Requirements of a Software Engineering Environment

The support requirements the design phase places on the software engineering environment are for the main part the same as the requirements and specification phases. However, to adequately support the process of design the quality and quantity of the support that environment provides must be significantly better than before.

What we mean is that in the design phase, the process is marked by a massive influx in the number of personnel that are involved. The environment is required to handle the increase without performance degradation. This may mean a necessity for the environment to be distributed across many locations. Furthermore, the environment is required to support the increased need for communication among all the new team members, thus mandating more management and organizational support.

Additionally, the software engineering environment is required to ensure the consistency of the information being developed. This means ensuring not only the consistency of the design with the specification, but the consistency with the original information created. With so many different parties now involved and all working off the same baseline information, the chance for not working on the latest design is very high. Therefore, the environment is required to provide a configuration management that is very robust.

The methods used in design are not as well defined as in the previous phases. Moreover, a designer's creativity is very important in attaining a good design. Therefore, the environment is required to provide very flexible and tailorable approaches for supporting different types of design techniques. The designer should also have the ability to check the quality of the designs through automatic analytical means using set evaluation criteria, so the environment is required to support this capability as well.

The techniques that currently exist use both text and graphical means, and the means to do both is required. A means to interpret the textual descriptions for syntactic correctness for methods like PDLs is required also. Again, the support of traceability, completeness, and consistency is necessary to be supported by the environment in this phase as well.

In summary, there are no unique requirements that the design phase places on the software engineering environment that were not encountered in the previous phases. It must however, support a greater number of people and a larger volume of information. Chapter Nine will describe how an environment supports the design phase.

5.4 Summary

In this chapter, we've investigated the general process of design, and reviewed some of the problems designers face when "confronting wicked problems." We've also examined some of the general techniques and approaches of doing design such as abstraction, information hiding, functional decomposition and data flow. We've also looked at some criteria which can indicate design quality, such as coupling and cohesion.

No standardized way exists for performing design. A designer's creativity and experience are paramount in successfully coming up with a good, workable design. Thus, it is important that a software engineering environment provide the following capabilities to support the design process. The environment should allow its users to:

- Formulate and conceptualize software designs and design changes;

- Express software designs in an unambiguous, structured manner indicating allocation of requirements to software components;

- Evaluate designs and design changes for internal consistency and quality;

- Evaluate designs and design changes with respect to traceability, consistency and completeness against the requirements and specifications;

- Capture the designs for automated storage, update and reuse by textual and graphic means in this phase and latter phases of the product life cycle.

In the next chapter we will review the implementation, test, and evolution phases of the product life cycle and for examination of how a software engineering environment can provide support to each phase.

FOOTNOTES:

1. Apologies to Descartes.

2. It also explains why many product developments skip the requirements phase, and go straight to design and implementation.

3. An interesting exercise is to take an organization chart of an ongoing software project and then draw the high-level design of the organization and compare the two to see if they match. This was first noted by Conway [BROOKS75].

4. Remember, each phase of the life cycle is an opportunity for introducing error. It does little good to have incredibly good specifications if the designers use them to create designs that the implementors can't use.

5. Yet remembering it, it's better to err on the side of detail if it means possibly leaving something out.

6. Note: Almost any separable entity in a design has been or is called a module. For example, sub-routines, procedures, functions, or related groups of the same, sequential or concurrent processes, load modules, etc., have all been called modules at one time or another. No strict definition exists. This is yet another example of the major problem that plagues software engineering, the lack of an agreed-upon vocabulary.

7. Note, though, Jackson has developed a Jackson Design Methodology which is made up of the Jackson System Development (JSD) method and JSP to address the requirements phase as well.

8. Some might disagree with this statement. Any method can be used anywhere, but driving a nail in a board with a hammer is much easier than using a banana. The point is to use the method in its most applicable circumstance.

9. It has been reported that greater productivity occurs in the implementation phase when the PDL and programming to be used are similar [GAFFNEY86].

10. Methods like Hierarchy, plus Input, Process, Output (HIPOs) diagrams and Nassi-Schneiderman structured flowcharts (NSSF) are highly graphical detailed design methods, but their usefulness is limited.

6. IMPLEMENTATION, TEST, AND EVOLUTION

"The program is almost 95 percent complete. Trust me."
Typical programmer's saying

6.0 Introduction

Implementation, test, and evolution are the last phases of the life cycle that a software engineering environment must support, as shown in figure 6-1. They are also the ones that have received the most attention over the years, for reasons which are obvious. First, producing code is very visible. One can escape from doing a formal design ("nobody is going to notice"), but it sure is difficult demonstrating how your computer-generated image display system works without producing the program to run it.

Second, the cost involved in not doing testing has climbed steadily over the past decade. The evolutionary costs of a product now consume approximately 70 to 80 percent of its total life cycle costs. Testing used to be an ad hoc affair, mostly the responsibility of the individual implementer. This is changing as software products have increased in size and complexity. The only way to test them is in an organized fashion.

By implementation phase we mean the efforts required in the production of a physical realization of the design that was created in the previous phase. The code produced in this phase should implement the design correctly and meet the resource, accuracy, and performance constraints defined in the specifications.

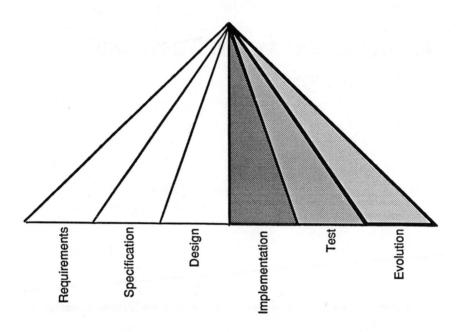

Figure 6 - 1   **Model of a Typical**
Software Engineering Environment

The process involved in the production of correct code has the longest tradition associated with computer science. It is also the process most difficult to describe precisely because its tradition is based upon an individual creating a piece of software. The process is informal, and not rigorously defined. This is somewhat suprising, since what an individual does during programming has been under intense scrutiny for the last thirty years. Although much is known about what implementers do in general, how this knowledge can be translated into a concise and precise description of the implementation process itself hasn't been determined nearly as well

Therefore, we will talk about the implementation phase from the same informal perspective of what should accomplished in the phase, and the difficulties encountered, rather than the steps one takes to actually produce a program.

Testing is the process of executing the physical realization we have created with the intent of finding errors. Testing is often considered as an aspect of the implementation phase, because the program is tested for correct execution by the programmer as it is being built. However, this type of testing is a localized affair, whereas we are more concerned with the testing of the overall product before it is released. Thus we will consider testing, as described in this chapter, to be different from what is commonly called debugging.

The evolution phase is what happens to the product after it has been accepted by the customer. It includes fixing errors in the code or documentation (which is commonly called maintenance) or adding enhancements to the product. These enhancements may be either predefined, such as those specified in incremental builds of the software product, or in response to the users' or customer's wishes. Evolution also implies the reiteration of each of the previous life cycle phases to some degree.

In this chapter we will examine each of these topics in more detail and investigate the requirements they place on a software engineering environment.

6.1 The Implementation Phase

The implementation process is the culmination of the totality of the previous phases' efforts being brought together to elaborate the "physical" form of the product.[1] The process, as shown in figure 6-2, represents the translation of the description of "how" the product worked (captured in the design) to "how" it will work within the constraints of the computer hardware it will execute on.

Recall that the output of the design phase was an abstraction of the product implementation [FREEMAN77]. It established the product's structure, its underlying data structures, its general algorithms, and the interfaces and control/data linkages needed to support communication among the various sub-structures established. The implementation is the physical realization of this abstraction. The implementation process, then, is simply a translation of the design abstraction into the physical realization using the language of the target architecture. If the design has been well documented and reviewed, this translation should be a relatively straightforward process. The use of a PDL which uses the implementation language as its basis is espe-cially useful in accomplishing this task efficiently.

Now, if it were only that simple.

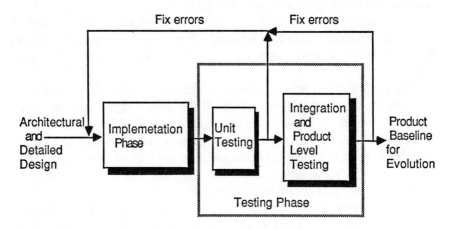

Figure 6 - 2 **Design and Test Life-cycle Phases**

Implementation Phase —The Reality. As anyone who has programmed knows, the translation process is not as trivial or straightforward as just described. It is a phase which is usually in a confused state, where management is having difficulty keeping track of everything that is going on, and where it seems there is always one more thing that has to be coded or fixed before the program will run. It's a phase, especially for large product developments, that can easily be termed chaotic or unstable. Most research and practical efforts today are aimed at making it less so.

One major problem that causes the instability lies in the difficulty of translating a design into an implementation. First, a design is never going to be an exact one-to-one mapping to the implementation unless the design is the implementation.[2] Thus, even with good designs, some effort has to be made to translate the design into an implementation, and that means a possibility of introducing error. Careful thought is necessary on the part of the designer to balance his or her needs in creating the design against those of the implementer who has to make it work.

Second, the translation process is made more difficult when a design isn't complete, consistent, or somehow doesn't communicate what was required in a way that can be understood. Design errors of omission or commision cause many implementers to spend their time solving the wrong problem [JENSON81].

Third, some aspects are just outside the designer's domain. The exact impacts and ramifications of using a particular operating system or programming language are beyond the scope of the designer, but definitely are a concern to the implementer.

Finally, the implementation itself is prone to be error filled, since creating it is an intensely human affair. A few examples can help illustrate some of the problems typically encountered in the implementation phase.

TRANSLATION PROBLEMS. As we stated, a problem which is inherent in the implementation phase concerns the translation process from a design into an implementation. Any translation process is prone to error, and the higher the level of abstraction that exists between the design and implementation, the more potential for error.

For example, consider the common use of abstract data structures in designs. From a designer's point of view a particular type may be seen as an ideal selection. The chosen data structure provides all the things required and is a perfect way to manipulate the data to be produced. Most designers, however, don't concern themselves with how much actual space is needed to store all the variables once the physical structure itself is programmed. This is left up to the implementation. Depending on the programming language used, however, and the physical size and partitioning of the real hardware's memory, it could pose serious implementation difficulties (data structures, especially ones with dynamic ranges, can eat up memory faster than a swarm of hungry locusts).

A similar problem to the data structure example is how will the implementation synchronize its various components. A designer may say that module A will communicate with module B and pass information C between them, but implementing this may not be so easy. For instance, consider an individual process module that in the design is designated to share information with a number of other modules.

First this module, a logical abstraction in the design, must be programmed into a physical entity, and must reside in some physical space in the architecture. The same is true of the other ones as well. The implementer must then use the specifications to determine how many times, and for how long, this module needs to communicate with the others. If these modules are time-critical; i.e., they must pass information that is needed in real-time, where any one of them ultimately resides [3] in the system may decide whether the product can meet the specifications.

Additionally, it is not only where an individual module is located in the network, but whether the communication timing is so critical that it must occupy physical memory all the time. Even if it can be non-resident, the issue of swapping it from secondary memory to primary memory and the increase in overhead that may cause then becomes a new issue to be resolved. The impacts of these issues may not be discovered until an actual implementation is done, regardless of how many prototypes were built previously.

The physical distribution of modules may not be a small feat either. If a module is about 100 programming lines long (a typically recommended "standard" size), in a system like Space Station with a 100 million lines of code, we are discussing possibly 1 million modules.[4] Now if these are spread across a network of computers, and if the majority of modules are time-critical, the poor implementer has a job that will keep him or her occupied for awhile just keeping track of what the names are, let alone where they are located. In addition, the requirement of creating the system in increments might necessitate the rearrangement of the modules for each new increment. Thus, new locations for the modules must be selected, which means a great amount more work. We can readily see why the implementation phase takes a long time and is marked by errors.

LOGIC PROBLEMS. Another problem which is a form of translation error is called an error of logic. In this case, an implementer interprets what the design is supposed to do differently from what the designer had in mind. This is a very frequent occurrence, and is one of the major sources of errors found in a product development [WOLVERTON84]. Overcoming this problem is not particularly easy, unless humans are completely removed from the process. That is why using methods that can express designs (and requirements and specification) in a rigorous, but understandable, manner are so important.

DOMAIN PROBLEMS. Implementers also have to worry about that which is not explicitly defined in the design (being outside its domain) but which must be taken care of by the implementation. Such an example is in trying to recover from execution errors. Since the implementer who can write perfect programs the first time and every time hasn't yet appeared, errors will likely exist in the product. One doesn't want the product to stop working because of these errors, so some way must be found to keep the program executing even in the case of errors. The SDI system is an example. It is estimated that it will have over 100,000 undiscovered errors in the deployed software, yet is required to be built in such a way to still accomplish its mission [ADAMS85]. A design can help in making recovery possible, by adding in redundant components, modules, etc., but it is up to the implementer to discover the details of all the possibilities the designer didn't think of.

Another issue a designer usually isn't concerned with, but which almost always impacts the implementation of the design, is how the system software (i.e., operating system, run-time executives, etc.) is used. A program doesn't exist in a vacuum and, when executing, is dependent on these supporting programs to manage resources such as memory, the processor, and the I/O hardware. The system software can, as much as the language being used to implement the design, impact throughput, timing, or efficient memory utilization. Again, it is usually left up to the implementer to determine how to make the design work within these constraints.

IMPLEMENTATION ERRORS. Even with all the above problems resolved, the implementer may still not use the language correctly. This means that time and effort has to be spent correcting the errors, which then delays other work that is required to be completed. Unfortunately, error correction has never proved to be an easy task. An implementer only has a 50 percent chance of successfully correcting an error if it can be narrowed to only 5-10 lines of code, and only a 20 percent chance if 40 to 50 lines are involved [BOEHM73].

TRADEOFFS. In confronting each of the problems above, an implementer is continually making a number of important tradeoffs, such as the maintainability of the product, its reliability, avalibility, etc., as shown in figure 6-3. Although many of these tradeoffs have been determined or at least constrained by decisions made during the previous phases, it is the implementer's ultimate responsibility to choose the correct degree of each. Most of the factors being traded off are non-functional in nature; thus, it is difficult to tell what will be the end result until the total product is completely built and tested. As Boehm said, it is these tradeoffs among the plurality of goals that is an implementer's hardest task.

The tradeoffs an implementer must make usually end up depending on: a) how effectively the design can be translated using the implementation language, and b) how efficiently it can be executed by the target architecture. For example, some programming languages seem more suited to certain applications then to others. If a language is not directly suitable, time/space

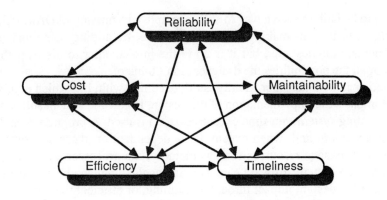

Figure 6-3   **Non-Functional Design Tradeoffs**

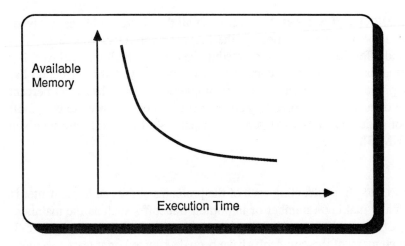

Figure 6 - 4   **Time/Space Tradeoffs**

tradeoffs might then have to occur, as illustrated in figure 6-4. These have their own ramifications, as the previous examples describing typical translation problems illustrated.

IMPLEMENTATION SUMMARY. The usual documents produced during the implementation phase consist of: (a) the programs themselves (both source and object), heavily annotated with comments that follow a standard format or convention; (b) software development folders, which describe an individual software module and exist throughout a module's life; (c) a software programmer's manual, which will describe the conventions used in the program, provides an overview of the implementation, describes any peculiarities, and describes how the support software interacts with the application, and; (d) any other documents which might be useful to describe the actual software. Of course, all the documentation from the other phases should be available also. The totality of this documentation (with the test plans, configuration management plans, etc.) should fully describe the software product. In fact, the documentation is the product. The quantity, quality, and timeliness of the document production is a sign of the health of the product development [FAIRLEY84].

The management aspects of the implementation phase are basically the same as in the design phase. Reviews are conducted to evaluate the quality of the programs. One aspect that starts taking on more emphasis is the configuration management of the program. The reason is that the product is in various stages of completion as the different implementation groups work on different parts of it, and no "whole" product may exist until system integration time. So more regularly than in the previous phases, all the work produced is gathered together and a baseline of the product is created and stored. The implementers will then work from that version. Configuration management and its purposes will be discussed in more depth in the next chapter.

In summary, the implementation process is a difficult one to categorize or describe. In it one can see the aspects of requirements analysis, specification and design. The implementer must decipher what the designer meant, how to use the language to implement it, and how to manipulate things to make the software design fit the operational constraints. It is also an iterative process, as the implementer tries to remove the errors that he or she created when developing the program.

Once the product has reached a stage where the various pieces can start to be brought together, the next aspect can begin. That is the testing of the product as a whole for errors.

6.2 The Testing Phase

Surprisingly, testing wasn't considered a discipline of software engineering until 1980 [MILLER84]. Probably a major reason was the confusion over testing and debugging.

Testing is not debugging. Debugging is concerned with an individual fixing errors in his or her product component that they are responsible to program. Testing, on the other hand, is concerned with executing a program with the intent of finding errors either by physical or logical means.

Two types of testing exist, informal and formal. Informal is usually done by the implementer to find errors in a particular product component. The approach taken here is to make the program perform the specified actions for that part of the product.

Once the implementer is reasonably certain that no errors exist, or can't be sure without having the other parts of the product available, then formal testing is usually conducted. Here, testing is concerned with showing precisely what the product will do, not in making the product do something as in informal testing [MILLER84]. Implied in formal testing are testing at the level of the unit (or module), and at the product level (either partially or fully complete). The latter type also is concerned with the integration approach needed to tie the product parts together into the final comprehensive whole.

A tested program is one in which the conditions that make it fail have not been found yet. This seems like a pessimist's attitude, but what it means is if the test result is consistent with the expected result, the component tested is deemed correct within the limited context of the test.

TEST CRITERIA. Testing is meant to find errors, not to prove a program is correct. However, it is currently impossible to completely test a program. Even moderately sized programs, just to completely execute each possible path, might take years of computer time [BOEHM73]. Thus a decision has to be made on how best to accomplish testing. Toward this end, Miller [MILLER84] has listed some of the major questions concerning testing which help form a testing strategy. They are:

- What components should be tested,

- How should they be tested,

- What is expected from the test?

In determining what should be tested, a number of factors stand out. One is the size of the product. Costs go up in a non-linear rate as the size of the product increases. This is caused by the requirement to test more items (the larger the program, the more ways components can interact), the need for a formal organization (more personnel and equipment are needed), and the time needed to fix the errors once found (its harder to localize an error). In large software products, both unit level and product level testing are required.

Another factor is the amount of change the software product may undergo in its lifetime. It may be more advantageous to formulate a strategy that concentrates on areas that will change the most often, rather than to test everything a little bit.

A third factor is the complexity of the product to be tested. Although complexity can be related to size, it is not necessarily true in all cases. For instance, a small real-time avionics product may be more difficult to test than a much larger business application that is batch oriented. Complex systems usually require a high level of testing.

TESTING METHODS. The methods to be used in testing will be discussed a bit later in the chapter, but they can be placed into two major categories: static and dynamic [MILLER78]. Static testing includes manual code inspections, structured walk-throughs, or other techniques that don't require the program to be executed. Dynamic testing is the execution of the product under controlled conditions to observe the results.

The tests themselves can be undertaken from either a white box or black box perspective. White box testing is based on the internal logic of the program. It requires an understanding of the program design, and emphasizes test coverage of the program paths and branches. It usually is used for unit testing.

Black box testing does not use any of the internal design knowledge of the program, instead requiring knowledge of what the external behavior of the product should be. Inputs are specified and outputs are observed. This type of testing is usually reserved for product level testing.

The expected results of the tests vary with the test coverage and type of testing. However, different types of errors can be found. Table 6-1 lists some of the types of errors that can be found through testing.

It is up to management to determine how much effort should be expended in testing. The criticality of the system is an important determinant in the amount of testing to be required. The more reliability requirements, the higher the necessity to thoroughly test, although totally error free software is economically unfeasible [MUNSON81]. In these cases testing costs can run as high as 45 percent of of the initial product development cost [MILLER84]. In

Logic	Mistakes when coding from the design
Overload	When data structures are filled to capacity
Timing	Coordination among parallel processes
Throughput	Processing speed
Capacity	Memory limits
Recovery	What happens when the system fails
System Software	Assumptions about the software

Table 6 - 1   **Errors Discovered by Testing**

other cases, it may be cheaper to wait for the users to find the errors than it is for money to be spent on testing. Management must decide for each individual product the best way to approach testing.

The process of testing begins back in the specification phase where the items to be tested were first determined, although in the requirements phase thought is given to how to test the product. The first formal plans were developed during the design phase, and refined as the design became more solid. As implementation takes place, detailed planning for testing should occur. The previous chapters list the documentation developed for testing during each of the specific life cycle phases.

What we have discussed so far about testing is a more idealized view of the process. In reality, testing is not done to the degree it should be [GLASS80]. It has been termed a "lost world," largely ignored by most practioners and academicians alike. The reasons are not hard to understand [MILLER84].

First, people don't like to test. It is seen as uninteresting, unimaginative, and places a person in the role of critic or "complainer." Second, it is also hard. The methods, automated or not, are difficult to apply, and their correct application requires a good understanding of how the product works. Finally, testing traditionally has not been seen as a critical item by management. They almost seem embarrassed by it. Naturally, people aren't going to flock to a job that no one considers important.

But testing is important, and should be considered a worthwhile occupation. As Miller points out, if any of the above attitudes begins taking hold within a project and reduces the amount of testing, it can turn a successful product development into a disaster.

6.3 The Evolution Phase

Product evolution is what happens to the product after it has been developed and officially delivered to the customer.[5] We have chosen to use the term "evolution" to describe the process instead of the more commonly used "maintenance." The reasoning is that the changes to the product   involve much more than just maintaining the system. They also include adding functional enhancements, increasing performance, etc. However, since "performing evolution" on a product is semantically doubtful, we will use the term maintenance instead, but the reader should keep in mind the more global implications.

For this reason we will categorize evolution into three basic types [SWANSON76]: perfective maintenance, adaptive maintenence and corrective maintenance. Perfective maintenance is the modification of the product in response to customer requests to make the product more usable, or implementer requests to make it more efficient. Adaptive maintenance is the incorporation of enhancements into the product that were previously planned, such as a change in the operating system used. Corrective maintenance is the fixing of errors in the product found after product release, or which were known at release but not yet corrected.

COSTS. The cost of maintaining a product is now accounting for approximately 80 percent of the total life cycle costs.[6] However, the amount of effort actually spent in correcting errors is the least, while modifying the product to make it "better" is the most. For example, the range of effort in each of the types of evolution varies, with perfective product evolution accounting for approximately 55 percent, adaptive 25 percent, and corrective 20 percent [SWANSON76]. The primary reason for this spread is the direct result of the conscious effort of developers to place more system functionality into the software than into the hardware [CLAPP81]. Software allows for a quicker change in system functionality (just change the software) and is cheaper than changing the hardware. An example is the case of the F-111 again, where two versions of a weapon system existed, one in hardware and one in software. Modifications to the hardware version cost 400 times more and took five times longer to complete than the same changes to the software version.

The high cost of maintenance cannot be solely attributed to placing more functionality into the software, however. For instance, it has been estimated that maintaining a line of program code can cost up to fifty times more than its original development [TRAINOR74]. Therefore some other factors have to be involved.

Some of the factors for the high cost can be traced to the original product development. Insufficient or incomplete documents, inconsistencies between the documents and the product, and an inflexible product design, among others, all contribute to making maintenance more difficult [RAMAMOOR-THY84].

Another factor is the limited quantity and quality of the personnel available [LIENTZ83]. Usually the maintainers are not the original implementers of the product. Further compounding the problem is the fact that the maintenance personnel are also typically the least experienced personnel on the product development. Additionally, with the high turnover rate that occurs in many organizations, the "corporate knowledge" that is needed to resolve problems quickly is no longer available to the maintainer. The mistakes that were made in the past are not visible to the maintainer to guide him or her when an error appears. The only thing that is left to depend on is the documentation, and that usually doesn't reflect the rationale as to why something was done, which is crucial to understanding why the product works the way it does [BALZER85].

The fact that corrective maintenance is performed on source code exacerbates the cost problem [BALZER85]. The implementer spent a great deal of time optimizing the program, making use of specialized knowledge about how the program operates. This diffuses or hides the knowledge of its operation, making it difficult for the maintainer to reconstruct what actually happens.

Costs in this phase also increases because in adaptive and perfective maintenance a "mini" software development occurs. New requirements are placed on the product, which necessitates updated specifications, modifications to the design, new code to be developed, integrated and tested. The cost of redoing the documentation alone is staggering. Add to this the fact, often overlooked, of yet another version of the product that must evolve and be maintained. After awhile, there may be only "one" maintenance effort, but it is taking care of ten different versions of the same product.

Another factor in the high cost of maintenance is that maintenance begets more maintenance. Fixing one error has a high probability, in the range of 20 to 50 percent, of introducing another [BROOKS75]. Moreover, as the product evolves, the various types of maintenance efforts on it destroy its structure to such a degree that it is either better not to maintain the system any longer, or to throw it away and start over [BELADY76].

The final factor contributing to the high cost is that maintenance, like testing, is not very appealing. As was once said, maintenance is like a penal system. You know it's necessary, but nobody wants to have to go there. Management isn't interested,[7] as it seems an admission of guilt that the product didn't work correctly originally. Since everyone wishes it would just go away, the resources to do it correctly aren't made available, which means certain errors aren't fixed, which causes other errors which also aren't fixed, etc.. The end is a very unmaintainable system, where every fix is expensive.

COST CONTAINMENT. Can anything be done to reduce the cost? Preventative maintenance has been suggested by a number of researchers [BALZER-85, BROOKS75, CLAPP81, RAMAMOORTHY84] as the best approach. They collectively suggest the following:

- First, specify the ultimate goals of the product development which will impact maintenance. For example, is the initial development cost to be kept low, the product to have high reliability, the product to be adaptable, or to have many planned enhancements? Determining how each will be traded off against each other will affect the ultimate cost of evolving the product.

- Second, plan the product to undergo at least corrective maintenance. This means keeping the documentation current as a minimum.

- Third, make management aware of the importance of evolution.

The last item is probably the most important. Most software efforts in existence are involved in the evolution of an existing system, not in its original development. Part of the problem seems to be in the mind-set that sees an incremental build of a product as a "new start," rather than as an aspect of evolution of the first increment. This perspective tends to wrongly separate adaptive and perfective maintenance from corrective, with the consequence that errors that were corrected once creep back into the product [BROOKS75].

In the next sections we will look at some of the methods available for implementation, testing and evolution.

6.4 Implementation Methods

As we discussed in Section 6.1, the implementation phase is concerned primarily with translation of the product design abstraction into another abstraction (the program) which represents the product. The methods[8] used in this translation process are meant first, to control the process, and second, to create the product.

There have been many methods touted to control the programming process. Three of the more commonly used ones in the past have been step-wise refinement [WIRTH71], structured programming [DIJKSTRA72] and program families [PARNAS76].

Step-wise refinement is the decomposition of programs into levels, with each upper level calling one or more subprograms in the next lower level. Structured programming, on the other hand, is the orderly and disciplined construction of programs as hierarchical, nested programming structures, sometimes called the non-GOTO approach. Program families instead view a program as consisting of a set of modules that will evolve over time. As a module changes, or a new one is added, a new program is created.

An interesting thing that has happened is these methods have moved up a level of abstraction into the design phase. This should not be too surprising, for if the design has been done properly, (a) the software should have been decomposed into modules using some step-wise refinement method, (b) possible program families should have been already identified, and (c) the basic algorithms, and data and control structures derived. But what has also happened is that these techniques have been embedded within the programming languages as well.

This has helped in numerous ways. First, it makes the control of the translation process more apparent to the implementer. The implementer knows where to begin, what to do next, and when to end. Second, the design can be captured more closely by the implementation. The mapping between the design and implementation is closer because the language to describe the two use the same "vocabulary." Finally, the software product has a better chance

Requirement	Feature Emphasis (Features)
Software Engineering	• Strong Typing (Data Types) • Data Abstraction and Information Hiding (Data Types and Packages) • Structured Control Constructs (Statements) • Concurrent Processing (Tasks)
Embedded Computer Systems	• Error Handling (Exceptions) • Machine Representation Facilities (Low-level Features)
Large System Development	• Separate Compiliation and Library Management (Program Library)
Reusable Software	• Generic Definition (Generics and Packages)

Table 6 - 2   **Ada vs. DoD Language Requirements**

to be reliable and maintainable because the controlling process is inseparable from the creation process. The Ada programming language is a prime example of this merging of implementation technique and language.

ADA. Ada [ADA83] is a modern-high order computer programming language which is the standard language[9] for writing DoD mission-critical computer software. Its designers were explicitly concerned with embedding the notions of structured programming required for large system developments into the language [LEBLANC82]. Ada was also designed with the understanding it would be the foundation of a programming environment, called an APSE (Ada Programming Support Environment), to help with other aspects of large system developments such as testing and configuration management. This will be discussed in more detail in Chapter 10.

Table 6-2 shows some of the features of Ada and how they map to the DoD requirement for supporting development of a software product. We will quickly review each one of these Ada features in the following paragraphs. Detailed information on the complete language and its practical application can be found in [WALLACE86].

TYPE. A *type* is a language abstraction which determines the values a variable or data structure may take on and how it is manipulated [SHAW84]. It is used for representing the form and behavior of real-world structures in the language. In other words, it serves as a blueprint to describe (not create) a set of values and the operations applicable to those actions. Ada has predefined types as well as user-defined types. The latter allows the mapping of concepts from the design domain to the the implementation domain [FAIRLEY84].

Ada is a strongly typed language. Strong typing means that operations are allowed only between objects of the same type. This is useful because it allows for error checking at compile time since the type of a variable remains constant once created. By strongly typing data structures, only valid actions are allowed when accessing data, thus aiding reliability and error detection.

An added feature in Ada is the addition of *private* types. Here, access to a variable of this type is even further restricted. This aids information hiding by keeping implementation details hidden from unauthorized or unwanted access.

PACKAGE. A *package* is a powerful abstraction mechanism for encapsulating a set of related information and isolating it from the rest of the program [SHAW84]. Consisting of a specification part and a package body, it is the primary method for structuring the system. The specification part contains the visible and private segments of the package, which is optional. Interface specifications for the data manipulating routines are separated in the visible segment, while the details of the data representations and manipulation routines are placed in the package body [FAIRLEY84]. These details are hidden from the users of the package.

Use of packages allows large systems to be composed of many small components whose interfaces are precisely defined, and whose implementations are hidden from each other. Packages are extremely flexible and can model any hardware or software interface. Moreover, changes to the package bodies can be made without impacting the rest of the program, as long as the interface definitions remain the same. This also allows the package body to be recompiled without recompiling anything outside the package.

Packages provide true physical and logical modularity without loss of flexibility or efficiency. The resulting structure is clean, and things are easy to find.

STATEMENTS. *Statements* in Ada provide logic control of specific actions. The language provides for basic actions (subprogram calls, assignments, etc.), flow control (if, case, loop and exit, return, etc.), and scope (begin, end), as well as controls required for real-time applications (synchronization, initialization, abort, etc.) and error control (exceptions). The different types of logic control, with the availability of packages, allows for tremendous flexibility to implement any design, check for errors, and recover from errors.

TASK. Another powerful element of Ada is the *task*. A task is defined as a program segment that can execute concurrently with one or more other program segments as long as the effects of the order of execution are independent. Conceptually they are very similar to packages, having a package body and specification part. The entry declaration is placed in the specification part.

Tasks allow for parallel threads of control to be expressed in the program execution. This provides the capability to execute independent code segments on different processors resulting in greater processing efficiency. The concurrency is real if the target architecture is a multiprocessor, and apparent if it is a uniprocessor.

EXCEPTIONS. Error handling in Ada is handled through *exceptions*. Exceptions are a mechanism for suspending the normal execution of a program. An exception stops sequential execution when a particular condition is reached, and transfers control to some known location where the condition may be handled. This is used when ranges on values might be exceeded, operations might be applied to illegal data values, memory is accessed outside of limits, etc. [FAIRLEY84].

Exceptions provide the ability for fault tolerant programming, thus increasing the system's reliability. Ada allows predefined and user-defined exceptions, and the user defined error handling routines.

LOW-LEVEL FEATURES. Ada also provides facilities to interface with the underlying target architecture or peripherals without having to leave the language through its *low-level features*. Machine representations, machine code insertion, low-level I/O, and the control of runtime checks are just some of the features. This facility increases the capacity of the program to represent the design in cases where the language itself may not be able to express it as succinctly.

COMPILATION. The last two features of Ada we wish to discuss are its separate compilation capability and generic facility. Ada *compilations* consist of one or more compilation units which are submitted together to the Ada compiler. This allows large Ada programs to be broken into pieces which are compiled separately. Typically, the program is decomposed into separately compiled subunits, which are then compiled after the compilation unit on which they depend. This facility provides for type checking across the boundaries of the compilation units, thus ensuring the integrity of the interfaces.

GENERICS. A *generic* facility allows the textual parameterization of an Ada procedure, function, package, or task [FAIRLEY84]. The parameters in a generic clause are replaced at translation time using macro expansion. The use of generics results in a single copy of a program unit, which promotes modularity and the possibility of software reuse.

The capabilities of a language like Ada allow for the close mapping of the implementation and design without undue machinations on the part of the implementer. It encourages, if not demands, that software engineering methods be utilized. The control of the translation process is obvious in the language features. The language also promotes testing of the the individual program units, as well as the program as a whole.

The trend in methods for implementation is to provide powerful languages, like Ada, that are targeted for specific application areas which can embody the control of the design to translation process within the program creation process.

6.5 Testing Methods

The number of methods available for use in testing is considerable, but specialized. For instance, most projects create their unique methods for testing depending on the product being developed. In this section we will cover some of the more generic methods that can be used for testing. As was discussed in Section 6.2 on the Testing Phase, test methods fall into two major categories: static testing and dynamic testing.

STATIC TESTING. Static testing is a disciplined review and analysis of the program design and code. Static testing methods are used almost exclusively for unit testing, where the program component is small enough to be readily examined. Dynamic testing is the execution of parts of the program to examine how well they compare with the specifications. Dynamic testing is used in both unit and product level testing.

Static testing is concerned with analysis of the structure of the code. It is useful for finding logic errors in a program, as well as questionable programming practices [FAIRLEY78]. A logic error might be an incorrectly initialized variable, where a variable initialized but never used might be considered a questionable practice (it definitely is a waste of space).

The methods used in static testing include manual code reviews, structured walk-throughs, and static path analysis. Code reviews and walk-throughs are useful for finding computational and logic errors. However, their coverage is not usually complete enough to find data definitional or program flow control errors. Path analysis helps in this area.

Static path analysis uses techniques from compiler theory to examine the flow graphs and call graphs of the program. Flow graphs are used to represent the flow of control of a program. The program is divided into blocks of code which represent integral units where the program control flow executes in a sequential manner. When the flow of control changes (such as a conditional statement or if a label is encountered), a block ends. An arc representing the flow of control path is drawn from the old block to the beginning of the new block of code, as shown in figure 6-5. The variables that are used with the code blocks and flow along the flow paths are analyzed for their usage. The types of information that can be gathered using this method include uninitialized variables, variables set but never used, infinite loops and unreachable code [GANNON79, AHO86].

Call graphs are similar to flow graphs, examining instead the calling invocations of program units (the main program, procedures, subroutines, functions, etc.) by other program units [FAIRLEY78]. The calling parameters and variables declared and used in the program unit are then analyzed. Possible misuses of parameters and global and local variables can be detected.

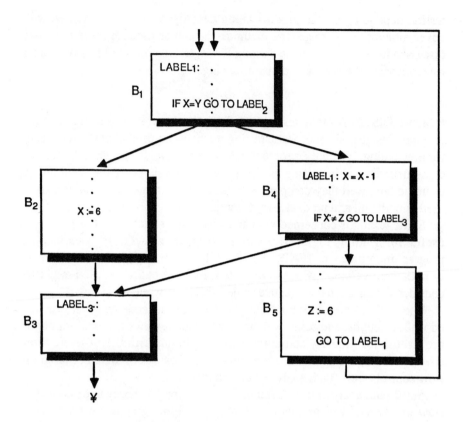

Figure 6 - 5   **Basic Blocks**

Static testing is useful to check for certain types of errors, but it is limited in its practical application. It is difficult to apply to large programs, and it does not give any information on errors that might occur during run-time, such as the evaluation of pointers or array references. One study suggested that as many as 25 percent of the errors may be undetected if path analysis is used alone for testing [GANNON79]. Dynamic testing can help provide better testing coverage.

DYNAMIC TESTING. Dynamic testing is concerned with execution of the program and the comparison of the results to the specifications. A well-defined test plan is usually a necessity when using dynamic testing as the tests are derived from the specification, and are checking for particular results. There are two general or different types of dynamic tests that can be applied, functional and logical.

Functional testing is intended to demonstrate that the program performs adequately under typical operational conditions. The test data is derived from specified functional requirements without regard to the individual program structure [ADRION82]. The program should compute the correct nominal output value for the specified nominal input value as shown in the specification [FAIRLEY78]. Functional testing is concerned about the external behavior of the program, i.e., from a black-box view.

Logical testing is concerned with how the program performs its computation. In this case the perspective is from the program's internal behavior; i.e., from a white box view.[10] In one aspect of logic testing, each indivdual program statement, decision, and condition is tested. This means that each statement is executed at least once, or each branch decision takes on all possible values, or each condition in a decision takes on all possible values. The testing can go a step farther and check all possible decision/condition combinations, although this is rarely ever done.

Logical testing can also be used for checking the data and control interfaces between program units. Data interfaces exist in the parameter passing mechanisms used by the program, while control interfaces exist in the invocation sequences of module entry and exits, as well as system routines. For instance a design may not allow access to certain variables or to a module itself by other specific modules (remember the concept of "private" in Ada), and these must be verified.

Timing is another area which is ripe for logical testing. Response times, excution times of routines, access times of variables, CPU times, statement execution frequency,etc., are just some of the items that can be obtained. The information obtained can show where inefficiencies exist in the program, such as where a 10 line loop is accounting for 90 percent of the execution time of a 200 line time critical module. Bentley shows how these types of problems can be detected and overcome [BENTLEY82].

The dynamic tests above can be applied to the individual modules for unit testing, or to the product in product level testing. In a product development, individual modules are usually tested at different time intervals. It is therefore hard to test the "complete" product at any particular instance. To overcome this difficulty, a number of different strategies have been developed which are lumped together under the term "integration testing." Integration testing is meant to assure that when the modules which have been tested individually are put together, they operate as a whole.

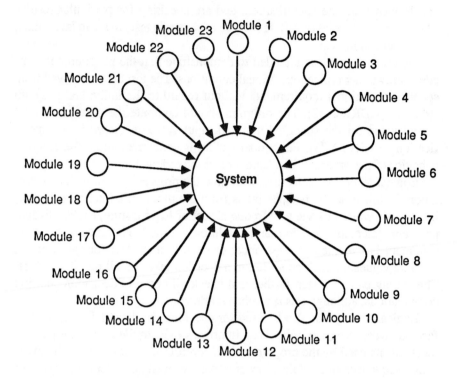

Figure 6 - 6   "Big Bang" Integration Testing Approach

INTEGRATION TESTING. Integration testing is the "complete" testing of the set of modules which makes up the product, using the previously unit tested modules to construct a product. One approach is to wait until all the units have passed testing, and then combine them into a conglomerate which is then tested, as shown in figure 6-6. This approach, sometimes called the "big bang" approach, is the oldest approach, and evolved from unstructured testing of small programs.

Unfortunately, the big bang approach has a number of disadvantages. Errors are difficult to isolate, since all the modules are interacting as one. Both hard and easy problems to fix appear the same. Fixing one error has a high probability of spawning others because everything is so tightly coupled. These types of errors cause a rippling effect which tends to spread new errors throughout the system. And finally, one is never sure when testing ends. There is no criteria for stopping since any error found means the product hasn't passed testing.

Another strategy is to construct the product in increments of tested units. A small set of modules (two or three) are integrated together and tested, to which another module is added and tested in combination, and so on. The advantages of this approach are numerous. Interface discrepancies can be easily found and corrected. Errors are localized to the new module and its interconnections. Fixing an error minimizes the spawning of new errors. The product development can be staggered, and modules integrated in as they complete unit testing. Testing is completed when the last module is integrated and tested. Integration testing can be accomplished from either a top-down or bottom-up approach, depending on the goals of the tests [FAIRLEY78].

When integration testing is complete, one more set of tests are run. These are called acceptance or certification testing. Here, the product is run with the actual hardware under operational conditions with the customer present. If the tests are passed, the product is officially complete.

The use of static and/or dynamic testing doesn't ensure that every error will be found. The practical limitations on testing, such as time and money, preclude that possibility. However, a well-defined test plan and integration strategy can go very far towards creating reliable products, and ultimately reducing the life cycle costs.

6.6 Evolution Methods

The methods used in the evolution phase are basically the same ones used in all the previous phases. The depth to which they are applied will vary depending on the type of evolution that is occurring.

In evolution that is marked by perfective maintenance, the current requirements and specifications are going to be changed. This will necessitate a repetition of each of the life cycle phases, but instead of starting over immediately, the output of each phase will be modified and estimates to how these modifications will affect the next phase outputs will be made. If the new enhancements are significant, then a decision may be to start a new product using the information gathered from the original one as input to the requirements phase.

If the evolution concerns adaptive maintenance, then the product is undergoing planned enhancements and all the same methods should be applied. The products of each individual phase are modified, but represent additions (or deletions) to the previous ones created. Notice that in both the perfective and adaptive case, if the documentation of the product at each phase is not up to date, then the amount of effort in reapplying the methods increases and the possibility of error also increases.

In the evolution marked by corrective maintenance, the testing phase methods are the ones usually first applied. Errors are reported from the user and documented by the use of trouble reports which describe the error, the operations being performed at the time, the product being used, and any supporting documentation such as the description of correct operation as specified by the specification or user manual. Depending on the severity of the error and the number found, a priority of fix will be given to the error. Errors that are fatal (ones that stop the program or keep a critical aspect from working correctly), or can cause damage to life or property are given the highest priority.

Depending on how well the error is described, the maintainer will try to repeat the error and document any symptoms that seem to foretell the error. Again, depending on the experience of the maintainer, a set of prescribed tests will be run, ranging from static test on an individual unit to product level tests using the full complement of dynamic tests. When (or if) the error is located, a judgment will be made on whether to fix the error. As was stated earlier, fixing one error might ripple many more throughout the system. If it is decided that the error should be fixed, a change is made to the program,[11] and the fix tested. Once satisfied that the error has been corrected, it is documented in the appropriate manuals, and a change notice sent out to current users of the product, and to either of the groups performing adaptive or perfective maintenance.

The updating of the documentation once an error is found is a source of much frustration. Ideally, every document that is affected should have the change incorporated. Unfortunately this is not easy, nor is it inexpensive, to do. No easy solution to this problem currently exists unless all documentation is available on-line, and any change that is made can be automatically traced to other changes that are also required.

One can begin to understand why no one wants to work on corrective maintenance.

6.7 Automation of Implementation, Testing, and Evolution Methods

The automation provided in these phases of the life cycle is substantial, varied, and well known, so we will only highlight a few. This does not mean the rest are of no interest in creating the software engineering environment, but as we will see in Chapter Ten, many environments targeted to support the implementation and test phases have been developed.

6.7.1 Implementation Automation

The automation of methods to support implementation has received the most attention. Again, the reason is that programming is very visible, and can be done without doing any formal design. It is also the logical place to start. The reduction of manual labor is the reason to use computers in the first place. What better place to start than reducing the efforts involved in manually setting switches that used to mark the earliest form of programming.

Current automation of the implementation phase includes all the items necessary to translate and execute the program that represents the translation of the design. These include compilers, linkers, loaders, operating systems, run-time executives, etc. This type of automation helps with the "clerical" aspects of implementation. The trend is now to aid the implementer's creativity in the creation of the programs themselves.

Automation used in the support of creativity comes under the general category of Program Transformation Systems [PATSCH83]. These systems are all meant to aid the implementer in developing programs. They range from simple editors to interactive transformation systems that use inputs from the specifications directly.

As an example, one simple kind of transformation system is the use of program composers or editors [TIETELBAUM81]. These are programs that are graphically oriented, and usually language specific, that have embedded within them the syntactic rules of the language. A visual representation of a language construct is shown on the screen in a template form. The key words of the language are in bold face, and the operand that requires manipulation is underlined.

The user calls up a construct for a particular language, such as an **If Then Else**, which then appears on the screen as **If** _____ **Then**_____

Else_____. The user then fills in the blanks with the operands he or she wishes. If it is illegal according to the language rules, then the user is notified. The operand is another statement, such as when nesting "If" statements, the new construct is created with all the correct syntactic definitions made. The level of sophistication of checking and helping the user depends on the individual editor. For instance, some allow partial execution (really interpretation) of the program developed so far, with highlighting showing the execution flow. When the program is complete, it may be then compiled and executed on the target architecture.

The advantages of this type of automation are obvious. The implementer does not have to worry about the syntactic elements of the language and can instead concentrate on composition of the program. Errors in language syntax are the most common ones made, and become greater as the language complexity increases. New constructs can also be tried out and tested before deciding to use them. This is also helpful in testing for errors. Finally, the productivity of the implementer, especially the inexperienced one, is increased.

Some of the more sophisticated transformation systems attempt to generate code automatically from the specifications, without programmer assistance [BALZER85]. Here, specifications are created, usually using a formal language of some type (like a PDL, or RSL in SREM), which is then processed and transformed into code. The crossing of the design gap is the major focus of research. The potential benefits are increased productivity, and enhanced product evolution, since only the specifications would have to be changed and retransformed.

6.7.2 Testing Automation

Automation in testing is aimed at reducing the clerical effort to conduct tests, and providing the capability to run more of them. For instance, static path analysis can be obtained in an automated manner from sophisticated optimizing compilers, which must perform the same types of analysis in their optimization procedures.

Software test drivers are another approach to automating the testing process. These automate the process of planning a test, setting up and running a test, collecting data, and analyzing the results. The test drivers are formal test procedures that are coded in a special test language. The test driver allows the specification of many different types of tests and test data. When executing a test, the test driver applies the specific test procedures to all or parts of the program. The result is that a program can be tested in a number of ways concurrently without the tester having to run a test, check the results, run the next test, etc. This saves time, as well as provides a record of where a program is producing errors. This is important, since simple errors are usually coupled to complex errors [DEMILLO78], and errors tend to cluster [BRANSTAD80]. By having a record of the errors and where they appear, predictions can be made on the likelihood of the program still containing errors.

There are generally two types of software test drivers: object-level and source-level. Object-level test drivers operate on the object-level modules, and are language independent. Source-level operates on the source code, and specifies tests that are based on the internal program structure. These are highly language-specific.

Other automated testing support has been applied to run-time profile generators and system performance monitors [PLATTNER81]. Run-time profilers provide services such as being able to sample the program during execution to find out which areas of the program are being executed the most frequently. A profile displaying the relative frequency of statement execution is then generated.

System performance monitors are similar to profilers except they normally embed extra statements into the source code to aid in the collection of data. For instance, they can count the number of executions of a single statement, such as a procedure call, to provide more exact information then the profile. They can extract how often and where procedure calls are made to systems services. And they also can provide information on which program paths have been executed based on specified input data.

Almost any test method can be automated, but it is usually up to the specific product development to determine whether this will occur. The reason is that most implementations of test methods are dependent on the product developed and the target architecture it executes on, and it may not be cost effective to spend the money automating the methods.

6.7.3 Evolution Method Automation

There isn't any automation in this phase that is unique. All the automation that exists in the other phases is useful for accomplishing evolution of the product. The real question is whether the automation will be provided to the groups doing evolution, since they normally don't have a high priority in the overall scheme of things. This will be addressed further in Chapter Twelve.

6.8 Requirements of a Software Engineering Environment

The life cycle phases of implementation, test and design re-emphasize the requirements placed on the environment by the other phases. The implementers must have consistent and complete information about the design available from which to code from. Moreover, they must have the capability to code and debug their programs rapidly, and have the capability to show how the resulting program meets the design. Thus the environment is required to provide these services.

The testing phase has many different techniques that are required. Static testing (path analysis), dynamic testing, unit testing, and integration testing are all required to be supported by the environment. In each of these cases the ability to show traceability between what code is being tested and what set of requirements the code is satisfying is necessary.

In evolution, it is vital to have all the methods and information that were used to create a product available on-line. Moreover, when a change or enhancement is made to the product, all the documentation requiring changes must be identified as a minimum and changed if possible. The requirement on the environment to perform evolution is an environment. Chapter Nine will identify the capabilities in the environment which will satisfy the above requirements.

6.9 Summary

In this chapter we have surveyed the processes, methods, and automation that make up the implementation, testing, and evolution phases of a products life cycle. We have seen that the process of implementation is not straight-forward, mostly because of the difficulty with translating a design into an implementation, and because the process of producing code is error prone. A software engineering environment must try to help in both these areas.

In testing, we have examined the various methods that can be used in testing. Each is targeted toward testing one aspect of the product, and to thoroughly test it many approaches must be supported by the environment. Moreover, the environment must support the rapid creation of tests and test data to remove much of the drudgery and difficulty involved in testing.

The evolution phase calls on all the processes, methods, and automation that exists to perform the tasks of adaptive, enhancement, and corrective maintenance. It requires all the information that went into building the product, as well as the information about the product itself.

To fully support the activities of these phases of the life cycle, a software engineering environment should provide to its user the capability to:

- Create and execute programs;

- Debug and test the programs;

- Evaluate the program for consistency and completeness against the design;

- Evaluate the quality of the programs created;

- Create and execute various tests on the program components during unit and product level testing using both static and dynamic means;

- Evolve the product using the information and methods that created it.

The next chapter is concerned with management activities and their requirements that a software engineering environment must support.

FOOTNOTES:

1. Physical form is somewhat of a misnomer. Software has no form, weighs nothing, and can't be touched. Yet it has a static form (the tapes, disks, or firmwire that represent the program) and a dynamic one as well (the program while it is executing in the system) which we can "measure."
2. Which is why many advocate the use of an implementation language with full syntax as a PDL.

3. In other words, which processor in the network the module is attached or assigned to.

4. This isn't exactly right. The 100 million lines aren't all application lines. So instead of a million modules, lets be conservative and say 100,000 instead.

5. This includes an incremental delivery of a product.

6. Caution is advisable in interpreting this number. A product evolution that changes the software may necessitate changes to the hardware as well [CLAPP81]. However, since a new product is developed from scratch only once, but evolved numerous times, the cost should be close to this ratio.

7. Instead of being in a "lost world" like testing, it is a "poor step-child" [LIENTZ83]. I'm not sure which is worse.

8. We are going to relax our definition of method for the implementation, testing and evolution phases. What exist are really more of a collection of techniques, rather than formal methods.

9. Fortran, CMS-2, Cobol and Jovial are also DoD standard languages currently in use.

10. White-box testing is very dependent upon having good documentation available.

11. If separate compilation is not available, then the whole program may have to be recompiled. This is not satisfactory in most cases, so "patches" to the machine code are made instead. At some future time, usually at regular intervals, all patches are compiled into the source code.

7. MANAGEMENT ACTIVITIES

"Ninety percent of the time things will turn out worse than you expect. The other ten percent of the time you had no right to expect so much."

Augustine's Laws

7.0 Introduction

Management is an activity that concerns both the process of developing a product and the product itself. The management of the process is directed inward, controlling how resources are being used to develop the product [BERSOFF84]. It is also directed outward, concerned with the product integrity and how the user and customer perceive it.

The people managing software development have the most important and difficult job of all. Because they can have the largest impact on the success or failure of the software product [BOEHM84a], every decision they make has the potential for making bad things better or good things worse. Unfortunately they start off work everyday with a definite disadavantage. It is the nature of things in the world that the probability of doing something wrong is higher than the probability of getting something right. For example, a manager can adversely impact the product development in all sorts of ways, like:

- Assigning too much work to one group, and not enough to another.

- Assigning the wrong people to the wrong job.

- Failing to listen to their technical personnel on technical issues.

- Choosing the wrong organizational structure for the task at hand.

- Neglecting to obtain adequate resources to create the product.

- Not fully understanding what the product is.

We shouldn't be too harsh on software management because it is a very complex undertaking in which a complex network of interrelationships and interactions exist [ABDEL-HAMID83]. The type of person who can do it well is rare. The ideal manager is one who can understand and balance the technological, economic, and social bases through which software is developed [SCACCHI84]. Moreover, he or she must be a pragmatist, knowing what can and can't be realistically accomplished [FOX76].

The best way we can describe it is that being a software manager is very much like being a coach of a sports team. Your function is to get everyone ready to play, i.e., obtain facilities and equipment, get them into shape, train them, select the proper positions for them based on their abilities, etc. When the game begins, you, as coach, influence the game by deciding the tactical strategy. How well the players implement it is beyond your direct control. If they do it poorly, there aren't a lot of options open to you. If you choose a poor strategy, then you are also out of luck. Thus, things have many more ways of going wrong than right. And in the end, the players get the cheers for a good play, and the coaches get blamed for their poor performance.[1] Which brings us to the points of motivation, responsibility, and accountability.

As any good coach knows, to be successful, the team has to act as a team and not as a bunch of individuals. For a software manager, instilling this teamwork idea into the developers is important to the eventual success of the product. This means helping define peoples' roles and functions or responsibilites. Furthermore, the manager must make it clear that the responsibilities such as reliability, quality, correctness, etc., don't exist in any one role or person, but are in all the project personnel. What must be avoided is the current trend in software management to shift accountability from the producers (i.e., developers) to the non-producers (i.e., management). Every person involved in the development must take responsibility for the product, and like in a game where one player is caught out of position, someone else must fill in to cover.

In this chapter we will examine some of the activities that we lump together as management activities, i.e., those things that management is ultimately responsible for in making the product successful. We have chosen to break them into three categories: Resource Management, Product Assurance (quality assurance, configuration management, verification and validation), and Reusability. Some of these categories are not traditionally grouped as management functions, especially reusability, but in the concept of a software engineering environment we believe they should be. The remainder of the chapter will try to explain why.

In the final analysis, management is concerned with people. After all, people produce the product.

7.1 General Management Activities

In the previous four chapters we concerned ourselves mostly with the process of developing the software products, not really very much with its management. As we mentioned in the introduction, management has the greatest potential for making a mess of things. The primary reason is that management is really concerned with decision making under uncertainty [BOEHM84a]. These uncertainties are caused by such things as incomplete requirements, changes in the scope of work, incorrect initial assumptions, and (negative) deviations in productivity [HOWES84]. They are also caused by the tradeoffs between reliability vs. efficiency, maintainability vs. efficiency, etc., that affect system effectivesnesss, development time and schedule, and life cycle maintenance. The resources or time required to put out the "perfect" product are infinite. Therefore, it is management's responsibility to make these tradeoff decisions.2 Management attempts to reduce the uncertainty by three general methods: planning, monitoring and controlling [SEEWG82], as shown in figure 7-1.

PLANNING. Planning is the activity which involves estimating what is needed to meet the objectives of the product development, and then organizing and allocating the resources to perform the work. Estimation must consider the size and complexity of the software being developed, the skill mix and productivity of the development professionals, the funding allocated the development, the time allocated the schedule, the potential problem areas, and the power and sophistication of the support resources, including development methods [WOLF85].

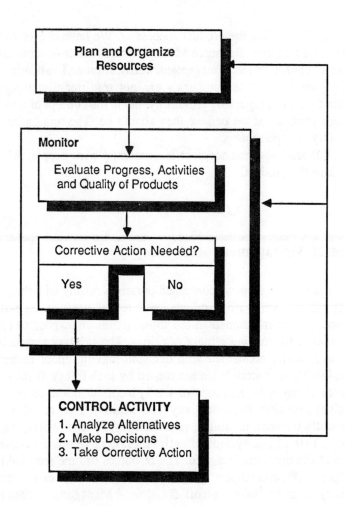

Figure 7 - 1   **The Management Process**

Plans must be made to develop an integrated approach toward the overall program, and to develop cohesive working relationships among all the support groups. Two very important issues that must be resolved in this activity are what is the product (i.e., what are its requirements) and what constitutes a successful product development and product [THAYER80].[3] Once estimation is complete and documented in a software development plan, the resources will be organized and allocated to do the work. We will discuss more about planning in Section 7.2, Resource Management, and Section 7.4, Reusability.

Criterion	Definition
TRACEABILITY	Those attributes of the software that provide a thread from the requirements to the implementation with respect to the specific development and operational environment
COMPLETENESS	Those attributes that provide full implementation of the functions required
CONSISTENCY	Those attributes that provide uniform design and implementation techniques and notation
ACCURACY	Those attributes that provide the required precision in calculation and notation
ERROR TOLERANCE	Those attributes that provide continuity of operation under nonnominal conditions
SIMPLICITY	Those attributes that provide implementation of functions in the most understandable manner (Usually avoidance of practices which increase complexity)
MODULARITY	Those attributes that provide a structure of highly independent modules
GENERALITY	Those attributes that provide breadth to the functions performed
EXPANDABILITY	Those attributes that provide for expansion of data storage requirements or computational functions
INSTRUMENTATION	Those attributes that provide for the measurement of usage or identification of errors
SELF-DESCRIPTIVENESS	Those attributes that provide explanation of the implementation of a function

Table 7 - 1   **Criteria Definitions for Software Quality**   *Source: [SQM79]*

Criterion	Definition
EXECUTION EFFICIENCY	Those attributes that provide for minimum processing time
STORAGE EFFICIENCY	Those attributes that provide for minimum storage requirements during operation
ACCESS CONTROL	Those attributes that provide for control of the access of software and data
ACCESS AUDIT	Those attributes that provide for and audit the access of software and data
OPERABILITY	Those attributes that determine operation and procedures concerned with the operation of software
TRAINING	Those attributes that provide transition from current operation to initial familiarization
COMMUNICATIVENESS	Those attributes that provide useful inputs and outputs which can be assimilated
SOFTWARE SYSTEM INDEPENDENCE	Those attributes that determine the software's dependency on the software environment (operating systems, utilities, input/output routines, etc.)
MACHINE INDEPENDENCE	Those attributes that determine the software's dependency on the hardware system
COMMUNICATIONS COMMONALITY	Those attributes that provide the use of standard protocols and interface routines
DATA COMMONALITY	Those attributes that provide the use of standard data representations
CONCISENESS	Those attributes that provide for implementation of a function with a minimum amount of code

FACTOR	SOFTWARE CRITERIA	FACTOR	SOFTWARE CRITERIA
Correctness	Traceability Consistency Completeness	Flexibility	Modularity Generality Expandability
Reliability	Error Tolerance Consistency Accuracy Simplicity	Testability	Simplicity Modularity Instrumentation Self-Descriptiveness

Efficiency	Storage Efficiency
	Execution Efficiency
		Portability	Modularity
			Self-Descriptiveness
			Machine
			  Independence
			Software System
			  Independence

Integrity	Access Control Access Audit		
Usability	Operability Training Communicativeness	Reusability	Generality Modularity Software System Independence
Maintainability	Consistency	Interopera- bility	Modularity Communication Commonality Data Commonality

Table 7 - 2 **Software Criteria and Related Quality Factors**
Source : [SQM79]

MONITORING. Monitoring is the activity used to gauge the progress of the work to date, the quality of the products to date, the quality of the development process, and the adherence to standards. Management must be continually aware of the expenditures of effort required to meet the project goals and the progress being made toward the scheduled completion dates for each product. Management must take corrective action on any expenditure which is not proceeding according to the plan, which may mean conducting policy impact assessments and analysis in adminstrative and technical areas.

By using product assurance techniques, the quality of each product is compared to a pre-established definition of quality as shown in tables 7-1 and 7-2. Products not meeting the standards will require reworking. Progress is periodically evaluated, and accomplishments are compared against the plan.

Technical progress and resources expended are matched against the budgets and schedules of the development plan, and any deviations discovered marked for correction.

Product assurance techniques are also used to evaluate the quality of the development process and adherence to standards. The techniques such as inspections, audits, and walk-throughs are used to show that each product developed during a phase is complete, consistent and up to date. Compliance to standards is important in that they are useful in preventing errors, finding errors early and making the developers more productive [POSTON84]. Section 7.3, Product Assurance, describes the monitoring function in more detail.

CONTROLLING. The management activity of controlling is concerned with maintaining control over both the development process and the products of the process. The control of the process focuses on meeting the goals and objectives (established in the development plan) through the use of all the available resources. Authority is delegated and responsibility assigned through the organizational structure to various groups so they may be able to execute their duties in a timely manner. Conflicts among the various organization structures are resolved, and communication channels are forced to remain open.

The control of products focuses on the products of each activity in the software development process. Configuration management protects products by creating a master copy ("baseline") against which controlled changes are made. This ensures the consistency of the evolving product as requirements are defined, specifications are documented, the design is developed and implemented, and changes made to it. Figure 7-2 summarizes the major activities of management.

DEFENSIVE MANAGEMENT. How planning, monitoring, and controlling are accomplished by management changes with each phase of the life cycle. The reason is that the perspective taken by management changes because the levels of the organization involved become lower as the product undergoes development. In other words, more technical and less senior personnel form the ranks of (lower) management. Table 7-3 illustrates some of the concerns of management in each phase.

Management also must be aware that the development process is not perfect, and that change is inevitable in the product, which means the process

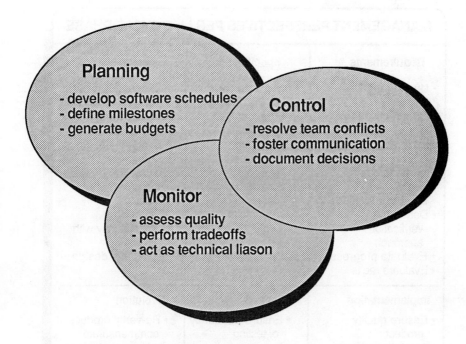

Figure 7 - 2   **Major Management Activities**

development is inherently unstable. Every decision is fraught with the possibility of causing more damage than good, as all the intangibles lurk out there in the distance waiting to foul things up. Thus, in this spirit we offer some words of advice which we call " The Rule of Defensive Management." They may seem a little paranoid, but as in driving, you have to watch out for the other guy. The rule is to ask the following questions before and after every management decision:

- What can go wrong?

- How and when will I know it went wrong?

- What will I do when it does go wrong?

- How am I going to prevent it from going wrong?

MANAGEMENT PERSPECTIVES PER LIFE CYCLE PHASE		
Requirements	**Specification**	**Design**
• Understand User req'ts • Communication and Concurrence of req'ts with user • Determine accuracy of resources • Evaluate risk • Establish baseline • Determine verification approach • Evaluate progress • Evaluate req'ts	• Evaluate spec's for testability • Form contract with user • Generate functional test data • Establish consistency with req'ts • Evaluate spec's	• Ensure complete design • Develop test plans • Evaluate design adequacy • Generate structural test data • Establish consistency with spec's • Evaluate design
Implementation	**Test**	**Evolution**
• Ensure quality product • Establish adequacy of implementation • Determine standards followed • Ensure consistency with design • Evaluate implementation	• Ensure adequacy of testing • Ensure product integrity • Sell product to customer	• Re-verify product commensurate with level of redevelopment

Table 7 - 3

In summary, the pragmatic manager will recognize that something, whether it be the requirements, specification, design, etc., will not be right or complete. Therefore, to operate in this environment of decision-making with incomplete knowledge, management should try to build schedules that recognize this fact, promote early identification of things that might change, and promote flexibility in the product design to accommodate future change [BUCKLEY84].

7.2   Resource Management

Resource management is concerned with managing the four major resources that a manager can apply to a software development: funding, time, personnel, and equipment. In this section we will be concerned with the first two more than last, mostly because the number of personnel and amount of equipment used are normally grouped together with funding as "costs."

Resource management begins at the start of the system development, before the actual software requirements analysis phase is initiated. A gross cost is determined for the software and a budget is given to the software program manager as an initial guiding point. These will be revised (usually upward) as the project gets better information.

Estimating resources accurately and determining a realistic schedule are still the major problems in successfully planning software developments [ABDEL-HAMID83]. The reason is that so many things can go wrong. Wolverton [WOLVERTON84] lists just some of the typical reasons why:

- Simultaneous unattainable requirements;

- Defective specifications;

- Overinspection and testing;

- Unsure customers;

- New technology/designs;

- Disputed interpretations of requirements.

Each of the above problems could have easily been attributable to almost every late or costly software project.

RESOURCE PREDICTION. Predicting costs and schedules is especially hard, and numerous models have been suggested. Table 7-4, for instance, lists only some of the ones that have been suggested. We won't attempt to go into any detail on these models, but will try to explain some of the basics involved. The literature is full of information of on models. A small sample is [HERD77, MYERS78, GOLDBERG80,BOEHM81, and WOLVERTON84].

• Experience Method	• Number of Instructions
• Constraint Method	• Quantitative Method
• Top-down Estimating	• Cost per Instruction
• Ratio Estimating	• Percent of Hardware Method
• Standards Estimating	• Putnam
• Bottom-up Estimating	• Cocomo
• Units of Work Method	

Table 7 - 4   **Methods of Cost Estimating**

The problem with all cost and schedule models that have been suggested is that they depend on past experience for calibration [ABDEL-HAMID83]. If the past data is poor, or if it was gathered only on small product developments, then estimating the schedule for large projects becomes suspect. These models come typically in two flavors: micro-estimation and macro-estimation [MYERS78].

Micro-estimation begins with fixing the size, start date, and duration of each phase. Adjustments are then made for personnel experience, product complexity, etc. For example, Brooks noted that utility programs are three times as difficult to write as application programs, and system programs are three times harder than utility programs [BROOKS75]. Therefore, dozens of factors are typically used as input.

Work breakdown structures (WBS) are often used to develop this type of information. Here, a product development maps out all the high level tasks that are required to be done in each phase. Then each of these is divided into sub-tasks, in an iterative process until the lowest level of granularity is reached. Each bottom level sub-task then has an associated cost, time, and manpower or other value which is then used to compute its parent and so on until the total cost, time and manpower is computed.

Macro-estimation uses more general information like manpower, time and effort that have been gathered over time and generates an expected curve of life cycle manpower vs. time. The macro model tries to give estimates

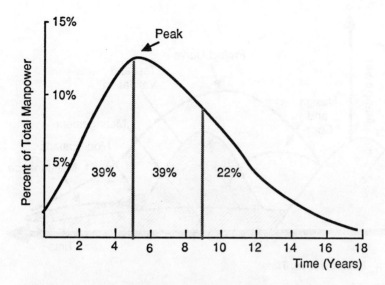

Figure 7 - 3   **Rayleigh Distribution of Manpower vs. Time
in a Typical Product Development**

based more on general case analysis. One macro-estimated model used is the Putnam model [PUTNAM78, MEYERS78].

The Putnam model is used to predict costs and delivery schedules. The model can use historical data to generate likely costs and schedules for future, or it can be used to predict cost and schedule of a product development as it is progressing.

The Putnam model assumes that all software projects follow a curve characterized by a Rayleigh distribution as shown in figure 7-3. What is predicted to occur is that the peak manpower will occur at about 40 percent of the total budget. This is then followed by the product evolution which then consumes approximately 60 percent of the expenditures.

To use the model, the manager plots the number of people in each phase of the development as a function of time, similar to that as shown in figure 7-4 [WARBURTON83]. Notice that the composite project curve is a Rayleigh shape, but has several sub-cycles. Each sub-cycle shows how the manpower will increase and fall off as the project progresses through each phase of the life cycle. Requirements, specification and planning work which are not usually included in the model are also shown.

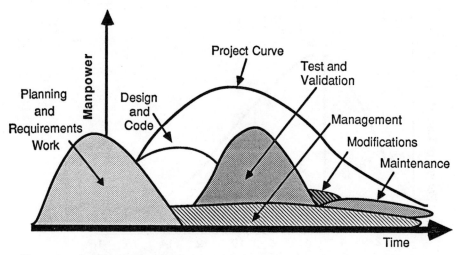

Figure 7 - 4   **Manpower vs. Time**

Both types of modeling have their place, but micro-estimation is harder than macro-estimation in that it requires much more information to obtain results than the macro method. Also, the results can fluctuate widely (up to 200 percent in some cases [MYERS78]) depending on the weight given particular factors in the model which may or may not be present in a particular product development.

The Putnam model seems to work reasonably well for very large projects, although a prudent manager doesn't do it once and forget about it. The inability to include all the front end information is a drawback for starters, as is the lack of precision of the estimates. Most likely the manager will not only want to continue to excercise the model throughout the life cycle, but also want to use at least one other model, such as the COCOMO model [BOEHM-81] for verification and to obtain a "warm" feeling about the numbers.

The Constructive Cost Model (COCOMO) model uses both micro and macro-estimation techniques. In this model, equations based upon studies of numerous projects are used to estimate the cost and schedule based on the delivered lines of source code. Effort multipliers, or cost drivers (see figure 1-15) are used to refine the estimates and tune the software equations and the resulting estimates. The cost drivers themselves can be be tuned depending on numerous other factors as well. The outputs of this model are usually reliable if the lines of code is reasonably well known and the multipliers can be chosen correctly.

ESTIMATION ACCURACY. Whatever method is used, care must be exercised when using the results of cost estimation models. It is often the case that external factors really drive the schedule. For instance, the OS/360 operating system was developed in two years because the hardware was going to be ready in two years [MYERS78].

Further, men and manpower are not interchangeable. It has been shown many times that although related, there is not a one-to-one corespondence between the two. The reason is the cat and rat problem. One cat may kill one rat in one hour, and two may kill it in half an hour. However, sixty won't kill it in a minute. What you'll have is most of the cats not even seeing the rat, and those that do are probably suffocated by the others trying to get at the rat. Result, one dead rat, and ten dead cats, probably taking five minutes. As has been noted, adding manpower to an already late project only makes it later [BROOKS75].

The management of resources is very easy, if the project development follows the estimates. If it doesn't, then it becomes very difficult. Many authors suggest the best way to attack the problem is to view the management process as a feedback control system [MYERS78, ABDEL-HAMID83, BERSOFF84]. Here, the development process is seen as having some "natural schedules," like those shown by the Putnam model. The trick is to learn what parameters can be tampered with to keep the development stable, and when something unexpected happens, what can be tuned to regain stability. For instance, if a schedule starts to fall behind: (a) the scope of the product requirements can be reduced, and/or; (b) resources can be reallocated from one task to another, and/or: (c) the schedule and manpower can be increased (within reason) or; (d) the project can be terminated.

However, the option(s) chosen must be done with care to avoid overcompensation and creating even more instability in the development. It seems that the schedule and organizational structure significantly influences the decisions of all the development personnel, and changing it changes their perceptions of the problem [ABDEL-HAMID83]. This might in turn lead to making uninformed decisions that lead to other compensations, etc.

MAKING A PLAN. The last element of the management of resources is the documentation of the master plan, or what is commonly called the software development plan (SDP) [COOPER84]. In this document are captured all the initial cost, schedule, personnel and equipment estimates and assumptions of

---

SOFTWARE DEVELOPMENT PLAN

1.0 Introduction
2.0 Furnished informaton, equipment, services, facilities
3.0 High risk areas
4.0 Software engineering standards, practices, procedures
5.0 Project organizations
6.0 Schedule and milestones
7.0 Design approach
8.0 Implementation approach
9.0 Integration and test approach
10.0 Software development practices
11.0 Product assurance management
12.0 Product release plans

Table 7 - 5   *Source: [COOPER84]*

the product development, like organization, design approach, etc. It is revised as necessary as the product progresses through the life cycle. The document is used by management to keep track of the development, as a means to get everyone involved in the development process to agree to an approach, and as a communication device to ask and resolve development questions. Table 7-5 is a typical outline of an SDP.

Automation to support resource mangement activity has not been extensive. Typically, what has been provided are automated WBSs, spreadsheeting types of programs, and a few of the cost models. One effort called the Manager's Decision Support System (MDSS), has been been under study at the Defense System Management College [BUEDE84]. It has planning aids for evaluating product development alternatives and ways of answering cause and effect questions concerning the development. Every organization seems to have its own planning standards, and therefore little in the way of standardized effortsto help in this area are being reported.

The activity we want to look at next is the monitoring activites that come under the general heading of Product Assurance.

7.3 Product Assurance

Product assurance is the activity that is concerned with product integrity, i.e., the construction of a product which closely matches the user/customer's real needs [BERSOFF84]. The product should be one:

- that fulfills user functional needs;

- that can be traced throughout the development life cycle;

- that meets the specification for performance;

- whose cost is as expected;

- whose scheduled delivery is met.

The responsibility of assuring product integrity rests with all the development personnel, but a number of groups are charged with the specific responsibility and authority to ensure that it happens. These are the Quality Assurance, Configuration Management, and Verification and Validation groups. Testing is also part of this group, but its formal role is concentrated in one particular phase of the life cycle, rather than across it. Moreover, realize that the terminology used in product assurance is used in a widely varying manner among participants. One person's quality assurance is another's test and evaluation [BRYAN84]. With these cautionary notes, we will start with Quality Assurance.

7.3.1 Quality Assurance

Quality assurance (QA) is an activity that tries to ensure that the product meets or exceeds specification [BERSOFF84]. It is defined by the IEEE Standard for Software Quality [IEEE81] as a planned and systematic pattern of actions necessary to provide adequate confidence that the items or project conforms to established technical requirements. In other words, it makes sure products adhere to a pre-established standard.

The quality of a product are the totality of features and characteristics that bears on its ability to meet user needs [BUCKLEY84]. The control of quality are the actions necessary to measure the characteristics of the product and compare them to the specification.

Quality can't be tested into a product, but must be built into it. The process must start at the very beginning of the life cycle and continue until the product is retired. The reason is simple . Each phase of the life cycle provides a new opportunity for error. Even if we produce quality requirements, this does guarantee quality specifications. And if we allow a poor specification to be produced and propogated, a poor design will result, as well as a worse implementation. As Mizuno points out, this "accumulation of errors" can lead to a product that is unfixable [MIZUNO83]. Figure 7-5 shows this process graphically. Table 7-6 illustrates the type of quality factors that should be measured in a software development and when, and the resulting impacts if they are not built in.

However, quality does have a price and not all factors can be attained simultaneously. Certain tradeoffs have to occur since some factors are synergistic in nature, and others are in conflict. Table 7-7 illustrates how some of these factors interact, and table 7-8 shows some of the tradeoff considerations.

QA TECHNIQUES. The techniques used for quality assurance are normally reviews [FREEDMAN82], inspections [FAGAN75], and walk-throughs [WEINBERG84]. Reviews are concerned with finding inaccuracies, omissions, and extraneous information. They determine the internal completeness and consistency of the product's requirements, specification, design, implementation, and test information. Reviews also assess the information produced with respect to consistency to its predecessor information.

Reviews are conducted by a broad range of personnel, including developers, managers, users, and outside experts. They are not a permanent body in the organization, but are set up as necessary and conducted as meetings. Each review group has specific objectives and questions to be addressed, depending on what type of review is initiated. The findings are returned to the proper development group for any action.

Inspections evaluate the correctness of the component level specification, design, implementation, test plans, and test results. They are more formal and more rigorous than reviews. Here a very focused set of questions are asked, such as going over a checklist of faults that might appear in the product.

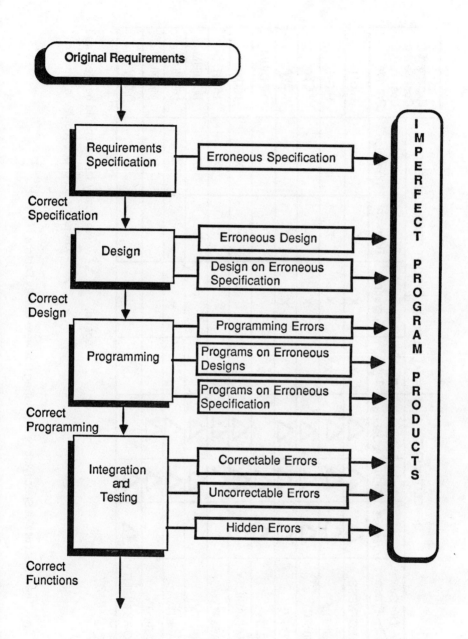

Figure 7 - 5   **Accumulative Effects of Error**   *Source : [MIZUNO83]*

Life Cycle Phases / Factors	DEVELOPMENT			EVALUATION		POST-DEVELOPMENT		Expected Cost Saved: Cost To Provide
	Req'ts Analysis	De-sign	Code & Debug	System Test	Operation	Revision	Transition	
CORRECTNESS	△	△	△	X	X	X		HIGH
RELIABILITY	△	△	△	X	X	X		HIGH
EFFICIENCY	△	△	△		X			LOW
INTEGRITY	△	△	△		X			LOW
USABILITY	△	△		X		X		MEDIUM
MAINTAINABILITY		△	△			X	X	HIGH
TESTABILITY		△	△	X		X	X	HIGH
FLEXIBILITY		△	△			X	X	MEDIUM
PORTABILITY		△	△				X	MEDIUM
REUSABILITY		△	△				X	MEDIUM
INTEROPERABILITY	△	△		X			X	LOW

Source : [SQM79]

Legend: △ - where quality factors should be measured

X - where impact of poor quality is realized

Table 7 - 6   The Impact of Not Specifying or Measuring Software Quality Factors

Factors	Correctness	Reliability	Efficiency	Integrity	Usability	Maintainability	Testability	Flexibility	Portability	Reusability	Interoperability
Correctness											
Reliability	○										
Efficiency											
Integrity			●								
Usability	○	○	●	○							
Maintainability	○	○	●		○						
Testability	○	○	●		○	○					
Flexibility	○	○	●	●	○	○	○				
Portability			●			○	○				
Reusability		●	●	●		○	○	○	○		
Interoperability			●	●					○		

If a high degree of quality is present for factor, what degree of quality is expected for the other:

○ = High   ● = Low

Blank = No relationship or application dependant

Table 7 - 7   **Relationships Between Software Quality Factors** *Source: [SQM79]*

Integrity vs. Efficiency	The additional code and processing required to control the access of the software or data usually lengthens run-time and requires additional storage.
Useability vs. Efficiency	The additional code and processing required to ease an operator's tasks or provide more usable output usually lengthens run-time and increases storage.
Maintainability vs. Efficiency	Optimized code increases maintainer's efforts. Using modules, instrumentation, etc., however, increases overhead.
Testability vs. Efficiency	The above applies to testing.
Portability vs. Efficiency	The use of direct, optimized, or utilities decreases the portability of the system.
Flexibility vs. Efficiency	Generality for a flexible system increases overhead.
Reusability vs. Efficiency	The above applies to reuse.
Interprobability vs. Efficiency	The added overhead for data conversion and interface routines decreases operating efficiency.
Flexibility vs. Integrity	Flexibility requires very general structures. Security may be harder to insure.
Reusability vs. Integrity	As above, reusable software provides severe security problems.
Interoperability vs. Integrity	Coupled systems allow for more paths that can allow either accidental or purposeful access to data.
Reusability vs. Reliability	The generality required by reusable software makes providing for error tolerance and accuracy difficult

Table 7 - 8   **Typical Quality Factor Tradeoffs**

The make up of this group is very specific, usually all having the same level of expertise.

Walk-throughs are different from inspections or reviews. Here the product is "walked through" (i.e., a lecture is given on it) by the person or persons responsible for the product. The reason is to convey as much information as possible to the widest possible audience. General improvements to the product are suggested in this type of "informal review."

These techniques are employed to give management unbiased information on the status of the product [WEINBERG84]. Development groups are known for being optimistic about their progress and quality, and it is important that an independent assessment be given. If problems occur, then management has the information from which to make logical and reasoned decisions.

Quality assurance techniques by their nature do not lend themselves to automation, although it could be used to help in showing traceability and consistency in performing reviews.

The next product assurance technique we wish to examine is configuration management.

7.3.2 Configuration Management

Configuration management (CM) is the aspect of product assurance that is concerned with identifying the configuration of a system at discrete points in time for the systematic controlling of changes and monitoring integrity and traceability throughout the life cycle. This helps management know what it is that they are supposed to build, what it is they are building, and what has been built so far. The following discussion is based on [BERSOFF84].

Configuration management has four components:

- identification,

- control,

- auditing, and

- status accounting.

IDENTIFICATION. Identification is the definition and recording of the product baseline.[4] A baseline is a snapshot in time of the existing aggregate of information which defines the product. When this information is updated and another snapshot made (called "freezing the baseline") the next (and newest) baseline is formed. Software identification is concerned with giving names to these baselines and tracing their parentage.

Identification is important because one baseline might be used as a basis (i.e., is a parent of) of a number of different modifications, each having its own baseline (i.e., are unique children of the original baseline). In large product developments where many enhanced versions of the original are being worked on simultaneously, ensuring integrity of each version is vital.

CONTROL. Software configuration control is an administrative mechanism for initializing, preparing, evaluating, and approving/disapproving all proposals for changing the baseline throughout the products life. The administration of change proposals includes: (1) documentation, called an Engineering Change Proposal (ECP) that is for the initiation of requests for change as well as the definition of the proposed change; (2) an organization for formal evaluation and disposition of change proposal called a Software Configuration Control Board (SCCB), and; (3) the procedures for the control of changes to the baseline.

Requests for change might come from a change in the requirements or from a documentation defect. However, not every proposal for change is accepted. An assessment is made of the technical feasibility of the change and its impact on schedule and budget. Considerations of the effects on future baselines, product maintainability, flexibility, etc., are also required. The change is approved or disapproved, based on its value and cost. If accepted, the baseline is modified once a fully verified change is created. The system is very autocratic, with the leader of the SCCB having final authority to disapprove or approve a change.

AUDITING. Software configuration auditing is the mechanism for determining how well the current state of the software product maps to the requirement and specification documents. It also serves as the mechanism for formally establishing the baseline. A document is not sanctioned to be baselined until after it has been audited. The same is true for updates to the baseline.

Auditing has two functions: configuration verification and configuration validation. Configuration verification is meant to ensure that what is intended for each configured item specified in one baseline is achieved in the next. Configuration validation is meant to ensure the configured item meets the customer/user's needs. These two together help ensure a quality product and raises any problems to management in a very visible fashion.

STATUS ACCOUNTING. Configuration status accounting is a record of the baseline and any changes made or approved. Since approved changes aren't instantaneously incorporated, it is important for baseline integrity and for future change proposal deliberations that the baseline be tracked carefully. Configuration status accounting provides a history of the three other configuration components as well.

Automation of configuration management is extensive, especially in the control component. Usually each component has its own set of automated methods which are tied together to form a configuration management system. For large software product developments, fully automated configuration management systems are almost a must. See [BERSOFF84] for a detailed description of CM automation.

The benefits of configuration management are high. It helps reduce errors in the product, helps ensure its integrity, and changes are made only to the areas that require it. Also a history of its development is maintained. The primary disadvantage is that it is not inexpensive to do. It is a difficult trade-off to decide how much current funding should be spent on configuration management vs. the amount of funding that will eventually be saved. One area that is usually not done with as much rigor is in the auditing component of CM. Sometimes management will just decide that next Friday, whatever exists will be the new baseline. This is dangerous, but it does given some level of traceability, and is inexpensive (if nothing goes wrong later) to do.

The final activity of product assurance we will examine is verification and validation. These are very similar to configuration auditing.

7.3.3 Verification and Validation

While both quality assurance and configuration management can trace their beginnings to the hardware side of engineering verification and validation (V&V) came into being expressly for coping with software and its development [BERSOFF84]. Verification and validation is concerned with how well the software product fulfills functional and performance requirements and provides assurance that specified requirements are stated, stated correctly, and interpreted correctly. The focal point of verification and validation is the customer and making sure that what is delivered is what he or she wants.

The IEEE Glossary of Software Engineering Terminology [IEEE83] defines verification as the process of determining whether or not the products of a given phase of the software development cycle fulfill the requirements established during the previous phase. This means that the products must meet prescribed goals as defined through the baselined data.

Validation is defined as the process of evaluating software at the end of the development process to ensure compliance with software requirements. In other words, does the product meet its objectives and do the right job.

Boehm states V&V informally as "Am I building the product right?" and "Am I building the right product?" [BOEHM84].

The evaluation criteria used for performing verification and validation are completeness, consistency, feasibility, and testability [BOEHM84]. Completeness shows that all product components are present, and all are developed. This means no TBDs, no non-existent references, no missing functions, or missing products. Consistency means that each phase component does not have conflicting interpretations with the previous phase output. This means the products are traceable. Feasibility means that the product will save more than it costs to build, regardless of the cost criteria. Testability means the ability to find an economical way to test the products that will show whether or not they meet the specifications.

V&V LIFE CYCLE COVERAGE. As with the other aspects of product assurance, the processes of verification and validation must span the life cycle as depicted in figure 7-6 [FERRENTINO77, SEEWG82]. The arrows reflect the paths taken and numbers indicate the activities described below:

1. Review the requirements for completeness, consistency, feasibility, and testability. Since requirements aren't usually defined rigorously enough, the arrow is is dotted.

2. If the criteria of completeness, consistency, feasibility, and testability can't be established at the requirements level, they should be established using the specification as the base.

3. Determine if the specifications correctly implement the requirements.

4. Determine if the design correctly implements the specification.

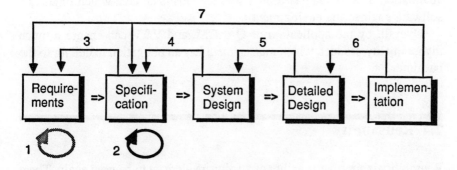

Figure 7 - 6   **Span of Verification and Validation**

5. Determine that the design decomposition does not violate the the product design.

6. & 7. Determine if each component of the product implementation reflects the detailed design and that the product correctly represents the implemented requirements and specifications.

V&V must be an integral part of the software development plan, and as in all the previous techniques of product assurance, be accomplished by an independent team.

The result of doing verification and validation is not necessarily the reduction of the number of errors created, but the reduction in the number of days to find the errors. This increases the probability of producing a higher quality product, but like configuration management, verification and validation is not inexpensive to perform.

The methods to perform verification and validation are the same ones to do quality assurance. The difference is in viewpoint. QA is concerned more with making sure the product adheres to pre-defined standards, while V&V is concerned with how well the product performs.

Automation in support of V&V is varied. Consistency and completeness can be aided in certain phases by the use of PSL/PSA, or if a method like Structured Analysis is used, by commercial products like Teamwork/SA.

Greater coverage is afforded by methods like SREM, but no complete automation of this area has been achieved. This is an area which requires a software engineering environment.

Overall, by the application of QA, CM, and V&V can ensure a much higher quality product, which management has an obligation to deliver to the customer.

7.4 Reusability

Reusability is simply the ability of a software element to be used again. There are a number of software elements that are candidates for reuse, which include reusable data, designs, requirements and specifications, programs and common systems, and code/modules [JONES84, HOROWITZ84].[5]

Reusable data are the basic elements of information that can be reused. It may include standard database information, optical, voice, graphic or music information. A standard data interchange format is necessary for this to work fully.

Reusable designs are designs such as compilers or sorting algorithms that can be used in a variety of ways, but implemented uniquely.

Reusable requirements and specifications are like designs, but represent the upper level descriptions. For many product developments of the same type of application, say for instance in a radar system, the general requirements are going to be the same.

Reusable programs and common systems include reusing complete products like operating systems or spreadsheets.

Reusable code/modules are parts of a product's implementation that can be used in other products. Subroutines or math functions are examples.

These reusable elements have also been categorized in another fashion to help clarify what reusable software consists of: those elements that can be reused in a number of applications (e.g., a math function); those that are used in successive versions (e.g., a new version of a product based on a previous one); those that are reused whenever the program containing the element is executed (e.g., a compiler); and those that are reused in a program (e.g., a subroutine) [WEGNER84].

WHY MANAGEMENT ACTIVITY? The question probably being asked is why is this a management activity? As one can see, there are many opportunities for software reuse that span the entire life cycle. There is also great benefit in reusing software wherever possible, with reduction in software cost, increased productivity, better reliability, etc. [CARD86]. However, the decision authority is with the manager to either build, buy, or reuse software and it is also his or her responsibility to encourage, conjole, threaten or beg the technical members of the staff to apply reuse whenever possible. This is not particularly efficient, but that's the current state of affairs.

What would be better is if the issue of reuse was viewed as the same as that of verification and validation. In fact, reuse should probably be just another evaluation criteria of V&V. At each phase a question should be asked whether the product or part of the product is a candidate for reuse. In this way reuse has the same visibility as each of the other items in V&V.

Now we don't mean to imply that reuse isn't being applied. In one application area, NASA for instance reused 70 to 95 percent of its existing software [SILVERMAN85]. This range for potential reuse has been supported by other studies [see JONES84].

From another perspective, this means out of the 25 billion lines or so of code that are produced each year, 75 to 85 percent is common but still is being recoded and paid for yearly [JONES84]. That's plenty of money. And the reduction of cost is a management responsibility.

PROBLEMS WITH REUSE. Given the fact that all this money is being wasted on redundant code, why hasn't reuse been overwhelmingly embraced by the software community? It is difficult to say really, but we suspect the trouble lies in both the technical and personal attitude domains.

Despite cases like NASA, for software to be truly reusable, information on its performance, characteristics, application domain, and abstraction level, has to be available [CHEATHAM84, MATSUMATO84]. In many cases it is. In most others it isn't, or isn't readily available, which really proves to be the impediment to reuse [SILVERMAN85]. In other words, for reuse to be technically useful it must support the use of components to build products from scratch, not simply reuse existing code. That is where the increase in productivity is required.

The other problem is with developer's attitudes. Everyone wants to do it their way. If it is a really hard problem, or real easy, or you don't know how to start or are stuck on a problem, then you begin to look around for something to steal from.[6] But unless it really is a problem, reusable components are just like program libraries. Things are always checked in, but never checked out. It is up to management to motivate their personnel to investigate reuse and make it a natural occurrence.

There is debate over whether Ada, especially with the use of generics, will help solve the problem [CHEATHAM84, LITVINTCHOUK84], but regardless of its outcome, unless management gets involved, reuse will probably continue to languish.

7.6 Requirements of the Software Engineering Environment

The management phase places a few more requirements on the software engineering environment than did the other phases. Since management is concerned with planning, monitoring and controlling the development process and the product itself, the environment must support these activities. For instance, two very important activities of management are product assurance and configuration management. To aid in the verification of products, the capability to trace requirements to specifications, specifications to design, etc., is a necessity. Similarly, the changes to the products throughout the life cycle must be able to be tracked and controlled. Moreover, the environment must do so from the very beginning of the life cycle.

An aspect of management that an environment must support is the gathering of information so that managment can make rationale decisions. This means that not only should the environment help with the creation of a budget and the track costs, but ways of analyzing the impact of changes to the budget, schedule or personnel is required as well.

Finally, the environment is required to support the reuse of components by aiding in the identification of where reuse is possible, and by keeping a library of reusable components. Chapter Nine will illustrate further how an environment can support the management activities.

7.7 Summary

In this chapter we have reviewed the activities associated with management. We have examined the functions of management (resource management, product assurance, and configuration management), and reviewed some of the techniques used in each. We have also argued for including reuse as a management activity, and why it should be applied in a similar fashion as verification and validation.

In summary, management is an activity that spans the life cycle. Poor management can cause a product development to be set back more easily than any other means. This implies that management must be cautious in its decision making, must have the right information from which to make a decision, and not overcompensate if a bad decision is made.

Moreover, management involves the manipulation of not only time and money but people. It is up to management to keep the organization functioning smoothly, and keep everyone and everything coordinated.

The next chapter examines some support a software engineering environment requires to meet all the requirements that have been imposed on it.

FOOTNOTES:

1. These same phenomena explain why successes in software projects never are heard about.

2. It's somewhat ironic that management's own decisions make their later decisions difficult.

3. Sometimes so much effort is placed in planning the development that the product is forgotten.

4. Note the difference between "baseline information" and "baseline". Baseline information is all the reference information that can be used to create any version of the product. A baseline is the specific version of the product. It is a subset of all the baseline information that exists.

5. The definitions for each element vary between authors.

6. "Software reuse has the same advantage as theft " [STANDISH84]. Calling reuse "stealing" would probably cause it to be used more. Reuse sounds too much like "hand-me-downs."

8. LINKAGES

"I don't want to be an alarmist, but I can see the day when millions of computers will be fighting, for some small piece of data, like savages."

Prof. Heinrich Applebaum[1]

8.0 Introduction

In this chapter we will explore just some of the issues that must be considered when implementing a software engineering environment. Up until this time, we have concentrated on the abstract elements that make up an environment, and the processes and methods that go into building a product. We now need to concentrate on how these concepts can be realized and integrated together to form a physical software engineering environment. Thus this chapter is concerned with the parts and linkages that are necessary to make this happen. The three elements we want to explore are the database, the environment system support functions, and the architectural hosts for the environment.

The database is probably the most critical aspect of a software engineering environment. It is the integration element of the environment, and in a sense gives it its meaning. Without a database, a software engineering environment ceases to exist. The database contains all the information that has been created by the automated methods, allows for the reuse of the information, the traceability of information, and the consistency of information. How well, and how easily the information can be passed among the various methods of the environment will determine how well the environment will attain the goal of creating a quality product.

The software engineering environment system support functions provide the necessary services to execute the software engineering environment

[262]

software, and provide services to the environment user to make effective use of the environment features.

The final element necessary is the software engineering host. It should be obvious that a software engineering environment is a total system, composed of hardware and software, and is not just a software product. The capability of the environment to build a product is as much dependent on the capability of the host to adequately support the environment as on the methods used to create it.

With these few words of introduction, let's turn our attention to the issues of the software engineering environment database.

8.1 The Software Engineering Environment Database [2]

Looking back over the previous chapters, we have seen as a recurring requirement the necessity of capturing the information created in one life cycle phase and reusing it in another. Not only that, but also a requirement to be able to ensure that when any information is used and changed, the changes are also reflected back in the original information. Other requirements that exist have also been the capability to check for the consistency of information across phases, and the ability to check on the completeness of a particular software product.

Upon examination, each of these requirements states basically three things. First, any information created by a method must be retained and available for use by any other that requires it. This means some type of repository must be available with access available to all methods. Second, the information retained must be "transparent" to each individual method. In other words, a method must be able to access and manipulate the information using its own viewpoint and media representation, not necessarily the ones originally used to create the information. For example, SADT creates output data information represented by graphics with text, while SCRS uses the exact same information using a template and text.[3] We want the information contained in two to be the same, and any change reflected in one to be noted in the other. And third, the software engineering environment must have a single focus; i.e., it must support the capture and manipulation of information required to create the software product.

How can these diverse requirements be satisfied? Well, it's pretty obvious that what is required is a database of some kind as a minimum. A very large, and very robust one at that. In the next few sections, we will examine the issues to be considered when building a database for a software engineering environment.

What is a database?   A database is just a repository of different types of information. There may exist text, graphics, or even optical data in the database. Whatever information is created by the particular methods used in the phases and management activities to support the creation of the software product will reside here. This includes the information required to produce the requirements document, the specifications, the design documents, test plans, management plans, etc. However, in an ideal software engineering environment database, the information is completely electronically stored. In other words, any paper documentation is created out of the information that is stored in the database. This also means that whatever is not created and stored in the database, does not exist.

The contents of the database are usually stored by category. Many categories are possible, but five major categories are basic to an environment [SEEWG82]. These are:

- Baselined

- Non-baselined

- Archival

- Measurement

- Support System Library.

BASELINED INFORMATION. Baselined information is any data object which is management "owned"[4] and controlled by the configuration management process (see Chapter Seven). This implies that baselined objects persist over the life of the software product and that changes to these objects are controlled very closely. This is also called a "persistent database" [MCKAY-86]. Changes to the database are the responsibility of the Software Configuration Control Board.

Baselined information is not only a product, such as a requirements document, but also the information that is part of that document. For example, if

SA is being used, it may be an individual diagram. The granularity of the data object stored is dependent on the method used to create it. We will return to this issue a little later.

NON-BASELINED INFORMATION. Non-baselined information is that which is temporary in nature. This is all the information that is currently being worked on. The information created may eventually become part of the baseline (which is created by reference-type automation), or just be information that is used for analysis purposes, such as that created by value-type automation.

ARCHIVAL INFORMATION. Archival information contains a history of all the products created during its development, and consists of all the baselined information of the final software product. This information is formed as a unit after the product is accepted for delivery. When the product undergoes evolution, this information is used as the basis for a new active baseline which is separately configuration managed.

MEASUREMENT INFORMATION. Measurement information are data objects of a quantitative nature that represent some quality or characteristic of the development process or software product. The information is gathered by the software engineering environment system support functions, which are not part of the development process itself, but help manage the environment. These are discussed in more detail in Section 8.2.

Measurement data might be used to evaluate how well the process of the development is progressing, such as the number of errors found, the number of changes being made to the baseline, the number of compilations, the number of tests a module has been given, or the amount of time a module has taken to reach compilation. It can also be used to report on the product, such as the number of software functions created, the number of modules created, or the number of lines of source code developed.

SUPPORT SYSTEM LIBRARY. This is the data that contains all the automated methods themselves, as well as the automated support system functions software. It is the repository of all the software required to implement the software engineering environment. This data is also considered baselined, and is under its own configuration management.

How is data accessed? So far we have described the types of information that are in a database, but not how it can be obtained. This capability is provided by a Data Base Management System (DBMS). A DBMS provides a set of capabilities that allows a user to deal with data in a very abstract way.[5] The DBMS is responsible for the serialization of requests for access to data, the admissibility of the requests (i.e., is a request valid), the consistency of the database, and its correctness.

We will use the terms database and DBMS interchangeably for convenience, but technically the database is the physical object, while the DBMS is a software support program that manipulates it. Before we can really describe how the data is accessed, we need to discuss how data is created first. So we will diverge for awhile and talk about the DBMS itself. This discussion is based on [ULLMAN82].

DBMS. The DBMS is a software program that acts as an interpreter to user requests concerning the data in the database. The user formulates these requests in a form of a query using a query language or data manipulation language (DML) of some type. The actual details as to what happens to the query and how it is processed are not really necessary to know at this time, so let's just say everything works and the requests are honored.

Now, there are many different users of the database and each views the database in a slightly different manner. So when a request is made, the DBMS has to be able to understand which user is requesting the data and how it is viewed. This is accomplished by providing each of these users with their own conceptual database, as shown in figure 8-1. (Note that each view's conceptual database is described and defined by its "own" DML interpreter.)

Examining the figure, we see that there are three levels of abstraction with which the DBMS must concern itself. At the lowest level is the physical database, which has stored in it the "raw" information, either in files, records, or some sort of data structure. A database manager takes care of interpreting queries into terms the file manager of the physical database can understand.

At the level above it, the DBMS has to worry about the conceptual database. This database is an abstraction of the "world" of which the users are

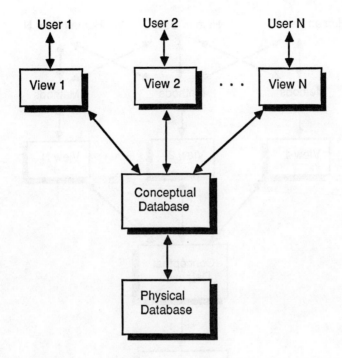

Figure 8 - 1   **Abstraction Levels in a Database System**
Source: [ULLMAN82]

a part, in this case, all the things that define the software engineering environment model. The DBMS provides the language to describe the model and
how to access the information in the physical database.

Above the conceptual database lie the views of the database. These views
(or subschemas) are abstract models of a portion of the conceptual database.
They allow the data to be accessed by users who have different needs, such as
a specifier wanting to know about the timing of a certain module, a designer
wanting to know how the module is interconnected, and an implementator
wanting to know about the code that is implemented in the module. Each
requires information about the module, but not all the same information.

Views can also be used to construct or derive information from the
conceptual database, but which is not actually a part of it. For instance, a
manager may request the current length of time the development of a module

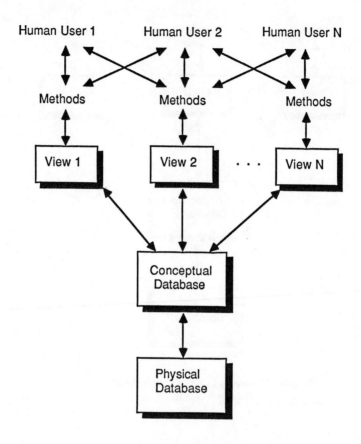

Figure 8 - 2   **Levels of Database Users in a Database System**

has taken. This is unlikely to be stored in his or her conceptual database because length of time would have to be updated daily. When the request was received for the length of time the DBMS would translate this request into "current date minus module start date," which is understood by the conceptual database, and the proper information could be accessed from the physical database.

We said earlier that the term user was used in a very general way. In a software engineering environment, we have two levels of users,[6] as shown in figure 8-2. At the very top, we have the human user who is trying to construct the software product. He or she must use the methods, which form the next lower level of "user," to access and manipulate the data. Now each human user views the data through their own conceptual framework provided through the methods, and we've seen that individual methods themselves use different ways to view the data. Moreover, recall that we want all the methods to be able to reuse any information that is created and resides in the physical database as well. A question that quickly comes to mind is how can all these views and levels of abstraction be mapped? One way is to describe the conceptual model in such a way that the data structures that are used to represent the physical data and the views seen by the methods are similar. This is done using an Entity-Relationship-Attribute (ERA) Model to help organize the various conceptual schemes.

ERA MODEL. The ERA model consists of entities, relationships, and attributes. An entity is a stable form about which we can gather information. It normally is something tangible, like a car, or chair, but it may also be something abstract, like an idea or process. An entity forms a part of the real world being model. Thus it is something that exists and is stable.

An entity class represents a collection of entities that share specific, stated properties. Those entities which exhibit those properties are considered members of an entity class. For example, Jack, John and Bob are all entities. If they all were employees of the same company, they would belong to the entity class "employee."

Each entity has particular properties that help determine to what entity class they belong. These properties are called attributes. An attribute is that information which can be measured or recorded about the entity. For example, a pen (an entity) may be red (an attribute). Like entities, a set or group of attributes can be collected to form an attribute class. An attribute class represents a collection of attributes that express similar measurements or evaluations of all entities in the given class. Thus, the entity class "office" may have the attributes values of 100 sq. ft., 290 sq. ft., and 500 sq. yds., which are gathered under the attribute class "office area."

The last element of the model are the relationships among the entities. A relationship is an association evident between two entities or entity classes. They are based on a purpose and viewpoint. Moreover, a single entity may have many associations with other entities. For example, John (an entity) is larger (a relationship) than Bob. The types of relations that can exist are one-to-many (John is related to ...), one-to-one (Gene is married to Jill), and many-to-many (AL West Teams defeat/are defeated by AL East Teams).

Given this conceptual model, we can begin to define the items that each method manipulates as an entity which possesses particular attributes and has relationships to other entities. These relationships can specify how one entity, say a part of a requirements document is related to other entities such as a part of a specification, or a design, or some source code. For instance, SCRS output data item template "Fire Command" is derived from an output data "Fire Command" on SADT diagram A21. In this manner, the capability to trace information created by one method and see how (and if) it is used by another is allowed.

The conceptual database (which models the software engineering environment processes, methods, and how methods can interact with one another) takes into account (via the DBMS) which methods need to use which entities. It also services queries for entities that reside outside a method's view, and generally serves as the integrating agent for the environment.

Unfortunately, this is not sufficient.

The ERA model does not have the flexibility to define or manipulate relationships that change dynamically. This is a capability needed if methods are going to be allowed to be used in different ways than those which were predefined. This ability is a requirement from the human user's view.

If the conceptual database is restricted, in other words, all allowable interactions between methods are predefined, then the problem disappears. But this severely restricts the ability of an environment to have more methods added to it, and constrains the human user from discovering new ways of creating the product.

A technique of handling this problem is by the use of the object model to describe the entities [COX84]. An object is an instantiation of a data abstraction which contains a collection of data and the set of operations that is defined on them [STANKOVIC84]. In this approach, every automated method operates on and views the world as objects. An object may be a text string, a document, a graphic, or even part of a graphic (an SA "bubble," for instance). An object has a name, a type and a value(s), and the operations that can be applied to it. When a method has created an object, and is ready to store it, it requests the conceptual database (via the DBMS) to create an appropriate entity, its relationships and attributes. These are uniquely specified by the view under which it operates. It is then mapped into the physical database via the database manager and file manager. The file manager also knows about objects, and stores the physical data accordingly. The process is done in reverse to retrieve an object.

The advantages of using objects as entities are that they encourage data transparency, encourage a uniform user interface (each method's media representation is seen, treated, and thought about by the human user in the same way), and they allow the view of the user and the view of the physical objects themselves to be closely aligned.

This all seems very complicated, and it is. A valid question to ask is why not just eliminate the ERA model and just consider the software engineering environment as having one gigantic, global database. In this way objects could be created and manipulated by the automated methods themselves. The operations contained in the objects could substitute for the conceptual database by describing which methods could use an object and how.

This is a possible solution if each method, upon creation of an object, describes every operation that can be performed on it by any other method, informs the other methods of the object's existence, keeps track of the object when it is being used by another method, responds to requests for the object, etc. In other words, do everything the DBMS system does. The bookkeeping has to be done somewhere, either in the methods themselves or in the DBMS. We have chosen to leave it in the DBMS.

There have been efforts to make the process of describing views and passing information between automated methods easier. Called the (proposed) Information Resources Dictionary Standard (IRDS) [ANSI85], it is aimed at trying to standardize the management of data to increase sharing of data, reduce the number of redundant programs, and simplify data conversion. It provides a standard framework for defining conceptual databases.

The IRDS uses the ERA model as its underlying foundation to define data.[7] An entity represents a "real world" concept, but not the actual physical data in the database. Relationships can exist between two entities, and are binary in nature, i.e., three or more relationships are not allowed.[8] Attributes are used to specify the entity type. Attribute-groups also exist, which are ordered sets of attributes.

Figure 8-3, which depicts the relationship between the IRD processes and IRD data, resembles that of the ISO communication protocol model. The IRD Schema describes the structure of the IRD. For every entity, relationship, attribute, and attribute-group that can exist in the IRD, the IRD schema will contain the corresponding entity-type, relationship-type, attribute-type, and attribute-group-type. The standard also proposes specific entity-types, relationship-types, attribute-types, and attribute-group-types that may be used. The proposed standard data entity-types and relationship-type are shown in table 8-1.

A Core System-Standard Schema is used to support intra- and inter-communication about information. This Schema, which is expected to be part

IRD PROCESSES   IRD "DATA" LAYERS

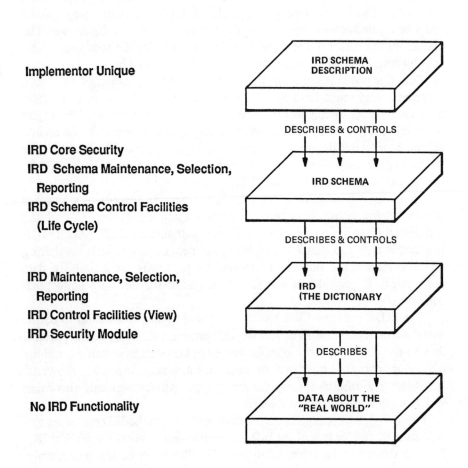

Implementor Unique   IRD SCHEMA
                                          DESCRIPTION

                                          DESCRIBES & CONTROLS

IRD Core Security
IRD Schema Maintenance, Selection,
   Reporting   IRD SCHEMA
IRD Schema Control Facilities
   (Life Cycle)

                                          DESCRIBES & CONTROLS

IRD Maintenance, Selection,
   Reporting   IRD
IRD Control Facilities (View)   (THE DICTIONARY
IRD Security Module

                                          DESCRIBES

No IRD Functionality   DATA ABOUT THE
                                          "REAL WORLD"

Figure 8 - 3 **The Information Resource Dictionary System**

DATA Entity-Types

DOCUMENT, describing instances of human readable data collections.

FILE, describing instances of an organization's data collections.

RECORD, describing instances of logically associated data that
belong to an organization.

ELEMENT, describing instances of data belonging to an organization.

BIT-STRING, describing abstract representations of strings of
binary digits.

CHARACTER-STRING, describing abstract representations of
strings of characters.

FIXED-POINT, describing abstract representations of exact numeric
values.

FLOAT, describing abstract representations of approximate numeric
values.

PROCESS Entity -Types

SYSTEM, describing instances of collections of processes and data.

PROGRAM, describing instances of automated processes.

MODULE, describing instances of automated processes that are either
logical subdivisions of PROGRAM entities or independent
processes that are called by PROGRAM entities.

EXTERNAL Entity-Types

USER, describing individuals or organizational components.

Table 8 - 1   IRDS System-Standard Entity-Types

of every DBMS conforming to the standard, defines the allowable contents of the IRD. The specific entity-types, attribute-types, etc. described above make up the core schema. Since the predefined types obviously can't define all possible types an organization using the standard might use, the core schema has the capability to be extended or customized. This means new entity-types, attribute-types, etc., are added to the schema. The core schema can support extensions to the functions and control facilities as well. Figure 8-4 illustrate the four data levels specified in the IRDS and an example of some typical information contained in each.

There are a few other issues that need to be discussed before we move on to the support system functions. First is the importance of view in defining the database for an ideal software engineering environment. The environment must support many different classes of people performing a wide variety of tasks. Each wishes to use the information contained in the database in the way that is most natural to him or her, i.e., see from their perspective. This may not (and probably is not) the same as some one else's view. Additionally, they manipulate methods which are automated and also have a view of the world, and represent it in many different fashions. Moreover, there are general management views that require support as well, like project, product version, release, etc. The resolution of all these views may be the hardest aspect of building an environment [NAVATHE86].

To keep the DML description of the environment from overloading the DBMS trying to support all these views, defined roles for development personnel might have to be adopted. This means you are a requirements engineer, a designer, tester, etc., and only have access to the aspect of the environment that supports that role. This is only one implication a software engineering environment can have on an organization. Chapter Twelve discusses others.

Second, we haven't addressed the problem of how data is secured from unauthorized access, or how all this data that is being reused is kept up to date and timely. This is especially difficult if the database is distributed across many locations. The use of the IRDS and object model can help some by keeping track of the information, incorporating time stamps, and defining allowable operations on the data. But this is a very hard problem, and the best we can do is say data should be secure, updated, and timely, and it's beyond the scope of this book to discuss it further.

Another issue is database performance. It is readily apparent that the performance of the database is critical if any work is going to be accomplished at all. Having it contain all the information about a product down to the level of granularity of a single graphic in a document, as well as storing all the

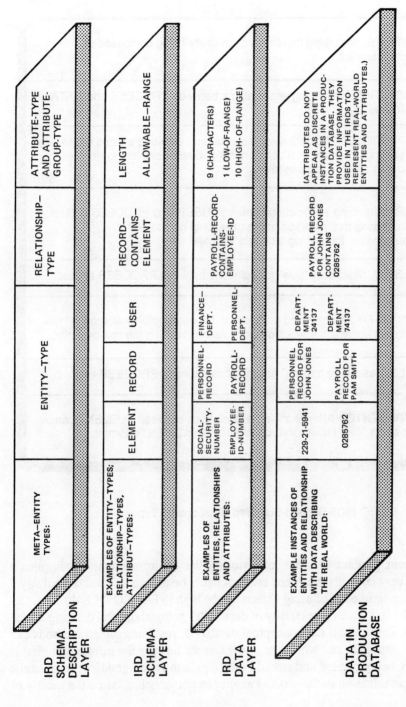

	ENTITY–TYPE		RELATIONSHIP–TYPE	ATTRIBUTE-TYPE AND ATTRIBUTE-GROUP-TYPE
IRD SCHEMA DESCRIPTION LAYER META–ENTITY TYPES:				
IRD SCHEMA LAYER EXAMPLES OF ENTITY–TYPES; RELATIONSHIP–TYPES; ATTRIBUT–TYPES:	ELEMENT	RECORD USER	RECORD–CONTAINS–ELEMENT	LENGTH ALLOWABLE–RANGE
IRD DATA LAYER EXAMPLES OF ENTITIES, RELATIONSHIPS AND ATTRIBUTES:	SOCIAL-SECURITY-NUMBER EMPLOYEE-ID-NUMBER	PERSONNEL-RECORD PAYROLL-RECORD	FINANCE–DEPT. PERSONNEL-DEPT.	PAYROLL-RECORD-CONTAINS-EMPLOYEE-ID	9 (CHARACTERS) 1 (LOW-OF-RANGE) 10 (HIGH-OF-RANGE)
DATA IN PRODUCTION DATABASE EXAMPLE INSTANCES OF ENTITIES AND RELATIONSHIP WITH DATA DESCRIBING THE REAL WORLD:	229-21-5941 0285762	PERSONNEL RECORD FOR JOHN JONES PAYROLL RECORD FOR PAM SMITH	DEPART-MENT 24137 DEPART-MENT 74137	PAYROLL RECORD FOR JOHN JONES CONTAINS 0285762	(ATTRIBUTES DO NOT APPEAR AS DISCRETE INSTANCES IN A PRODUC-TION DATABASE. THEY PROVIDE INFORMATION USED IN THE IRDS TO REPRESENT REAL-WORLD ENTITIES AND ATTRIBUTES.)

Figure 8 - 4   **Information Resource Dictionary System (IRDS) Contents**

CONTAINS, describing instances of an entity being composed of other entities.

PROCESSES, describing associations between PROCESS and DATA entities.

RESPONSIBLE FOR, describing associations between entities representing organizational components and other entities, to denote organizational responsibility.

RUNS, describing associations between USER and PROCESS entities, illustrating that a person or organizational component is responsible for running a certain process.

GOES-TO, describing "flow" associations between PROCESS entities.

DERIVED-FROM, describing associations between entities where the target entity is the result of a calculation involving the source entity.

CALLS, describing "calling" associations between PROCESS entities.

REPRESENTED-AS, describing associations between ELEMENTs and certain other entities that document the ELEMENTs' format.

Table 8 - 2   **IRDS System-Standard Relationship Types**

different product versions, and storing the environment itself, implies a very, very large database, and one that better be able to be accessed quickly.[9] The overhead costs of using objects can be high [STANKOVIC84].

The last issue is the quality of data. After going about and defining all the views, defining all the conceptual databases, resolving which methods can share what data and when, etc., how can we be sure the information that is finally being created and stored in the database is any good? Unfortunately, you can't. It is up to the product assurance personnel to assure the quality of the product is acceptable. The one good thing is that the integration of information allows the product assurance team to do a better job than it could before.

8.2   Software Engineering Environment System Support Functions

The software engineering environment system support functions are all the components required to support and manage the environment. They form the infrastructure of environment, much like a run-time system does for an executing program, and provide a wide range of services. For example, the DBMS is an element which supports the retension and manipulation of data. Some of the other support functions are project communication support, environment invocation and usage support, environment guidance support, and metrics gathering support. Each is "outside" our model of a software engineering environment, but each is required to exist for the environment to exist.

PROJECT COMMUNICATION SUPPORT. Project communication support includes all the functions that are necessary to keep everyone involved in the product development in communication with one another. Communication can take place in many ways. For example, communication between individual members of the development team, between management and the developers, and between development personnel located at different sites. Communication doesn't only occur between human personnel either, but also among all the computers that will make up an environment. For instance, the software engineering environment should be able to communicate to other software systems such as financial systems, mockups, trouble reporting systems, etc. to either obtain information or provide information. We won't consider the latter type of communication further, but recall that it does exist.

The dissemination of information to all the development personnel is extremely important to the smooth running of a project. Without it, the project can flounder due to a lack of direction and bad morale. Communication within an organization is a social function and necessity, and with the software engineering environment being the one aspect of the project everyone will be using on a daily basis, it must support the communication process well.

The information that is required to be communicated in a project may involve all the personnel (changes in the organization structure, where the company picnic is going to be held, etc.) or just small groups "hey, when is project review meeting?" They may also be formal or informal. The communication support function needs to support all the different kinds of communication. Two ways of doing so are to provide for the sending of mail and for the posting of bulletin boards.

The mail function should support the notification of mail received to the recipient, support mass mail deliveries, support certified and urgent mail capability, support timestamping, etc. The bulletin board should be open to any developer who wants to post notes about different subjects.

The communication support functions should also help the individual developer manage his or her time by providing personal time schedulers and calendars. A capability to insert a request for a meeting on other person's calendar is very important since going to meetings often takes up a great deal of time and arranging one is always difficult.

The final aspect of the communication support is document creation. Since documents are the major form of communication to the user and sponsor of the product, a means to create documents easily is necessary. This function must be defined with a careful understanding of what information the methods create, what has been currently created and stored in the database, and what is required to meet the specific document organizational formats each type of document requires. The support function should support checking of document standards, the creation of standard document formats, perform spelling, checks, etc.

ENVIRONMENT INVOCATION AND USAGE. The environment invocation support functions are those required for a user of an environment to sign on and off, access methods, and access other support routines. These support functions provides the normal security functions associated with gaining access to the software engineering environment, keeping track of users and their file space, their access rights, their tie-in time, etc. These are all the things that no one except the support system manager worries about, and the user when he or she can't access something.

The usage support functions also interpret the commands issued by the users when using the environment. The command language should be standard across the environment, not only to access support functions, but within each individual method as well. This means supporting text and graphic manipulation. In other words, there should exist a friendly human interface.

ENVIRONMENT GUIDANCE SUPPORT. The environment guidance support consists of navigation aids, method-oriented help commands, and method coercers. Even with a friendly interface and user manuals, it is unlikely that a user of the software engineering environment will know all the ways to utilize it efficiently or effectively. Moreover, users having different levels of experience will also be accessing it, thus some form of guidance is mandatory.

The on-line navigation aids are detailed "maps" of the environment, giving information on the methods, what they are, what they do, how they do it, what other methods they interact with, examples of their use, etc., as well as how the support functions operate. This function is meant to allow both the experienced and inexperienced user to see the structure of the environment, and navigate around it.

The method-oriented help commands are associated with each method. This information is similar to what is in the navigation aids, but at a much more detailed level, more in line with being a tutorial. At any time in the use of a method, a user should be able to ask questions about its use. More detail is provided by the methodology coercers.

The method coercers are support functions that have detailed knowledge about how a method should be applied, and how the data it is creating is be used by other methods. When using a particular method, the user can either query the method coercer about what to do next, and what are the results of taking certain actions, or let the coercer lead the user through a session in using the method. The coercer also knows how the data is used by other methods, and can provide a path to the other methods to see how it is being used.

The level of guidance is only limited by ones imagination, but the point is that it is extremely important for many levels of guidance be provided to the users of the environment if it is going to be used effectively.

METRICS GATHERING SUPPORT. The final support function to examine is that which is needed to gather information about the functioning of the software engineering environment and the quantitative information that gives indications about the progress of the product development. The information about the environment performance; i.e., its use, availability, responsiveness, etc., and identification of possible bottlenecks.

The information about the product is concerned with the quality of product and the effectiveness of the the environment methods to increase productivity. Some aspects that should be measured are methods used, data created, errors involved and traced to methods, number of lines of code, number of errors found, etc. The list is almost endless. However, gathering information about the effectiveness of the environment is important to find out how to make it work better, and what contributes to making a better product.

There are many other support functions that exist in an environment, like the operating systems, run-time executives, communication packages, etc. that we haven't addressed. But the list above provides an indication of all the things that are needed to make an environment run. The last aspect we need to examine is on what is the environment hosted on?

8.3   Software Engineering Environment Hardware Characteristics

The software engineering environment is a very sophisticated software product in itself, one that requires equally sophisticated hardware support. A software engineering environment for a large product development will likely not have one central computer that will host the entire environment. The environment will likely be networked or distributed across many computers that are tied together. Some of the issues this raises are that distributed databases must be supported; data must be able to pass between the various host computers; if the hosts are heterogeneous, then format conversions may be necessary; communication protocols for checking the reliability of the network must be supported; and balancing of the processing loads of each host must be supported.

The software engineering environment hardware must support both the environment software itself, and the products being developed on it. Although we have discussed an environment from a single product development perspective, an environment will probably be supporting many different products simultaneously. The load on the environment can be very high. And good execution performance on the part of the environment must be perceived by its users. It is critical for its acceptance and use.

This performance can be enhanced by spreading the processing through the use of workstations, intelligent terminals, and the like, but the partitioning of the functions of an environment is not a trivial task. Just the requirement to support all the different types of peripherals will test the underlying operating system's I/O and file capability, not to mention its processor and memory management elements.

It is inappropriate for this text to go into more detail about the architectural support needed to host an environment because it is very dependent on the specific one being built. Needless to say, however, the hardware chosen to support the software engineering environment is extremely critical to its eventual success or failure.

8.4 Summary

In this chapter we have tried to convey just a few of the issues that must be given consideration when constructing a software engineering environment. The most critical is the definition and creation of the database. It is the glue that ties all the other elements together, and the capability of the environment ultimately rests in how well the database is constructed. The understanding of all the views is fundamental to its construction.

We've also discussed some of the support functions that are necessary for the environment to operate. Like the database, these provide the services necessary to allow the user to make maximum use of the environment's capability.

Finally, we touched on the issue of hardware support of the environment. As in the database and support functions, the performance of the environment is critical to its success, and even with a good database, if it is slow, the environment's worth decreases.

FOOTNOTES:

1. From "The Great Data Famine," Art Buchwald, 1976 .

2. In the discussion on the environment database a central database is implied. Please understand that a database can be physically distributed, but logically it is seen as one.

3. We are going to ignore for the moment the issue of how a method might have to be extended to use the information created by another. This issue will be discussed in Chapter Eleven. For now, let's assume it can be done.

4. Management owned means management has approved the process of creating the data object. The approval is implicit in which methods are available, and how they are tied together, in the environment.

5. The term "user" is used in its most general form.

6. A method can also mean methodology.

7. No implementation of the DBMS is implied in IRDS.

8. True in the core standard. User extensions are possible.

9. It also implies that you should invest in makers of disk drives.

9. PUTTING IT ALL TOGETHER

"First you pillage, *then* you burn."

Hagar the Horrible

9.0 Introduction

You will recall, back in Chapter Two, that we stated this book was primarily concerned with the development of mid- to "Probably Won't Work Today" sized software products, and an "ideal" software engineering environment to support their creation, as illustrated in figure 9-1. By ideal, we didn't mean "nirvana," but an environment that has the minimum required to accomplish its goals. Remember, these goals are to:

— reduce software costs,

— reduce the variation of practice, and

— increase productivity.

If these goals can be attained, a software engineering environment will meet the definition of being "ideal." Again, what is wanted for an environment is something like the DC-3, which was the result of a shrewd combination of technology, cost, time, and market, and is still being used 50 years after it was developed.

So far in the book, the discussion has focused on the individual phases of the software development life cycle model and their ramifications on our

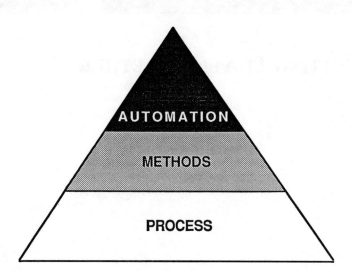

Figure 9 - 1   **Model of Software Engineering Environment**

general model of a software engineering environment. In this chapter, we will gather the different requirements that were surfaced in each phase and extract from them the basic structures needed to build an "ideal" software engineering environment.

9.1 Life Cycle Phase Review

Before we examine all the physical elements that must be part of an ideal software engineering environment, it is important to maintain the proper perspective. Remember, when building a software engineering environment, the concentration must first be on the products that are required to be delivered during the development, not on the methods and automation of the environment. If we don't do this, the reasons why environments are built will be lost among all the fuss of adding this method or that. It is easy to lose sight of the fact that an environment is there to support the building of products, and not an end in itself.

To refresh our memories, the typical products that are created during a software development are again shown in table 9-1. Recall the process of how

• Requirements document	• Specification Document
• System Description Document	• Test Specification
• Software Development Plan	• Test Procedures
• Functional Design Document	• Test Reports
• Detailed Design Document	• User Manual
• Verification Plan	• Source Code Listings
• Trouble Reports	• Object Code Listings

Table 9 - 1   **Typical Components of a Software Product**

each was derived, and the methods available to create them. If you can't remember, that's all right because we will be reviewing the processes in a moment.

Second, given this reminder, we do want to make full use of the power available through using computers to reduce the clerical work of drawing pictures, keeping track of information, tracing it, comparing it, etc. Thus, the software engineering environment (i.e., the methods that substantiate the process and all the other activities management requires) should be automated as much as possible.

This implies that the environment must be built with the focus on providing the general support necessary to accomplish automation. We will do this by identifying the generic types of automation necessary to support the methods used in a phase. For instance, say two methods like SA and SADT were going to be part of the environment. They both are graphical in nature, have rules for applying the graphics to a problem, and have information that can be extracted and checked for consistency and completeness. To be automated, they would require as a minimum, a graphics editor, some type of consistency and completeness analyzer, and a way of putting that information into the environment database.

Thus, we will try to extract the essence of the types of methods required in each life cycle phase, and identify the generic type of automation required. In the example of SA and SADT, tailorable graphics editors would be specified. It is assumed that the automation provided, like graphic editors, could be used by other methods in subsequent phases, and therefore will be specified only in the phase they first appear.

The type of automation provided, reference-type automation (RTA) or value-type automation (VTA) will also be noted. Recall RTA is used to create information for the baseline, while VTA creates non-baselined information. The applicability of the automation to other phases also will be specified.

In the next several sections we will review each of the phases of the life cycle and review the generic requirements each places on a software engineering environment. We will then describe the types of automation support necessary to fulfill each these requirements. Finally, we will gather all the information together and show how it all fits together.[1]

One last note before we begin. The automated support listed for the software engineering environment is not meant to be all inclusive. It is only meant to show the minimum types required. One more automated method can *always* be added, no matter how large the list.

9.1.1 Requirements Phase

PROCESS. The process of performing requirements analysis is divided into two sub-processes: concept formulation and requirements analysis and definition. Concept formulation is the exploratory analysis which is meant to define what system requirements have been given to the software to the satisfy. Requirements analysis and definition is the continuation of the concept formulation process. The requirements are further interpreted and their feasibility and risk analyzed. The results of the analysis are formally documented in the form of a set of preliminary requirements. A requirements document, an operational concepts document, an interface document, and a users manual are the primary outputs of this phase.

METHODS. The methods that are useful in this phase support semantic information capture, semantic analysis, and feasibility and risk assessment. Semantic information capture is the capture of requirements in the form of a semantic model involving the identification of key terms, categorization of the terms, term definition, and identification of relationships between terms. The capture of the semantics information creates a formal recording of the semantic model of the requirements which becomes part of the baseline.

Once the requirements are expressed in the context of a semantics model, the model relationships can be used for a systematic analysis of the completeness and consistency of the requirements. Traceability may be later established through reference relationships between requirements and specifications, design, code, etc. The relational analysis can also be used to assess the impact of the requirement changes on the baselined products. Finally, the semantic analysis model aids in the identification of requirements incompleteness and inconsistency.

The requirements are also evaluated for feasibility and risk. Feasibility is assessed from the perspectives of design, performance, and cost. Design feasibility demonstrates that there is at least one design that can satisfy the requirements. Use of prototyping is appropriate to perform this task. Perspective performance is also modeled as part of the design feasibility. Cost is estimated and analyzed for the product development and evolution phases.

The methods that are used to support requirements analysis can be characterized as being highly graphical in nature, have formal rules to apply the graphics, support consistency, completeness, and traceability, and require simulation support of some kind.

AUTOMATION. The generic types of automation which the environment should provide to support the requirement process and methods are:

Problem Expression Editors (RTA) — These tailorable editors permit the capture of formal expressions of the problem in text and/or graphics form. The formal expressions obey language-like rules which can be processed by the semantics language processor. The formal expressions are defined by an individual method, and include the rules describing which information created is used by other methods.

    — Applicability also to the specification, design and implementation phases.

Semantics Language Processors (RTA) — A semantic language processor performs syntax checking and recording of the semantics information. The results are available for later analysis or retrieval. The information resembles a data dictionary augmented by relations. These are tailorable to support each formal language.

— Applicability also to the specification and design phases.

Semantics Information Analyzers (VTA) — A semantics information analyzer uses the relational information kept in the semantics processor to check for consistency and completeness of the requirements. These are tailorable.

— Applicability also to the specification and design phases.

Semantics Information Manipulators (VTA) — A manipulator performs storage and retrieval of the semantic information created. It might be part of the DBMS or separate from it.

— Applicability also to the specification, design and implementation phases.

Prototypers (VTA) — A prototyper supports a number of different modeling techniques to conduct feasibility and risk analysis. It can execute queueing models or simulation models based upon information extracted from the semantics language processor, or in a standalone mode. Other techniques could be supported as appropriate.

— Applicability to all phases.

Resource Estimators (VTA) — A resource estimator consists of a set of models that can be executed to help perform cost feasibility of the product and product development. Information on schedule, manpower, computer resources required, etc. would be used as input.

— Applicability to all phases.

Error Reporters (VTA) — Error reporters gather information on errors found and develop trouble reports that are passed to the developers for non-baselined data, and the configuration managerfor base-lined information.

— Applicability to all phases

Document Generators (VTA) — A document generator is a set of routines to extract information from the software engineering environment database to create different types of documents. The document generator has embedded within it a set of tailorable rules to determine document content and format based upon documentation standards. These rules are flexible enough to be tailored by a human user, or can be based upon a particular method's language rules. The document generator operates on information at the level of an individual object.

— Applicability to all phases.

9.1.2 Specification Phase

PROCESS. The specification process should transform the requirement descriptions into a precise statement of the software product's external behavior. The two key sources of information used for this transformation are the semantic information captured in the requirements and the information from where they were derived. The specification process is one of refining the requirements to a point where they are testable. The outputs of this phase are the "final" requirement documents and software specification.

METHODS. The methods used in the specification phase are aimed at formally recording the information developed in the requirements phase in a manner to aid the checking for consistency and completeness. Information about system performance is gathered, and again prototyping is performed to gain a better understanding of the software product.

The methods used in this phase concentrate on manipulating the syntacs that are used to capture the semantic information in the requirements phase. They can be characterized as low graphic intensive, requiring usually the manipulation of tables or templates, or the use of formal textual descriptions.

AUTOMATION. The generic types of automation which the environment should provide to support the specification process are much the same as provided in the requirements phase. A problem expression editor can be tailored to allow expression of a specification using text as in PSL or text and graphics as in SCRS. A semantic language processor for each can check for errors in the notation, while the semantics information analyzer can check for consistency and completeness. The only additions are:

Inter-Method Information Traceability Exchanger/Analyzers (VTA) — The inter-method exchanger has the rules for passing information between particular methods embedded within it. When information is created in one method, it can be automatically transfered to the other method in correct format.

The analyzer is used to ensure traceability, completeness and consistency of information between or among methods. The semantic information created by a problem expression editor in the requirements phase should be reused by the tailored editor creating the specification. The analyzer is used to trace how the information is reused (helping in verification), and can be used to see where gaps in the specification are.

— Applicability to all phases.

Inter-Method Impact Analyzers (VTA) — This analyzer is used in conjunction with the inter-method information analyzers to assess the impact of changing or deletion a part of a specification. All possible changes to the requirements documents and specification documents are identified. The costs resulting from the changes in terms of schedule, funding, and manpower are also provided.

— Applicability to all phases.

9.1.3 Design Phase

PROCESS. The design process is involved with the creation of an abstraction of the software product. This abstraction is a software architecture that maps to the implementation. It represents a formal, well organized representation of what the program is supposed to do.

The design process is very iterative in nature, and consists of two sub-processes. The first, architectural design, creates the overall structure, interfaces, and interconnections of the software product from the specifications. The detailed design process which follows refines the architectural design and produces specifications from which the implementers can program. These may include abstractions of the data structures and algorithms to be used.

The planning for tests that must be conducted to verify and validate that the product meets the specifications is also begun in this phase.

The outputs of the design phase are many and varied. They include test plans, life cycle support documents, top level and detailed design specifications, and interface specifications.

METHODS. The methods used in the design phase concentrate on mapping the abstract design that exists in the specification into a software architecture. In architectural design, the structure of the design is expressed in modules or similar components. The interfaces and interconnections of the modules also are defined. Prototypes and simulations are used to obtain more detailed knowledge of potential software performance bottlenecks. Design metrics such as coupling and cohesion are applied to get rough estimates of the quality of the design.

In detailed design, the methods aim at defining the high level algorithms and data structures which will be implemented in the next phase. Psuedo-code is used to develop the implementation structure and to define the internals of the interfaces.

The methods used can be characterized as both graphic and language intensive.

AUTOMATION. Again, much of the automation provided the previous two phases can support design as well. For example, the problem expression editors can be tailored to support any of the design methods that use graphics or PDLs. Also the traceability of the design back to the specification and requirements can be accomplished by the inter-method analyzers. The types of automation that are more specific to the design phase are:

PDL Interpreter (VTA) — The PDL interpreter can be used to execute a design before it is actually programmed. The input is a PDL with sample program input data and the output shows the results of applying the input. The PDL interpreter is tailorable, and the PDL has to be an executable subset of an implementation language.

—Applicability only to the design phase.

Design Complexity Analyzer (VTA) — This analyzer applies metrics to the designs to evaluate the quality of the design with respect to coupling, cohesion, modularity, interconnections, etc. It uses information about the design from the problem expression editor to perform its evaluation.

— Applicability also to the implementation phase.

9.1.4 Implementation Phase

PROCESS. The implementation process is concerned with producing a physical realization of the design that was created in the previous phase. It should implement the design correctly and meet the resource, accuracy, and performance constraints defined in the specification documents.

The outputs of the phase are source code and listings.

METHODS. The methods used in the implementation phase concentrate on mapping the specification to the program, and on approaches to produce code that is reliable and maintainable. Most of the methods, like structured programming, are embodied in the programming languages used for implementation. The methods in this phase are mostly textual in nature, with graphics appearing only in template-driven approaches.

AUTOMATION. The generic types of automation which the environment should provide to support the implementation process and methods are:

Program Template Builders (RTA) — Program template builders construct fill-in templates of a particular language and all its constructs based upon the rules of the specific language and standards for documenting programs. Partial execution of the program templates for debug purposes is included. The output is a ready-to-execute program. These are tailorable to different languages. The template builder can be used as standalone or input can be received from the editors in the form of a PDL.

— Applicability only to the implementation phase.

Compilers/Assemblers (RTA) — Compilers that support a wide variety of high level languages are necessary. They should also provide code generation to target architectures that are not the host architecture. They should produce output listings, cross reference maps, etc. Assemblers might be needed for specific hardware architectures. Input is from the editors or template builder.

— Applicability only to the implementation phase.

Linkers/Loaders (RTA) — These programs provide the capability to resolve external references among separately compiled or assembled programs, and create load modules for execution. Input is from the compiler/-assembler.

— Applicability only to the implementation phase.

Debuggers (VTA) — Debuggers should be at the source level. When the source is executed and an error is encountered, information useful for analyzing the error such as line number, values of variables, input data, etc. should be made available.

— Applicability also to the test phase.

Data Extraction/Reduction Monitors (VTA) — These are routines that instrument an executing program and allow information on dynamic performance and accuracy to be extracted. The data is reduced to identify potential bottlenecks and poorly performing sections of the program.

— Applicability also to the test phase.

Standards Checkers (VTA) — Standards checkers perform static analysis of the program to identify standards violations. Input is from the problem expression editors.

— Applicability only to the implementation phase.

Simulators (VTA) - Simulators are programs that simulate the execution of a program of target architectures other than that of the host machine. They are used to test the product implementation on the host before it is executed on the real computer.

— Applicability also to the testing phase.

Path/Control Flow Analyzers (VTA) — These analyzers can analyze the path and control flow of a program to look for undefined variables, incorrect calling sequences, unexecuted code, etc.

— Applicability also to the testing phase.

Run-Time Support Analyzers (VTA) — These are all the routines that support the analysis of the program run-time requirements. These include: dependency analyzers which identify the run-time libraries that are required by a program; run-time storage analyzers, which provide insight into the static and dynamic program storage requirements; and run-time tasking analyzers, which evaluates tasks for interaction with other tasks, and evaluates possible deadlock conditions.

— Applicability also to the test phase.

9.1.5 Testing Phase

PROCESS. The process of testing is the execution of the physical realization of the software product for the purpose of finding errors, either logical or physical in nature. It is also meant to show that the product satisfies the performance parameters defined in the specification. When errors are discovered, the developers then correct the errors and any changes required of the documentation. These changes must be reflected in all documentation that references the section of the software product implementation that was changed.

The outputs of the testing phase are the test results.

METHODS. The methods used in the testing phase are varied. They can focus on either the unit or module to be tested, or on a partial or complete product during integration testing. Static testing methods are used to examine the static program execution looking for information such as data flow, or call paths. Dynamic methods execute the program under controlled conditions looking for anomalous behavior such as computational errors.

The methods use mostly text, and very little in the way of graphics.

AUTOMATION. Testing uses many types of automated support. The software engineering environment should provide many different types of automated testing methods. Some were already identified in the implementation phases. Only a representative few are listed below:

Test Harness (VTA) — A test harness provides the framework for unit testing of programs. The tests can be defined, test data prepared, an instrumented test executed, and the test results displayed, all interactively.

— Applicability only to the testing phase.

Black-Box Test Generators (VTA) — These generators are used to create functional test skeletons based upon input from the specification documents. Details are are later added by the tester.

— Applicability only to the testing phase.

Verifier/Assertion Analyzer (VTA) — These analyzers verify that the program correctly implemented specifications by checking the truth of assertions (embedded in the program) against actual program execution.

— Applicability only to the testing phase.

Test Data Generators (VTA) — Different testing strategies are embedded in the generator (such as path testing). Given a testing stategy and the program, it will automatically generate test cases.

— Applicability only to the testing phase.

Test Results Comparators (VTA) — These comparators use the specification documentation and test results to compare and analyze if the testing matches the specification.

— Applicability only to the testing phase.

Performance Monitors (VTA) — These monitors permit measurement of product performance parameters, such as response time, algorithm processing time, channel utilization, etc.

— Applicability only to the testing phase.

Test Coverage Analyzers (VTA) — These analyze the testing status of a software component as it progresses from unit testing to product level testing.

— Applicability only to the testing phase.

9.1.6 Evolution Phase

The software engineering environment is crucial to the support of the evolution phase. The information created and documented forms the corporate memory of the software product, and is the basis for all later changes. In fact, using an environment to create the product initially is extremely important to reducing the cost and increasing the reliability (and potential lifetime) of the product. Recall that a software product currently spends over 80 percent of its life in evolution.

There are no unique elements that a software engineering environment must support which are dictated by the evolution phase. All the processes, methods, and automation provided are usable, although every method may not be for every change.

9.1.7 Management Activities

PROCESS. The process of management spans all the phases of the life cycle. It is concerned with the planning, controlling, and monitoring of the software product development. The management process consists of resource management, product assurance (quality assurance, configuration management, verification and validation), reusability coersion, and documentation/standard enforcement.

Resource management is concerned with allocation of resources (time, money, people, and facilities) before, during and after a product is initially developed. Product assurance is making sure the product is the right product, and that it works correctly. Reusability coersion is trying to make sure reusable components are used whenever possible in the product. And documentation/standards enforcement is meant to assure the product is developed to the documentation and standards of the development organization.

METHODS. The methods used for management are dependent on the type of management being performed. In resource management, estimation techniques are prevelant. In product assurance reviews, audits, and change control are used. In reusability coercion, the availability of libraries of reusable components and guidance on how to apply reusability are necessary. In documentation and standards enforcement, the methods are dependent on organization policy. There is no one way to characterize all management methods.

AUTOMATION. The automation support necessary to support management permeates the environment in all phases. Some, like the resource estimators, document generators, standards checkers, inter-method impact analyzer and test result comparators (the last two useful in product assurance) have already been identified. The other generic types of automation that should be supported by the environment to support the management activities are:

Automated Precedence Network Analyzer (VTA) — This analyzer creates precedence network charts and identifies critical development paths based on inputs on projected milestones and precedence relations.

— Applicability to all phases.

Automated WBS / Schedule Generator (VTA) — This generator helps create budgets and work breakdown structures, as well as schedules, organizational responsibilities, etc. It uses information from the automated precedence network analyzer.

— Applicability to all phases.

Past Resource Analyzer (VTA) — This analyzer uses information from past product developments, along with a description of the current one, to create resource estimates for the product. If the information is kept current, it will estimate resource utilization and compare to current expenditures.

— Applicability to all phases.

Reliability Modelers — These modelers use information from the design quality analyzers, the trouble reporters, past history, and internal simulations to predict the reliability of the product, and to predict potential errors in the product components.

— Applicability to all phases.

Change Request Tracker (VTA) - The tracker logs change requests when submitted, tracks them through the approval cycle, and records their resolution.

— Applicability to all phases.

Configuration Managers (RTA) — The configuration managers keeps track of the baselined information and archives. All modifications to the baseline information have to be done through the manager. All modifications are kept track of, and old baselines archived. Modifications are recorded, and the results to the modules are reported to the various resource estimators.

— Applicability to all phases.

Reusable Component Generator/Analyzer (VTA) — This generator/ analyzer assists all members of the development team in the search for reusable components from the reusable component library. When one is found, it helps analyze the component for usability (cost to develop, size, applicable documentation, assumptions, etc.) in the product. A reusable component can be tested out using some of the other automated environment support, such as PDL Interpreter.

The generator part helps create a reusable component (requests all the pertinent information which describes the component) and then places it in the reusable component library. The format of the information is standardized based on specific component categories (document and type, code, test, etc.) to ensure consistency of component information.

— Applicability to all phases.

Reusable Component Library (VTA) — The library retains and manages all reusable components. Provides information to the reusable component generator/analyzer. Interacts with configuration management system to obtain copies of past software products.

— Applicability to all phases.

9.1.8 Support Functions

The support functions are all the functions that are needed to make the software engineering environment execute properly. The major aspects cover the database management system, project communication, metrics gathering, user guidance, and user interface to the environment. The automation provide by the environment is:

Database Managers/Processors (VTA) — These managers provide the necessary support to the database, including structuring the data, controlling the access to and updating of the data, serializing requests, communication to other databases, etc. The processors handle all the queries and interpret the data manipulation language.

— Applicability to all phases.

Schema Generator (VTA) — The generator allows for the generation of new schemas for the database. The generator also analyzes present schemas, and can test out new schemas produced before transferring them to the database manager/processor.

— Applicable to all phases.

Invocation/Command Language Interpreter (VTA) — The interpreter is used to process all the user commands in the environment, including sign-in, file manipulation, etc.

— Applicable to all phases.

Metric Data Gatherers/Analyzers (VTA) — Metric data gatherers are used to gather information on all aspects of the development. Each gatherer is tied into one or more of the other automated methods to obtain information on errors, compilation runs, component sizes, reusable components used, etc. The data is then analyzed for trends such as productivity increases or decreases in order to provide management or developers insight into the product development. It is also needed to evaluate the usefulness of the process model being used to produce the product.

— Applicability to all phases.

Project Communication Enhancers (VTA) — These are all the automated methods needed for project communication and personnel communication. It includes electronic mail, bulletin boards, personal time calenders, etc.

— Applicability to all phases.

Environment Usage Aids (VTA) — These helpers provide the guidance necessary to use the various parts of the environment — the methods, the command language, etc. It also contains the methodology coercers and tutorials on the environment's methods.

— Applicability to all phases.

9.1.9 Automation Summary and Usage Scenario

Figure 9-2 lists all the generic automation described above and depicts what phase of the life cycle they pertain to. We have tried to provide at least one generic type of automated method in each phase to provide a minimum level of coverage. We have also tried to keep the same level of detail in choosing them, so some like "menu managers" might not appear.

Some may feel the automation presented is beyond the state of the art, but almost everything presented exists today either as a product or as a working prototype. Only in the reusable component area has the state of the art not become state of the practice. What has not been done is the integration needed among the various methods. This is a major step required to truly provide the automated support required of a software engineering environment and attain the real reductions in software cost. The short scenario in the next section should point this out further.

SCENARIO. To help put all the automation in perspective, we will present a short scenario on how a product could be developed using the automation provided. Recall, however, the focus in an environment is not on the automation provided, but on the methods used to create the product. The automation allows it to proceed quicker, and provides a capability like performing traceability that may not be possible without it.

Let's follow the path a typical product might take if it were to be created by the software engineering environment we have just described. We will assume a single person is creating the product, and is just getting started.

First, the user signs onto the environment, with the command language interpreter taking care of all the details of the signing in procedures. The user, not knowing where to start, uses the environment usage aids general tutorial section to investigate some of the methods available for requirements analysis, or possibly a methodology that can help with developing the full product. If the user decides to structure his or her own methodology, the methodology coercer aid will help with the selection of the method or methods in each phase of the life cycle that can be formed together into a methodology. Let's assume a preselected methodology is chosen.

The user leaves the environment usage aids and selects the properly configured problem expression editor supporting the requirements method selected from the methodology. The user creates his requirements using the editor using its sophisticated graphics capabilities. During the creation process, the user can consult the tutorial guides on how to use the requirements method, as well as step-by-step guidance on what to do next. At any time, the user can consult the semantic information analyzer to check for consistency and completeness of the requirements. Items that are undefined as well as inconsistent usage are flagged. Hard copies of any part of the requirements developed so far can be obtained. The user may also wish to consult the reusable component analyzer to see if there is anything in the component library that is useful in creating the product. If there is, it is retrieved and integrated into the requirements. Assuming the creation of requirements has been satisfactory, the information is baselined, and the specification process is begun.

The user will again use the editor to create the specifications, but since a methodology is in place, part of the specification has already been completed. The inter-method information exchanger/analyzer knows which information in one method can be used in another, and has already captured that information in the appropriate format. Information not readily exchangeable is flagged. As the specification is created, the analyzer portion checks for

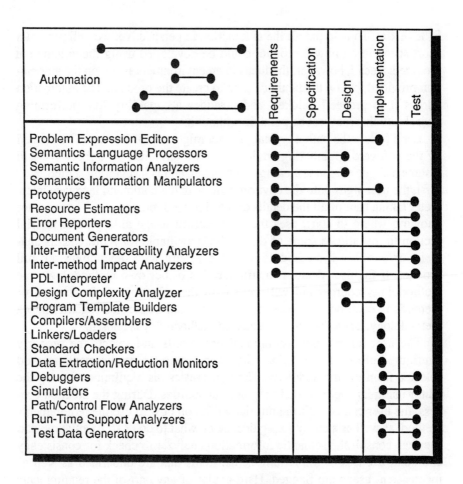

Figure 9 - 2   **Automation vs. Life Cycle Phase Summary**

consistency and completeness between the methods. The inter-method impact analyzer can be used to check to see what must be changed in the specification or requirements, and how much it will cost to do. A prototype of the product might be appropriate at this stage, so the requirements and specification information is sent to an appropriate prototyper to test the feasibility of the requirements and specifications.

Once satisfied, the user may want a printout of all documents required by the specification phase, which the document generator does by requesting the database to access the properly marked information. When it is sent to the

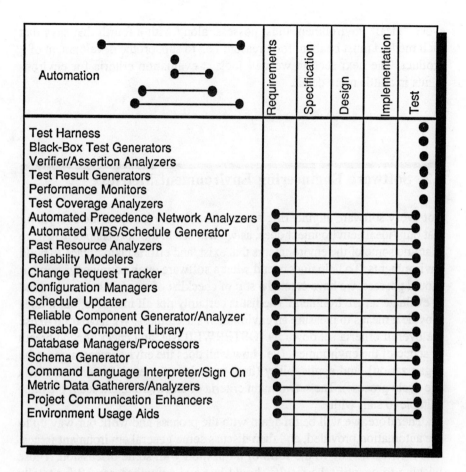

Automation	Requirements	Specification	Design	Implementation	Test
Test Harness					●
Black-Box Test Generators					●
Verifier/Assertion Analyzers					●
Test Result Generators					●
Performance Monitors					●
Test Coverage Analyzers					●
Automated Precedence Network Analyzers	●				●
Automated WBS/Schedule Generator	●				●
Past Resource Analyzers	●				●
Reliability Modelers	●				●
Change Request Tracker	●				●
Configuration Managers	●				●
Schedule Updater	●				●
Reliable Component Generator/Analyzer	●				●
Reusable Component Library	●				●
Database Managers/Processors	●				●
Schema Generator	●				●
Command Language Interpreter/Sign On	●				●
Metric Data Gatherers/Analyzers	●				●
Project Communication Enhancers	●				●
Environment Usage Aids	●				●

Figure 9 - 2   **(continued)**

document generator, it is formatted according to the documentation standards required, with any missing information annotated.

This process continues through the design, implementation and test phases. The software engineering environment aids the user in building the product, and helps in the maintaining traceability, consistency, and completeness of the product as it moves from phase to phase. The information is always timely, and the impact of changes is always available.

Notice, however that to accomplish these things, the information had to be available to all methods, the methods had to be integrated, and they had to be able to be automated. These three things are the basic requirements that every "ideal" environment must possess, along with a fourth that says that each method must be there for a reason; i.e., to support the development of a product. The next section we will look at evaluation criteria for environments in a little more detail.

9.2 Software Engineering Environment Metrics

Not every software engineering environment is going to provide everything that our "ideal" environment does, as we will see in the next chapter when we examine some of the environments that exist, and efforts taking place to build environments. To help understand what a software engineering environment should possess, we have created a sort of checklist of metrics that can be used to evaluate an environment. The list is certainly not all inclusive, but it does provide a means to measure an environments usefulness. We have tried to use the overall criteria set down by [OSTERWEIL81], and check for the breath of scope of the environment (i.e., how well does the environment support the organization), and applicability (how well does the environment support a life cycle process). These two main criteria of an environment seem the most suitable to start with.

Therefore, we will begin again with the process and work our way up to the automation provided, and then discuss some general environment issues. The metrics will be in the form of a question with some discussion. Those wishing to quantify the results should just add a number, say 10 for totally fulfilling the requirement, 0 for not, and somewhere in between for other answers.

PROCESS METRICS. These concentrate on the underlying process itself.

— Is the life cycle process well defined?

— Is there a specific development process?

— Is there a specific management process?

— Are the two related?

DISCUSSION

If the life cycle process is not well defined, then building an environment to support it will be difficult. Instead of being able to target the building of an environment, one that is tailorable must be built instead. The latter sounds like a better approach, but remember an environment is software, and if its requirements are poorly spelled out, then a poor result should not be unexpected.

— Is each process that occurs in a particular phase of the life cycle well defined?

— Is every product defined (contents, formats, etc.)?

— Are there explicit process exit criteria?

— Are there product assurance criteria?

DISCUSSION

It is not enough to simply have a life cycle model. Each process has to be defined in detail. This is especially true if it is to be automated to any level. Moreover, the process (development and management aspects) must be aimed at developing high quality products. If the products can't be defined in detail, how can methods be expected to produce information? Otherwise, what's the purpose of the environment? Finally, we need to know when we are finished. Without that, we really can't define what a product is.

METHOD METRICS. These should be asked for every life cycle phase.

— Do the methods support the process?

— Is a method usable in building a product?

— Is a method usable in increasing product integrity?

— Is a method usable with any other method?

DISCUSSION

It is important that the methods used have a reason for existing. Just "being there" clutters up the environment. An individual method must either help build a product or part of a product, help build a better product, or be usable with another to do either of the first two. Moreover, the methods available should be applicable to the product under development, i.e., have the correct viewpoint, domain, media, etc.

— Is the process fully supported by methods?

DISCUSSION

This is the inverse question. Are there enough methods to fully support the process? If there aren't, then something is not going to be automated, and the information will reside outside the environment. This will increase the difficulty of doing automatic traceability, consistency, and completeness, although if the process is well defined, then the problem has a chance of being solved using manual means. If not, information can slip away.

AUTOMATION METRICS. These should also be asked at every life cycle phase.

— How many methods are automated?

DISCUSSION

This is meant to refine the question of how much support is given each phase. If there are methods available, but they aren't all automated, then the potential capability of the environment for consistency, completeness, etc. is reduced.

— How many automated methods are integrated together?

DISCUSSION

The fewer the number that are integrated, or have the capability to be integrated, the less capable is the environment to provide the services that really make a difference to productivity and quality. This question could have alternately been stated as what is the degree of information coupling?

— Does the integration of methods appear seamless to the user?

— How easy are the automated methods to use?

— Is there guidance provided?

— Are there uniform user interfaces?

— What is the quality of the automation?

— Is the automation reliable?

— Is the automation performance adequate?

DISCUSSION

These concern the appearance of the environment to the user. If the user must worry about what is automated and what isn't, then it will detract from its usefulness. There are probably a hundred more that can be asked about the user's view of the environment.

GENERAL DISCUSSION ISSUES. Other questions that can be asked about the environment are more general in nature. For instance, what is the size, type and complexity of the product which is to be developed? A very good environment that doesn't match to the application type or size is not going to be terribly effective. To resolve this issue, a close examination of the life cycle process is required, as well as the methods available to support it.

Another question is the efficiency of environment implementation. In other words, is the environment performance adequate? A slow environment is an unused environment.

A third question is how stable are the methods? In other words, have they been used a much in the past? If not, the quality of the product might be suspect.

Which brings up the question what is the quality of the product developed by past uses of the environment. Has it been good, poor, or what would be expected without one? A corollary is; was it produced affordably by the environment, i.e., was the cost of using the environment worth it?

Finally, does the environment support peoples roles in a development? This goes back to the life cycle process model. The development and management models should reflect the development of a product based upon an organization's viewpoint. Remember, the model is an arbitrary representation, and must match the organization's way of doing business or it won't be too useful. The other possibility is that the organization will have to match the environment.

Asking each of these questions should provide some insight into the capability of the environment to produce a quality product.

9.3 Summary

An ideal software engineering environment is the minimum one needed to support the development of a software product. This chapter has presented a realization of an ideal environment and a scenario of its use. Also, a number of metrics that can be applied to evaluate existing environment were presented. In the next chapter, we will examine some of the efforts currently underway to build software engineering environments.

FOOTNOTES:

1. Much of this work is the result of studies conducted under [SEEWG82, MCKAY86].

10. SOME SOFTWARE ENGINEERING ENVIRONMENTS TODAY AND IN THE NEAR FUTURE

Usus est optimum magister

— Latin Proverb[1]

10.0 Introduction

In this chapter we will take a brief expedition around the world to see what efforts are being made in the area of software engineering environments. By studying what is currently available and the directions being taken by the various research tasks underway, we can gain a better understanding into the issues of building and using software engineering environments. Where appropriate, we will use our ideal environment as a basis against which to compare some of these efforts taking place.

Most, if not all, of the concepts incorporated into our idealized environment currently are being explored, tested, and/or prototyped in numerous government, commercial, and academic laboratories throughout the world. Major private and government software initiatives are occurring in the United States, Japan, the United Kingdom, and Brazil, only to name a few. Almost every industrialized nation, as well as third world nations which want to move into the first world category, have begun efforts to improve their nation's capability in producing software.

The reasons why are simple. As was shown in Chapter One, most of the industrialized world is becoming increasingly dependent on computers, and the capability to exploit the computer's capacity to do work cheaply, reliably, and more productively makes it literally an issue of economic survival. To poorer nations of the world, computerization of their industry is a way of leapfrogging into modern, industrialized nationhood. We predict the capacity to produce software technology and the control of information technology will be the major global economic goals of the 1990 s. In the next century, a country that cannot compete in it will be left behind .

A major aspect of most of the initiatives is the construction of some type of software engineering environment. Why all the interest? By now it should be clear that if software engineering environments like our ideal (or alternative) ones can be built, the quality and reliability of the software will increase, and the resulting cost of the software product will decrease. In this age of extremely intense global market competition, low price and high quality wins the largest market share. Therefore, it is economically prudent to invest in environments.

Second, we also know that we can't build software products of the size of 100 to 1000 million lines of source code without some sort of software engineering environment, and by the mid-to-late 1990s these are the system sizes that are going to be routinely specified for the twenty-first century. The ability to build large systems again provides an advantage in the marketplace over those who can't. Even if the technical issues confronting the building of environments for these sized systems mean they don't work as well as we would hope, the efforts spent provide spin-offs in ways of building smaller software products more cheaply and reliably.

Finally, software engineering environments provide a focus to all the software engineering technology efforts taking place. Major concerns often voiced about software engineering research and its application are that it is very diverse, is aimed at solving toy problems, and one research result can't be used with any other without a tremendous amount of effort. An environment helps solve these problems by directing research into providing practical solutions to the software problem by forcing the answer to the question,"How can this be used with X, Y, and Z methods that already are in the environment?" In some ways, this is the greatest benefit of developing an environment.

In this chapter, we will begin our look at the efforts taking place with software engineering environments in the United States, and then proceed to the efforts occurring in the rest of the world. Unfortunately, space limitations prevent more than a cursory look at each major activity (even trying to identify every environment project is difficult), but whenever we can, we will compare on-going or planned efforts with the ideal environment presented in Chapter Nine.

10.1 Software Engineering Environment Efforts — United States

In the United States, software engineering environment research and development is taking place in academia, commercial, and government sectors. We will give only a very brief overview of what is happenning in the academic sector, and then examine the other two more thoroughly.

10.1.1 Academic Environments

The academic efforts have concentrated more on the construction of program generation environments, in other words those that provide support mainly to the implementation phase, and sometimes to the design and test phase phases as well.[2] Limited budgets, lack of full-time personnel available to work on environment development, and the basic aims of research have been the major determinants in this limiting their range of work.

Some of the more well known implementations or prototypes are: the Gandalph environment at Carnegie-Mellon University, Pittsburgh [HABER-MAN80], an Ada-based support environment used to explore Ada concepts; the Program Development System (PDS) environment, at Harvard [CHEATHAM81], which is a collection of language-oriented tools for programming and evolution, with an emphasis on validation; the Precise Interface Control (PIC) environment at the University of Massachusetts, Amherst [WOLF85], another Ada-based system which is in the prototype stage aimed at supporting large system development; and Andrew, a distributed personal computing environment at Carnegie-Mellon [MORRIS86], aimed at investigating the automation of new software engineering methods, among other things.

None of these environments provides the level of coverage of that of the ideal software engineering environment. Each is focused on the production of smaller sized products (possibly with the exception of PIC), and none

NAME	Rqt's	Spec	Dsgn	Impl	Test	
Bell Lab. UNIX				●	●	[KERNIGHAN81]
Xerox XDE				●	●	[REDWINE84]
Bell Lab. PWB			●	●	●	[DOLOTTA78]
Hughes AIDES			●	●	●	[WILLIS81]
TRW SREM		●	●	●	●	[ALFORD85]
ITT PSE	●	●	●	●	●	[REDWINE84]
GTE STEP	●	●	●	●	●	[GRIFFEN84]
TRW SPS	●	●	●	●	●	[BOEHM86]

Table 10 - 1   **Partial List of Commercial Environments and Life Cycle Coverage**

provides much help in the requirements and specification area. None have seen application to any mid-to large-size software developments, either. Again, the concentration has been on trying to help the individual programmer, not large programming projects. However, they do provide the framework to explore interesting concepts, such as new user interface designs and new modularization techniques, which can be incorporated into future environments, as the Andrew and PIC projects are doing.

10.1.2   Commercial Environments

The commercial sector in the United States has been developing software engineering environments for a long time. They cross the spectrum from programming environments like UNIX™ [RITCHIE74, KERNIGHAN81] to software engineering environments like STEP [GRIFFIN84], with all sorts appearing in between. An (incomplete) list of commercial environments, their life cycle coverage, and references for further information are shown in table 10-1.

Up until recently, most of the development of software engineering has occurred within private corporations, but now a number of companies have formed software consortiums to attack software technology issues with greater capability than any one company can bring to bear. Specific areas of concern for these consortia are software engineering environments.

In order to give a flavor of what is happening in the commercial area in regard to environments, we will begin our examination with the UNIX environment. It is one of the oldest and most popular environments used and is available to the public in many different versions. It concentrates on providing the programmer with a "hospitable working environment." We will then move on to look at STEP, which is a very robust software engineering environment being used at GTE. Then we will look at what is going on at the two software consortia that have been formed, MCC and SPC, and see what they plan in software engineering environments.

10.1.2.1 UNIX

The UNIX environment is a different sort of software engineering environment than most we will examine. From one perspective, it is an operating system which can host a wide variety of application software ranging from word processing to embedded software development. From another perspective, it is a programming generation environment [REDWINE84]. The reason for this dual nature is rather interesting.

UNIX was developed in 1969 by two individuals (Dennis Ritchie and Ken Thompson), having no predefined objectives of what they were going to do. Their only goal was providing programmers like themselves with the tools they needed to make their job easier; i.e., providing themselves an "hospitable environment" in which to work [RITCHIE74]. They set out to accomplished this task by basing their environment on the idea of an operating system where, for the sake of programming convience, all operating system file functions and user programs would appear alike.[3] This eliminated the need for cumbersome access routines and extraneous control structures which were then the usual practice in operating systems. The result has been the most popular and influential programming/operating system in existence, with 40 installations in 1974 [RITCHIE74] growing into over 3000 in 1981 [KERNIGHAN81].

UNIX provides facilities for running programs and a file system for the managing of information. However, it is the file system that is the foundation of UNIX. Files have no type or internal structure, being considered only a sequence of bytes. This means all files look alike to the operating system and can be treated without worry of any special cases arising. This means a program and file are not distinct. The advantage of this is that data produced by a program and stored in a file can be used by another program with no or minimal inconvenience.

This also is enhanced by the fact that basic system interfaces for I/O provides for homogeneous treatment of the files, I/O devices, and programs. This means a program really doesn't have to care about where the data they operate on or produce comes from or goes to. Moreover, all operating system functions, like directory listers, are implemented as ordinary user programs. They are accessible to all users, who, if dissatisfied with their operation, can change them.

The way a UNIX user interfaces with the system is through what is called a "shell." The shell is nothing more than an interpreter for user commands. All commands issued by a user are viewed as requests to run programs. There exist a number of system programs to help the user create programs, manipulate files, create documents, etc. To use them, the user simply issues a command which executes the appropriate file(s). In UNIX System III, over 200 programs (called "UNIX tools") are available.

The philosophy in UNIX is to separate functions that are necessary to create programs and provide system services, rather than combining them into "monolithic" system routines that may not be flexible enough to do all the tasks a user wants done. Each of these functions is defined as a tool.

Although not every tool can can interconnect with every other tool in UNIX, the user can string many of these together (using "pipes"[4]) to create a specific function. Programs, in the usual sense of the word, are created by stringing UNIX functions and user created functions together to perform a particular task.

The order of execution can vary, and the user can create functions of almost any order of complexity desired. The user also can create his or her own tools to supplement the standard UNIX tools, or modify the existing ones to interact in new ways. This provides a very powerful, flexible, and simple mechanism in which to develop programs.

ADVANTAGES OF UNIX. The advantages of UNIX are numerous. Programs are easily and rapidly created and tested. The user doesn't have to create a lot of code, but can simply string together a number of pre-existing tools. With an extensive support library of functions available, UNIX encourages reuse, rather than reinvention.

The provision of so many tools encourages the UNIX user also to be creative. With many interconnections possible, the user can implement a program, understand the implications, and then look for ways to make it more efficient.

Debugging of the code is also much simpler. Since programs are these interconnections of functions, each function can be "pulled apart" one function at a time until the error is discovered.

One of the areas where many tools have been provided is in documentation. Very simple to very sophisticated documents can be created using UNIX. These tools have been expressly created to reduce the cost and trouble of documenting a product being implemented.

UNIX obviously provides for a high degree of data integration with its "file transparency" mechanism. This allows for traceability and consistency of data to be maintained, which increases the capability for conducting product verification.

DISADVANTAGES OF UNIX. UNIX also has some disadvantages. Each of the UNIX tools is in a sense "method fragments," without the method being specified. The best choice of tools is not obvious in every case. Thus only a fairly sophisticated user will be able to utilize the full power of UNIX with all the tools available.

Similarly, there is no method to process link. Although UNIX is very flexible, and can support most life cycle models in general, to support a specific process model would require a lot of work. Moreover, UNIX provides no support for requirements analysis and specification, or for high level design. However, it has been used in detailed design, and is especially useful for implementing data flow diagrams directly [KERNIGHAN81].[5]

Mid-size and greater product development is also not well supported in standard UNIX. The requirements of supporting a large development team, configuration management, use of standards, consistency of methods used, etc. are almost directly opposite of the UNIX "individualist" approach to product development. UNIX installations primarily support small teams of programmers working on a single program, not large groups working on many programs and geographically spread out.

Some work has been done to rectify this problem, primary under the UNIX Programmer's Workbench (PWB) [DOLOTTA78]. The PWB is a version of UNIX specifically for use in a computer center environment for the purpose of supporting a large number of users. It provides for source code control and supports project communication very well through an electronic mail system. But it still lacks the capability to support all the functions of a large product development.

SUMMARY. UNIX is a very powerful program generation environment. It appears to be a very integrated environment, but in fact isn't. The ability to transfer data in a transparent manner, and interconnect many tools, gives it this appearance. The ideal software engineering environment uses the same concept with its use of objects and standard automation packages that are tailored to the individual methods. The difference between the two lies more in the requirement for the ideal environment to be constructed from the process on up, while UNIX tries to match the process from the top down. The automated methods used in the ideal environment can be thought as similar to UNIX tools.

The other differences between the ideal environment and UNIX are in the support the environment provides across life cycle, and the specific support for organizing, managing, and developing mid-sized and larger projects such as product assurance, communication support, use of a standard process model, etc. The ideal environment supports all the needs of an large organization, not a small team. Again, UNIX wasn't created with this in mind, and now it has a harder time expanding to incorporate this particular view. The shaded portion of figure 10-1 shows the coverage standard UNIX provides verses our ideal environment. Many tools and methods only indirectly are supported, and a process model even less so.

However, we will see that the basic ideas used in UNIX are used in all the software engineering environments that follow. It has set the standard for all others to be measured against.

10.1.2.2 Software Techniques of Engineering Projects (STEP)

The Software Techniques of Engineering Projects (STEP) environment was an outgrowth of the GTE desire to provide automated support to some of its

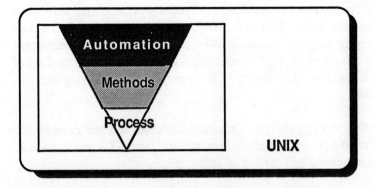

Figure 10 - 1   Unix Coverage vs. Ideal Environment

$400M research and development involving computer software [GRIFFIN-84]. The commercial applications that STEP supports development in include switching systems, communication and control systems, and networks.

STEP was developed differently from UNIX. The environment is based on a corporate methodology of building software; i.e., a process model and the methods that are needed to support the process. The major aspects of the methodology as described by [GRIFFEN84] are:

- A standard software architecture for all systems is described. It is represented as a hierarchy of logical components, each level being a decomposition of the preceeding higher level (like a task WBS structure), which includes a dynamic interpretation of the logical components as well as a static one;

- A tailorable, company-wide standard GTE software life cycle development model (with rationale described) which covers the full-life cycle ;

- An explicit description of the management aspects of the life cycle model, especially product assurance, and;

- A list of the necessary documentation for each phase of the development process.

The GTE software process development model was supported through a methodology consisting of ideas from Warnier, Yourdon, and Jackson as well as others developed in-house. In 1978, an environment was constructed to mechanize the methodology wherever possible with an integrated set of automated techniques. The result, STEP, provides the following services [GRIFFEN84]:

- Offers an integrated set of automated methods and techniques built around a portable database management system for configuration management and sharing of information;

- Enforces a set of standards throughout the product development;

- Ensures documentation is current, and;

- Provides management reports on project status.

STEP currently emphasizes automated support in the implementation, testing, and product assurance areas, with the front end not as heavily populated with automated support. Future plans include the incorporation of a requirements processing system and test plan generator. It does, however, provide for users to create their own automated methods and use them in conjunction with those provided in the environment. The concept of integrating functions/files as in UNIX doesn't really exist (functionality in each automated method is still at a much higher level than UNIX and integation takes place through the database), but there is an indication that this direction will be followed more in the future.

ADVANTAGES OF STEP. The advantages of using STEP at GTE are many. First, the environment directly supports a standardized corporate way of doing business. GTE has software engineering groups that constantly review the model, assess how well it performs on projects, and make suggestions for changes. Major changes have been incorporated since its inception, which has made a more robust model, bringing it closer to an ideal model. The tailorability allowed also let's the model cope with situations which are unusual, which keeps the process from being overly constrained.

The support of the process by selected methods used within GTE also is a distinct advantage. Training time is decreased, everyone involved knows the process, and concentration can be given to building the product, not about how to use the methods. Using identified methods also makes it easier to construct STEP, and probably enhances its reliability.

STEP directly supports the products GTE is involved with, which are mid-sized and greater. This is an advantage because the problems of managing the development was built into the environment from the start. It can be expanded as the product sizes expand (as is currently happenning). Moreover, the methodology has allowed both managers to communicate with each other because there exists a single vocabulary with which to describe the product and its development.

Finally, STEP has been used on many projects and has been reported to increase product reliability.

DISADVANTAGES OF STEP. There are few disadvantages in the STEP environment or approach. One is the use of a standard "template" in which all products must fit. This is fine for the particular business areas GTE is in, but it may not work well on all types of product developments (this area was one where changes have been made).

Another is that it appears that the database doesn't support data transparency as well as in UNIX or in our ideal environment. Automated methods are not part of the file system as in UNIX, nor is all data directly usable by any other automated method.

The lack of complete automation of all the methods which compose the methodology is also a problem, since some information is contained in the database, and some is contained on paper. However, STEP is an evolving environment, and additions are being made to make it fully automated.

Other disadvantages reported have to do less with the environment, but more with the fact of getting people to use it. Although care was taken to incorporate many of the techniques used across the company, not everyone is yet in STEP, so some users would still rather use other means to develop products. Another is that the performance of the implementation of STEP is not particularly speedy. Some of GTE's groups have been hesitant to use it for this reason. Reluctance of users and environment performance issues as detriments to environment use will be discussed further in the last two chapters.

SUMMARY. STEP is a very advanced software engineering environment that takes the same basic approach to building a software engineering environment as did our ideal environment. It supports a process model, provides

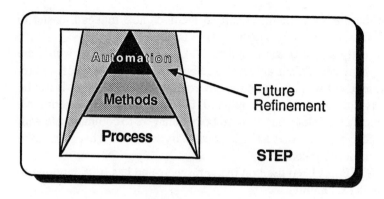

Figure 10 - 2   **STEP coverage vs. Ideal Environment**

methods to support the process, and provides automation of many of those methods. In comparison to an ideal environment as shown in figure 10-2, it comes very close. Notice the difference compared to UNIX in figure 10-1.

Overall, GTE's STEP, and similar environments like the Software Productivity System (SPS) at TRW [BOEHM84b], and represent the current state of the practice in the United States.[6]

10.1.2.3   Microelectronics and Computer Technology Corporation (MCC)

The Microelectronics and Computer Technology Corporation (MCC) [BELADY85, MYERS85, FISHETTI86] is a new, joint commercial research venture consisting of 21 shareholder corporations and 13 associates dedicated to advance the state of the art and reduce it into practice, across the spectrum of computer technology. Formed in 1983, and located in Austin, Texas, and armed with a $65M dollar budget contributed by the member companies for 1986, it is investigating the areas of semiconductor packaging, VLSI/CAD, parallel processing, AI and knowledge-based systems, database systems, human factors, and software technology.

The software technology area has two major objectives: develop technology to improve software productivity and quality, and transfer that technology to the sponsoring companies.[7] The work is viewed as long term research, and the goal is finding a basic, and possibly revolutionary change in the discipline of current software engineering. The thrust of development is specifically aimed at supporting the needs of large-scale product developments, especially those found in the requirements analysis, specification, and design phases.

Productivity gains above the 4 to 7 percent levels seen today, and the 7 to 12 percent needed to stay even, are required, although no target increase has been publicly stated as a goal of the research. To ensure that this level of productivity can be reached, the user must have access to the power of personal workstations, the capability to create applications that can take advantage of parallel processing, and access to a computer-aided software design environment that helps organize and automates most of his or her tasks. This environment is called Leonardo.[8]

LEONARDO. Leonardo will be a complete software engineering environment when it is completed. The draft specification is due in 1987, with building and refinement starting in 1988. Although there is no environment per se to discuss at this time, one can get some indication of what it might look like by examining the thrusts of the research taking place to support the effort.

The research for Leonardo has been partitioned to four groups. The first is the design process group which is concerned with complex design processes. It is responsible for identifying activities and the communication that people and organizations are involved with as they create a complex system. The group will elaborate the activities of developing large systems, investigate new models of the process, and it will attempt to understand how to bring design information out of the mind so it may be conceptualized and automated.

The next group is the design information group. Its responsibility is to determine how the information that is captured in a development can be organized, and reused. One of their goals is to determine what information should be kept during a development.

The third group is the design interface group. Its responsibility is to increase the visualization of the process. How information is presented and visualized is very important to its understanding, and one of the ways being explored is through animation.

The last group is the design environment group, which will build Leonardo. It is responsible for identifying its major components and integrating all the work of the other groups into a working software engineering environment.

The Leonardo software engineering environment may not resemble our ideal environment much at all. The process model they wish to use is one that represents a revolutionary, not evolutionary, change.It will be interesting to see what environment is eventually created out of these efforts.

10.1.2.4   Software Productivity Consortium (SPC)

The Software Productivity Consortium (SPC) is a limited partnership of 10 to 15 primarily aerospace companies from the the U.S. defense contracting arena.[9] The objective is to improve the productivity of the development of mission-critical computer (MCC) software. Started in late 1985, and located in Fairfax County, Virginia, it is budgeted for $41 million over its first three years. The thrusts of the work are in knowledge-based systems, software prototyping, reusable software, and software systems engineering.

Due to the newness of the program, there is not much information on the goals of each of the four areas. However, what is known is that research into methods and automated support to improve productivity is a key objective in each, and software engineering environments will be investigated. Moreover, since the work is directed at MCC software, from our discussion of the MCC software characteristics in Chapter One, we can postulate that the research will be directed towards helping produce real-time embedded software systems of massive size. A concern is not to duplicate efforts within each firm, but instead to leverage off all the work currently being performed.

10.1.3   U.S. Government

The efforts in software engineering environment construction and use in the U.S. government have been centered mostly around the Department of Defense (DoD). DoD has been in the software business from the beginning, and is the largest single procurer of software in the world. Thus, its interest in ways of increasing productivity and lowering software costs, involving enviroments, is keen. One such environment is the Navy's Facility for Automated Software Production (FASP) [STUEBING84]. It has been operational since since 1975, and is currently supporting over 15 million lines of source code for various Navy airborne electronic systems. The programs produced are of a higher quality and produced twice as quickly than that of the industry average.

Although software engineering environments like FASP exist,[10] most of the environments are specialized to supporting one platform, one project, or at best, one service. Also, like most current environments, they don't support the front end life cycle processes very well, where the real future costs in evolution can be contained. The major problem in DoD systems currently being produced are being traced back to requirements that aren't being properly formulated. The recent cancellation of the Sgt. York air defense gun because it couldn't fulfill its requirements (after $2 billion was spent) graphically illustrates the point.

The Department of Defense has, however, taken a number of steps to combat the high cost due to the duplication of efforts and lack of requirements support to develop systems, especially in the software area. Over the past dozen years it has moved toward controlling the proliferation of computer architectures and programming languages, by standarding on a few of each. It has developed a standard development life cycle model, DoD STD 2167, and is now involved in efforts to create software engineering environments to support it.

In the next few sections we will examine these software engineering environment efforts, as well as take a brief look at the efforts going on in NASA's Space Station Program.

10.1.3.1 DoD Software Initiatives

The efforts to control the cost and production of software has been gathered together under an umbrella effort called the DoD Software Initiatives. The program is run out of the Office of the Secretary of Defense, and is managed by the Director of Computer Software and Systems, who reports to the Deputy Undersecretary of Defense (Reasearch and Advanced Technology).

The software initiatives are focused in three areas of concern. The first is the programming language area. To help ensure the production of more reliable, better quality, timely, reusable, and cheaper MCCR software, development and standardization on Ada has occurred. Now efforts are aimed at its introduction into DoD.

The second area is in the development of software engineering technology to help automate software production, increase software portability, and
move the current state of the practice closer to what is needed in the future.
This is been the concern of the Software for Adaptable And Reliable Systems
(STARS) program.

The last area of concern is in stimulating the transfer of software engineering technology from the state of the art as practiced in research com-
munities into the state of the practice used in DoD. This is the function of the
Software Engineering Institute (SEI).

We will review the efforts occurring in each in the next three sections.

10.1.3.1.1   Ada Programming Support Environment (APSE)

One of the components of the DoD Software Initiatives is the support of the
Ada programming language. An Ada Joint Service Program Office (AJPO)
exists to control the language specification, validate Ada language compilers
to insure they meet the specification, and promulgate the language within
DoD and the U.S. government. An aspect of that support has been the
development of a specification called STONEMAN [STONEMAN80] which
describes the requirements for software support environments to support
Ada.[11] These are called ASPEs.

Three efforts have been undertaken by the DoD to implement subsets of
an APSE called a Minimal Ada Programming Support Environment
(MAPSE). A MAPSE is the minimum automated support thought necessary
to provide the capability to implement, debug, and manage Ada programs.
From this core come more components (called "tools") to increase the coverage of the MAPSE toolset in supporting design, specification, and requirements in the front end, and testing and integration in the back end of the life
cycle model. The point is to turn the MAPSE into an APSE.

The three efforts, one called the Ada Integrated Environment (AIE),
another the Ada Language System (ALS), and the third the Ada Language
System/Navy (ALS/N), have been sponsored by the U.S. Air Force, Army,
and Navy respectively. There are three efforts because each service has different computers that require different code generators, and each service
feels that it has requirements that have slightly different needs than the other
two. The AIE is being built by Intremetrics, Inc., and has been delayed due to

funding problems. The ALS was built by SofTech, Inc. and was delivered to the Army in early 1985. Funding for continued ALS development was stopped by the Army in June, 1986. The ALS/N is based upon the ALS, and is currently under development by a team headed by Control Data Corporation. Rather than examine each one, we will instead just review the ALS, remembering though that each of the others are slightly different.

ALS. The ALS [WALLACE84] is a programming generation environment that provides full support of the capabilities of the Ada language. Using the ALS, programmers can develop, test, run, and maintain programs written in Ada for use in dedicated, embedded target computers.

The ALS provides facilities for testing, documenting, management, and maintenance of developed Ada programs. All information on a project throughout its life cycle can be stored by the ALS in a database under full configuration control.

In addition to programs coded in Ada, the ALS is designed to accept programs written in target computer assembly languages. These assembly languages are intended to be used for writing special subprograms that can access capabilities of the target computers that cannot be reached from Ada.

Figure 10-3 illustrates the ALS. Since a requirement on an APSE is high portability, the ALS interacts with a host operating system called a Kernal APSE (KAPSE). The KASPE provides a set of services which allows ALS host-resident tools to be host hardware and operating system independent. The KAPSE serves as the exclusive interface between host operating system and host resident tools. In addition, the KAPSE provides a set of services for maintaining the ALS environment database.[12]

The ALS has over 70 different tools included with it. They are broken down into roughly 9 categories. Each is shown in figure 10-3. They are briefly described below.

The *language processing tools* provide for the translation of source code, linking of object code, and creating a loadable image functions of the ALS. In addition, these tools provide for the maintenance, examination, and modification of Ada program libraries.

The *program analysis tools* support the interactive symbolic debugging of Ada programs. They also provide generation support for various reports and listings without the need for recompilation, linking, or excecution of a program.

The *configuration management tools* support direct configuration management of software developments by providing a disciplined approach for describing and controlling the creation, history, and status of a program.

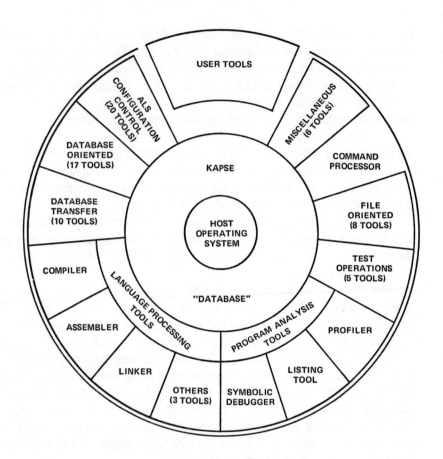

Figure 10 - 3 **ALS Tool Set**   *Source [WALLACE85]*

The *database transfer tools* support the ALS system administrator in the installation and general maintenance of the ALS environment database. This includes archiving and unarchiving files, creating backups of the ALs database, transmission and reception of a portion of a database to/from another ALS, etc.

The *database oriented tools* provide the ALS user a set of services that allows the examination and modification of the contents of the ALS database. The contents manipulated are the associations, attributes, and structure of the database, but not the data portion of the individual files.

The *file oriented tools* provide a set of services that allow the user to examine and modify the data portion of the files that make up the ALS database.

The *text operation tools* provide the main interactive text entry facilities for the ALS. Text may represent source code or support textual documentation. General formatting services are also provided.

Miscellaneous tools provide the user help and tutorial information.

Finally, *user supplied tools* are intended to allow the individual projects or organizations to extend the basic facilities provided by the ALS. The ALS makes no distinctions between pre-defined and user-defined tools.

The ALS operates in a manner similar to UNIX.[13] A user issues requests in a command language which is interpreted by a command language processor to perform certain functions. Unlike UNIX, the functions are at a higher level of granularity, and piping per se is not performed to create programs. The stringing of commands together is allowed, and it gives the appearance of a pipe to perform higher level ALS functions.

ADVANTAGES OF ALS. The advantages of the ALS is that it provides robust support to the implementation of Ada programs. It meets the basic goals spelled out in STONEMAN, which are to provide the capability for portability of user programs, and portability of the toolset. Everything a user needs to implement Ada programs is available. Information created by a tool is accessible to all other appropriate tools.

The configuration management aspect of the ALS is probably its greatest advantage because all data can be automatically configuration managed if required. There is no need for a separate group or system to do it. Moreover, the tools can be tailored to enforce the management policies and practices of the organization, thus providing for flexibility in its application.

DISADVANTAGES OF ALS. The disadvantages of the ALS are more a matter of time than anything else. Right now it supports the implementation phase very well, but no effort has been made to push it past this point. Part of the problem lies in its greatest capability, the configuration management. If everything in the system is being kept track of, the system overhead is very high, which results in slow performance. It is further exacerbated by the large amount of storage taken up by performing configuration management, which further increases system overhead. The other part of the problem lies in the KAPSE approach which adds overhead to every operating system call.

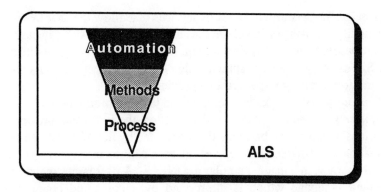

Figure 10 - 4   **ALS Coverage vs. Ideal Environment**

Another disadvantage of the ALS is that it wasn't built to support a life cycle model because the DoD had none at the time.

SUMMARY. The ALS is a fairly complete programming generation environment which provides the framework for building APSEs. It is in use at many sites, and is being hosted and retargeted for Japan's NTT DIPS computer by SofTech. The comparison between our ideal software engineering environment and the ALS is shown in figure 10-4.

10.1.3.1.2   Software Technology for Adaptable and Reliable Systems (STARS)

The STARS program is the second part of the DoD software inititative. Started in 1983, and funded in 1986 for $42 million, its primary objective is to reduce the gap between the current state of the practice and future software engineering requirements by developing new software technology and achieving its widespread use in DoD.

The STARS program is divided into six thrust areas, namely Methodology, Measurement, Human Resources, Business Practices, Applications, and the Software Engineering Environment (STARS-SEE). The STAR-SEE is a cornerstone of the STARS program. It is the focal point of all the efforts occurring in the other areas, where new software technology can be incorporated. Approximately $25 million was slated for the STARS-SEE effort out of the 1986 budget.

The status of the STARS-SEE was that it is currently specified, with draft copies of the Operational Concept Document and Specification having been released to industry for review and comment [STARS85,86]. It was envisioned that sometime in 1986 or 1987 a competitive request for proposals would be announced so that the environment could be built, with a scheduled introduction in 1991 or 1992. However, due to program restructuring, it's current status is unclear. A brief summary of the STARS-SEE as described in [STARS85,86] is given below.

STARS-SEE. The STARS-SEE is meant to support the development of any sized software product that the DoD chooses to implement. It will be a common automated software engineering environment for the development of MCCR software from which service and project specific environments can be configured. A high priority of the STARS-SEE is that it be tailorable to accommodate all the services' requirements.

The STARS-SEE will provide automated coverage of the full life cycle model as presented in DoD STD-2167 (see Appendix A). It is a goal of the environment to increase software productivity by an order of magnitude by the 1990s.

A key aspect of it is that the structure of the environment provide for evolution. Therefore, the STARS-SEE will be built in stages, and be based on the services MAPSEs. The importance of this lies in the fact that the environment must support all aspects of MCCR software development, which are on the whole, more comprehensive than any commercial development requires.

The STARS-SEE effort is currently involved in trying to determine how these various issues required to develop MCCR software can be integrated into the environment. Some of the major issues are:

- multilingual support (i.e., how can all the programming languages used across DoD be supported?);

- database exchange (i.e., how can all the data developed in various projects be made available to others?);

- multilevel security (i.e., how can the environment handle confidential, secret, and top secret information simultaneously while multiple levels of classified personnel are using it?);

- distribution and networking (i.e., how can an environment be distributed across many sites that might be involved in the software development?).

The STARS-SEE is expected to be one of the most comprehensive environment efforts ever to be undertaken. With it, DoD will finally start to bring some order to the chaos that currently marks DoD software development.

10.1.3.1.3   Software Engineering Institute (SEI)

The Software Engineering Institute (SEI) is a U.S. Federally Financed Research and Development Center (FFRDC) located in Pittsburgh, Pennsylvania. Started in early 1985, and funded for $103 million for five years, the SEI has a charter [DELAUER84] to:

- Accelerate the reduction to practice of modern software engineering techniques and methods;

- Transfer software engineering technology to and promulgate its use within the DoD community, and;

- Establish goals of excellence for software engineering practice.

The charter calls for 60 percent of the effort of the SEI be spent in transferring technology, 20 percent to provide support to DoD, 10 percent for enhancing software engineering education, and 10 percent for basic research.

The long range goal of the SEI is achieving technology transfer [BARBACCI85]. To accomplish this goal, the SEI requires a basic understanding of software development, an understanding of what constitutes the best methods, and the capability to make the use of the technology. The latter point can be accomplished either through the automation of individual methods, or by the creation of a software engineering environment, called by the SEI a Software Factory.

The Software Factory effort has just been started and the concept has not been cemented as of this writing. However, the environment that seems to be envisioned is an open and integrated one that supports the creation of large MCCR software products. An open environment is one which has an ability to incorporate tools, methods, and technologies very easily. An integrated environment is one where the components of the environment work together, share information, have uniform interfaces, etc. Acheiving these two goals simultaneously in an environment is difficult, because integration implies a detailed knowledge of how other methods work, while openness implies that this knowledge is not required. Since the Software Factory is only in the formulative stage, it is too early to speculate on the outcome.

10.1.3.2   NASA Space Station

The last software engineering environment effort we wish to briefly review is the NASA Software Support Environment (SSE) for the Space Station Program [GARMAND85]. The NASA Space Station, funded at $4 billion to $8 billion, is the next major space project for the United States. It is intended to be a permanent orbiting laboratory and factory which will also act as a "base camp" for future space missions. The Space Station is scheduled for an initial operational capability somewhere in the early to mid 1990s.

The computer software necessary to control the Space Station and all the ground sites is enormous, both in size and complexity. The initial estimates of the amount of all the software necessary to be developed is in the range of 75-100 million lines of source code, and up to four times that much will be needed to support future missions. Needless to say, the whole Space Station Program is highly computer intensive.

The Space Station Program currently has three major computer components defined. The first is the Space Station Information System (SSIS). The SSIS consists of both flight and ground data processing elements that support the operation and preparation of the Space Station activities. Application software for the Space Station is slated to be programmed in Ada.

The second computer component is called the Technical and Mangement Information System (TMIS). The TMIS consists of both the management and engineering information systems that support the management, design, development, and integration of the Space Station.

The last computer component is the Software Support Environment, or (SSE). The SSE is the set of automated methods and information required to provide a common development and maintenance environment for all applications software developed for the SSIS. The SSE will provide coverage of the full life cycle, and support product assurance and configuration management to a high degree, due to the critical nature of the software. The SSE is required to support the development of Space Station applications throughout its total life (over thirty years) which means it must be extremely flexible and allow for growth. The SSE is currently scheduled for operation in 1989-90, with the actual building of it to begin in late 1986 to early 1987.

10.2 Foreign

Commercial and government sponsored software engineering and software engineering environment activities are occurring not only in the United States, but all over the world. In the next several sections we will present a brief overview of the efforts in Asia, Europe, and South America.

10.2.1 Asia

In 1981, the Japanese government announced its plans for developing the Fifth Generation computer. Planning to spend over $450 million during the next ten years, the Japanese were aiming at making revolutionary gains in micro-electronics, parallel processing, and other supporting technologies to create the intelligent machine of the 1990s. Five years later the jury is still out on whether they will accomplish their goals, but they have been the catalyst for most of the computer technology efforts in the United States and elsewhere. For instance, it is directly responsible for the creation of the MCC and SPC in the U.S.

Since that time, Japan hasn't been the only Asian country moving in this direction. Both Taiwan and Singapore are starting software engineering efforts of their own. In the section, we will look at some of the current efforts in software engineering environment in Japan, and give overviews of what is occurring in Taiwan and Singapore.

A review of the Japanese Fifth-Generation Computer Systems Project can be found in [MOTO-OKA85].

10.2.1.1   Japan

As we mentioned, Japan has been the catalyst for most of the organized efforts occurring in software engineering technology. Although the Fifth-Generation Computer Project is by far the most visible, it is not focused on software engineering environments. This work has been proceeding along two complementary lines of work. One line of work is supported within Japanese industrial organizations like NEC, Toshiba, Fujitsu, and Hitachi [KIM83] who are in the mist of creating Software Factories. The other line of work is supported by the Ministry of International Trade and Industry (MITI). This effort is called the Software Industrialized Generator and Maintenance Project [SIGMA].

JAPANESE INDUSTRY. The Japanese software industry has long recognized its weakness in the creation of software, especially technologically advanced software. To compensate for this weakness, the Japanese have returned to the successful strategies that have worked in the automotive and electronics industry and have concentrated on building high quality software first, inexpensive software second, and technologically superior software last [TAJIMA81]. There is no such thing as a quality vs. price trade off in Japanese software. The Japanese believe that by building quality into the product they can achieve a low cost by reducing corrective maintenance to a minimum. A fundamental tenet of their software development is that one must fix all program bugs in existing code before more programming can begin. Moreover, they feel that building reliable software will allow them to compete in markets against sophisticated, but unreliable, software.

The Japanese software industry has started a program of building what are commonly called Software Factories in their plants [YEH85]. These Software Factories are strategic corporate enterprises organized like manufacturing facilities. They are usually specialized to support whatever business the organization participates in. The basic traits [KIM83,YEH85] of all these factories are that:

- They are based on standard methodologies which are precise and consistent;

- The methodologies are used corporate-wide;

- Deviation from the standard is not allowed;

- Automation support is totally provided and directly focused on implementing the methodologies, and;

- Product assurance is a prime component of the methodology.

These traits may seem overly constraining to an American programmer, where individuality and ownership of code is a source of pride, however the Software Factory concept does work. Toshiba reported average programmer productivity in 1983 was 10 times the U.S. average for real-time Fortran and Pl/1 code [KIM83]. Although a recent survey [ZELKOWITZ85] seems to indicate that the majority of software in Japanese industry has not reached the level of Toshiba, the trend toward using software environments in corporate organizations is stronger than in the U.S.

The Software Factory concept in Japan is aimed at bringing a very disciplined approach to programming. As mentioned, recently SofTech signed a contract with NTT to move the ALS to their computers. It will be interesting to see what will happen as the Japanese build Software Factories around the Ada programming language.

SIGMA. The SIGMA Project is a $100 million, five year Japanese government supported/ industry cooperative project to create a nation-wide computer network. The network will support a UNIX environment servicing 10,000 workstations. The workstations will be capable of using compatible software production systems.

The project includes plans for software service centers to develop and distribute software tools and create a standard software engineering environment. The project started in late 1985, and detailed specifications for the environment are not available at this time.

SUMMARY. The Japanese are moving rapidly in the software engineering environment area. Although their environment, like their software, may not be as sophisticated as that being projected in the U.S., their industry, unlike most of the U.S.'s, has many automated environments currently in place.

10.2.1.2   Taiwan

The Taiwanese Software Initiative [YEH85] is not on the scale of that of Japan or the United States. Taiwan has formed an Institute for Information

Industry (III) which is funded by government and private donations. The goals of the III are to promote the Taiwanese computer industry, conduct massive training of the Taiwanese in computers, help develop technologies that Taiwan can compete in, and transfer technology to Taiwanese industry. Although no software engineering environment work is specifically called out, efforts in this area are likely soon.

10.2.1.3　Singapore

In Singapore, a Regional Center for Information Technology has been established under the Joint Software Engineering Program (JSEP). Possessing a five year $44 million dollar budget, the center is focusing on three thrusts areas: software productivity and quality, office systems integration, and AI. One of aspects of the program is the development of a computer-aided software development (CASD) environment using Ada as a standard language. Again because of the newness of this effort, a detailed description of the CASD is unavailable.

10.2.2　Europe

The European community has, like the U.S., been moved to form a number of software initiative efforts to compete with the Japanese. One which encompasses almost all of Europe is the ESPRIT (European Program for Research and Development in Information Technology). Started in 1983, ESPRIT is both government and industry funded but organized under the European Economic Community (ECC) banner.

The goals of ESPRIT are to attain a competitive advantage in information technology, promote a rapid transfer of technology from labaoratories to industry, and promote the use of common standards for information technology within the ECC.

ESPRIT is funded for five years at $1.3 billion, and has over 250 projects currently underway throughout Europe. The major components of the program are the development of a fully integrated project support environment, development of a life cycle process which supports rapid prototyping, and the specification, development, and support of reusable software components.

ESPRIT is not the only software initiative effort in Europe. The United Kingdom has also has a project called Alvey which we will briefly discuss in the next section. Other software efforts are beginning to be organized in France and West Germany, and it is expected that within five years, all the European nations will have some type of formal software initiative in place.

10.2.2.1 United Kingdom

The Alvey Programme is a $470 million five year govenment and commercially funded software initiative begun in 1983 to advance the state-of-the-art in information technology. It is aimed at developing the tools and methods necessary to support the production of high quality, cost-effective software. The main thrusts are in the development of formal methods, software reliability, software metrics, and intelligent integrated software engineering environments based on UNIX. No published information on the environments is yet available.

10.2.3 South America

South America, specifically Brazil, has also begun a software initiative. Called the Software Plant Project [YEH85], its aim is to develop a structure for the industrial production of software to support the improvement of software productivity and quality. The main thrusts of the program are to develop a software technology base, and transfer this technology to the Brazilian software industry as rapidly as possible. A standardized software production environment, the Software Plant, is the project's main component. The Brazilian government is funding the project, but the amount and duration is unknown at this time.

10.3 Summary

The significance of software and software engineering environments is widely recognized around the world. As one can readily see, most of the initiatives have very similar objectives and thrusts. UNIX seems to be a favorite starting place for most of the environments currently contemplated, and this shows how little is really understood about the process models and methods required to develop software products. Ada-based environments are beginning to appear, but it probably will be another five to ten years before they become common. Hopefully, given all these world-wide efforts, new life cycle paradigms and new ways to automate them will be found, and be shared by all.

FOOTNOTES:

1. "Experience makes the best teacher."
2. A programming generation environment is one that is aimed at the implementation phase. A programming support environment includes support for the design and test phases. A software engineering environment includes requirements and evolution phase support. These are *general* categories we will be using to distinguish among the many things called environments.
3. Another crucial aspect of this decision was they were interested in exploring ideas and concepts in operating systems, and no one was there to tell them different.
4. When a program is run, a temporary file is created with the results. Another program can use that file as input and create another temporary as output to be used as input, etc. Rather than having the user specify all these temporary files, a pipe can be used which links the output of one program directly into the input of another.
5. But the data flow diagrams still had to be created originally, and were done so by users knowledgeable in the area.
6. There are many other large commercially developed software engineering environments that also exist in companies such as Boeing, CSC, Hughes, IBM, ITT and McDonnell-Douglas, which are either proprietary or about which literature is not readily available.
7. In the software technology area there are ten sponsoring companies: Bell Communications Research, Control Data Corporation, Harris Corporation, Lockheed, Motorola Inc., Sperry Corporation, Rockwell International Corporation, RCA Corporation (General Electric Co.), and NCR Corporation. MCC is basically made up of mainframe computer manufacturers and aerospace companies.
8. The name Leonardo is a trademark of MCC.

9. The companies are as of this writing: Allied/Bendix Corporation, Boeing, Ford Aerospace Corporation, General Dynamics Corporation, Grumman Aircraft Corporation, Lockheed, McDonnel Douglas, Northrop Corporation, SAI, TRW, United Technologies, and the Vitro Corporation.

10. None more successfully, either.

11. Technically, Ada environment work is not directed by the AJPO, but by a specific service. However, all the services cooperate with the AJPO through their service representative in the program office.

12. Another effort, called CAIS (Common APSE Interface Set) is underway to make these interfaces more transparent and compatible to encourage tool portability between different KAPSE's. See [CAIS84].

13. The concept of the ALS was based heavily on the UNIX model.

11. THE FUTURE OF SOFTWARE ENGINEERING ENVIRONMENTS TECHNOLOGY ISSUES

"One should be careful about predicting, especially about the future."
— Chinese proverb

11.0 Introduction

In the final two chapters, we want to explore some of the technology and introduction/transition issues associated with software engineering environ-ments. Thus far, we have examined a model of an environment, taken it apart, and then put it back together again in the form of an "ideal software engineering environment." However, questions still remain whether an envi-ronment like the one postulated can, or even should, be built, and if so, will anyone use it?

Much of what was presented in Chapter Nine about our ideal software engineering environment is speculative, because no one has built an environ-ment of that sophistication level yet. Efforts like GTE's STEP, the STARS-SEE, and NASA's SSE are all moving in that direction, but there are still many unknowns to be resolved. The ALS was the first real MAPSE, and it took much more money and time than anyone thought it would, and its coun-terpart, the AIE still hasn't been completed. Building environments appears easy, but it is not. Currently, the state of understanding of environment technology is at about the same point as compiler technology was in the mid-1950s, just before the first FORTRAN compiler was introduced. What exists today are all the component parts that are necessary to build one; it is just that no one as yet has figured out how to make them all work together.

COMPILERS AND ENVIRONMENTS. The parallel between compilers and environments is very appropriate (and remarkably similar) for a number of reasons. Today's program generation environments (PGE) play much the same role assemblers did in the early 1950s. At that time, assemblers represented the current state-of-art to most practioners. Even though they were available, their use wasn't very widespread. The basics of what an assembler had to do were understood well enough, but the basic theory was still a little fuzzy.

Just lurking off in the distance were the "automatic program generators" (i.e., compilers) that were going to make everything better (just like software engineering environments promise today). The vision touted in the early 1950s was that a programmer would just have to describe the problem in a high level language similar to English and "presto," out would pop a program. (Using software engineering environments is claimed to do the same thing, except one needs to substitute the word "software product" for the word "problem.")

Well, we know the rest of the story. The language was English-like, programming was made easier to do, but as far as automatic code generation, well, things haven't worked out quite as planned. It is thirty years later and we are still waiting. However, in the meantime, we have developed a very robust theory of compilation, and the construction of assemblers is done now in high school computer classes. Whether we will have to wait thirty years to understand software engineering environments as well as assemblers is un - known. There is, however, much research and debate about what should be in a software engineering environment, just as there were debates about what automatic program generators should look like.

ACCEPTABLE ENVIRONMENTS. In this book, we have presented an ideal view of what an environment should look like, but the translation of it into the real world is not so clear (see figure 11-1). In our ideal world, a number of assumptions are made, such as the problem being solved is well-defined, management will always make the correct decisions, the development personnel know what they are doing when performing requirements analysis, specification, design, etc. , and there are no intangibles to cause any problems in the development (like a cut in funding, or the only person who knows how a particular module works quits, etc.) In the real world, none of these things

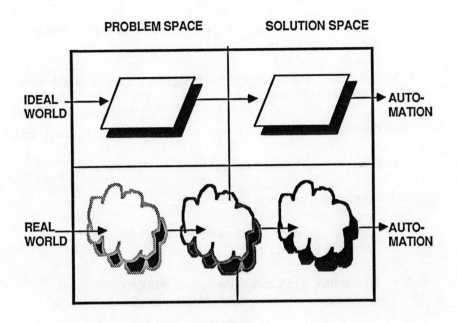

Figure 11 - 1   **Ideal World vs. Real World**

holds true. So one tries to find a solution that fits, but which may need a number of iterations before it becomes truly acceptable (*not* ideal). Even then it may be difficult to tell when the solution has been found.

The debates over software engineering environments center around what are the acceptable solutions, and how can they be obtained. The arguments involve the process models used, the methods available, and the proper use of automation. As we mentioned in Chapter Two, if there has been one difficulty in discussing environments, it is they can mean so many different things to people. Thus to satisfy everyone's desires, they have to include everything anyone can possibly want. An example of this syndrome are the characteristics a good environment should possess that are sometimes listed [MAGEL84, STARS 85, 86]. A software engineering environment should be:

- General, which means it should support the whole life cycle;

- Adaptable, which means it should be able to be implemented on many different types of computer architectures;

- Tailorable, which means it must be able to be tailored to different life cycle processes;

- Extendible, which means it should support the ability to add more methods and/or tools easily;

- Consistent, which means it should appear "seamless" to a user, and;

- Efficient, which means it should have good performance.

The environment should also provide for:

- Aggregation, which means methods should be able to be integrated together,

- Traceability, which means the path used in the creation and manipulation of a single item of information can be traced;

- Abstraction, which means as many of the internal details of the environment's actions are hidden from its users, and

- Recovery, which means the environment should protect the user from hardware or software errors.

And the list goes on and on. For the remainder of this chapter we will examine some of the technical issues involved in trying to attain these desirable characteristics, and see what they mean to the building of an environment. We don't pretend to have the final answers to any of them, and merely will be content to present them for discussion. Some of the issues also overlap one another.

11.1 Software Engineering Process Issues

The central issue of debate in software engineering and environments rages over the process model of the software development. As we noted in Chapter Two, there are basically four types currently supported: the Waterfall, Rapid-Prototype, Operational, and Knowledge-based. The arguments concerning them basically are over which one is best for developing software products. Unfortunately, these arguments miss the fundamental point of whether they are acceptable, and whether they model the process of develop - ing a product at all.

PROCESS AS SOCIAL ACTIVITY. The development of mid-sized or larger software products is a massive undertaking. It really is a large group social activity and should be viewed as such first. It involves people inter- acting and communicating together. They compete for resources as groups and/or as individuals, with the competition occasionally erupting into open "warfare." Real product developments are confusing, and human error is inherent in the process. In fact no one really has produced a study of what really happens during a large product development.[1] None of the process models really make these aspects very explicit.

Each of the current life cycle models describe the development of soft- ware as a rather antiseptic process where nothing like group dynamics is involved. When one compares where the models of software development and actual developments don't match, it is in this area. This leads one to ask whether many of the efforts to refine the current process models are useful or not.

In the MCC Leonardo environment effort discussed in Chapter Ten the opinion is that they are not and a new, revolutionary software engineering paradigm is needed if productivity is to really be enhanced. For example, even if coding were done for free, the cost of a product would only be reduced by about 10 percent during its development, and only 4 to 6 percent over its entire lifetime. Moreover, since the current life cycle models don't model the development of large sized products in today's terms very well (the Waterfall model was developed during the late 1960s), something else is thought to be needed. The need to model the development of software systems, not programs, is crucial [FOX85], and the impact of a new model on an environment will likely be profound.

ACCEPTABLE PROCESS MODELS. Even if the current models are not really very acceptable, they work de facto at least to the minimal acceptable level. After all, billions of lines of code have been developed and managed using the Waterfall model, and billions more undoubtedly will be in the future as well. Thus, the evolutionary improvements to the other process models based on this model are still important.

We know where the models need to be corrected,too. These are graphically illustrated in figure 11-2,which shows some of the problems perceived by the DoD in trying to apply the Waterfall life cycle model to defense software production in 1975 [APL75]. The problems have been in trying to correct them.

The Rapid-Prototype and Operational approaches have been responses to this need. Of course, a question comes to mind whether we want to model what is happening, or do we want to model what we want to happen during the software development process. The answer to this is very crucial, for it will determine how it will eventually be built and used. Let's consider a few points.

There have been arguments, some of which we have discussed in the individual phase descriptions, that the specification phase is really part of requirements phase, that design is really part of specification, that implementation is part of design, and that testing is really part of implementation. If all these are true, then testing and requirements analysis are the same thing! Regardless, building an environment to support any one of the possible combinations will influence how well methods are integrated. If specification and design phases are merged, then the products created will be different than the ones if they were separate. And so will the methods and automation needed.

The second point is that if any of the combinations above are chosen, then this is the view of the development that will be imposed on the environment user. This can be good or bad, depending on how strictly one wants to control the development process. If one wants stricter control, an environment can be used to constrain how the automated methods interact with each other or are integrated. A high degree of integration or low degree of interaction can restrict the user to doing things in a few prescribed ways. If one wants looser control, then the methods provided interact in many ways, with either a low or high degree of integration.[2] Whichever direction is desired impacts the way an environment will be built.

ENVIRONMENT CONSTRUCTION APPROACHES. For high integration and interaction, the software engineering environment has to be built in a top down fashion, i.e., the process has to be defined first, then the methods, and then the methods automated (although the ultimate goal of automation will determine which trade offs are necessary in each element). In the case of an environment which is not so tightly controlled, one can build it by automating many methods or techniques and having them support the process model, but not be derived from it. GTE's STEP is a general example of the first approach, while UNIX is an example of the second. The ALS is somewhere in between. Our ideal environment tries to take the best from both approaches, deriving the methods from the process, but allowing the methods to interact either in a restricted pattern, or allowing them to be "free" form, depending on the user (or project manager's) perogative.

The difference in the results of using each of the various approaches is in how much traceability, consistency, and completeness (and implicitly quality) one wants between the products completed in one phase with those produced in another. The more methods which are integrated, the more ability to provide these capabilities. In the end, the trade off is between user freedom to be creative vs. the requirement for a disciplined approach to developing software products. As the products become larger, the need for more discipline is apparent, but then there are more people involved who want the flexibility to do it "their way." The push/pull between what is good for the product vs.what is good for the developers is a constant battle.[3]

The reason why so much work is in trying to integrate phases is to try to eliminate some of the problems above. If, as we remarked, the requirements and testing phases were one and the same, then there would be less of a problem (although there wouldn't be much flexibility either!).

The general direction currently being taken in defining process models seems to be the same approach that was taken with compilers. In compilers, there are set definitions that describe generally what has to be done in each of the compilation phases. Interfaces to each phase are then rigorously defined, which allows whatever appropriate method desired to exist in a particular phase. Moreover, some phases can be removed, such as the optimization phase. This permits a trade-off between possibly less efficient code, against possibly faster compilation time. Understanding how to model a similar idea for the evolution process, where an enhancement is being made to a software product but where there is no need to redo the whole life cycle, would be extremely helpful.

In summary, the foundation of all technical issues concerning a software engineering environment eventually revolve around the process model used for software development. How acceptable one particular model models the development process will determine the quality of the product developed more than any other factor. A good process model should help the understanding of the process so that those participating in the product development know their roles and what to do, and the managers know what criteria to use to make decisions. Defining the right model is a difficult process.

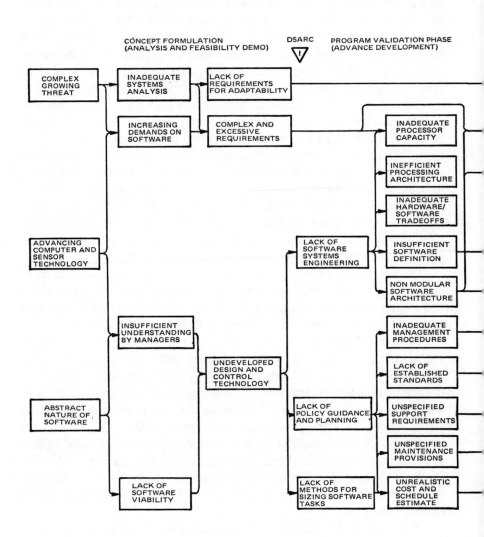

Figure 11 - 2 **Problems in the Software Life Cycle**

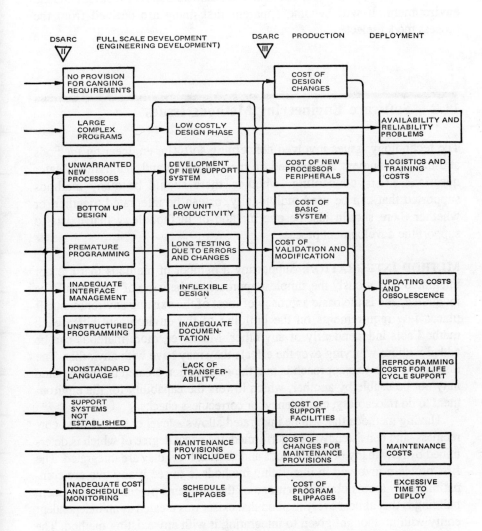

DSARC   FULL SCALE DEVELOPMENT   DSARC   PRODUCTION   DEPLOYMENT
  II   (ENGINEERING DEVELOPMENT)   III

The next section is concerned with the technical issues of methods and the environment. It will become apparent that many are derived from the process model selected.

11.2   Software Engineering Methods Issues

The technology issues involved concerning software engineering methods and the environment are focused on their selection and integration. Major questions exist concerning whether there should be many methods supported that can be used individually, or can be integrated together, or whether there should just be one method or methodology that exists to support the development process.

METHOD INTEGRATION. Supporting a number of methods that are not integrated is obviously the simplest approach to the issue of what should be integrated, and is the basic approach of most of the existing environments. It places few requirements on the building of the environment since each method acts independently of any other. Moreover, more methods can be added without worrying over the effects they may have with any other. The disadvantage to this approach is that the information created by one method may not be usable by another, which lowers the capability for the environment to do traceability, consistency, or correctness checks.

Having methods that can be integrated allows a level of traceability, correctness, and consistency to be performed, the exact degree of which is determined by how many of the methods and at what level they are integrated. The first problem involved in integrating methods is to see if any two are compatible. This seems obvious, but one of the problems plaguing environment building is that almost every method that exists was created as an independent entity with no thought given to integrating it with any existing method. The problems of the methods' individual viewpoints, representations, media and guidance all come into play.

Then, if one can find two that seem compatible, does one or the other (or both) have to be extended to interact with the other. This means that one has to check to see if the underlying foundation of a method is going to be affected, and whether by integrating it with something else lessens its usefulness.

Method integration has two separate approaches as well. One aspect is to integrate information only, in other words, the data created by one method is usable by another, but each method is used separately. The other is to merge the two methods. Using one then isn't useful without the other. The degree to which the integration takes place can be traded off, depending on the methods used.

As more and more methods are integrated, the greater the complexity of the integration. Notice though, that the information that is being produced and created by the methods must somehow be stored and identified as to which method created it, and which others can manipulate it. The importance of a database that can handle this job becomes readily apparent, as does the usefulness of having one view of the data, like that provided by objects. If a single view is not provided, then interfaces between each method must be defined. Each new method increases the number of interfaces necessary by N-1, where N represents the total number of methods being integrated. The addition of methods that are integrated to some degree increases the capability of the environment, but also increases the complexity involved in building it.

Also, if not all the methods are integrated, at least at a sharing of information level, then some work is going to have to be performed to reuse information created by one set in the other. Partial integration of methods additionally means that the user of a particular method must know which others it can be used with. This is more of a burden on the user than knowing that no method can be used with another.

One can reduce the complexity caused by partially integrating methods together by utilizing a completely defined methodology. Here, all the methods are fully integrated together, and the steps to use them are fully specified. The advantage to this approach is that it makes an environment easier to build because everything is defined, the database doesn't have to worry about what is or is not integrated, and the user needs to know only one "method," not the intricacies of many different ones. Traceability, consistency, and completeness among the various elements of the methodology are able to be supported to the highest degree possible.

The disadvantage is that one can't really start in the middle of the method to try something out. One needs the information that precedes any specific point in the methodology, so one must always start at the top. This obviously reduces some flexibility. Moreover, if the methodology does not match the application very well, then its usefulness is severely limited. Finally, a new method can't be added to the methodology without likely perturbing everything in it because the dependencies between the methods already used are so strong.

Overall, the environment designers must make a number of trade offs among ease of construction, degree of flexibility of method use, and the benefits accrued by the environment in being able to build quality products.

METHOD INCLUSION. Another aspect of how methods can affect the construction of the software engineering environment is the issue of which methods should be included. Obviously, one wants methods that will help cover the entire life cycle, but to what degree?. As we mentioned in Section 11.1, should the methods support the process directly, indirectly, or be somewhere in-between? Using a methodology that covers the entire life cycle provides one approach, while partial integration or no integration may provide less robust coverage. This is an important issue because if the methods don't support the process in some fashion, then something else must fill in the gaps or that part of the process probably won't get done (which is the usual case).

Additionally, if the software engineering environment is only partially integrated in some way, the methods which get selected first to be integrated in a software engineering environment will likely determine the way the environment views the development process. For example, if the first methods chosen language are a compiler and design method, and the construction proceeds outward, then a language view may dominate. On the other hand, if a requirements and a specification method are chosen first, then a product view may dominate. The first path, which is bottom up, is trying to look at specifying data objects from the point of view of the implementation language to be used and the mappings between methods in each phase will be colored by the language's view of the world. The other path, which is top down, uses products that are created in each phase, and the mapping in between method uses this perspective.

Whether or not the end result is the same in both approaches is unknown, but a bottom up approach definitely is difficult when many programming languages are required to be supported in an environment. However, if a single language is to be used, this approach might provide for less problems in trying to leap the conceptual boundary that exist between implementation and design as described in Chapter Six.

METHOD DEFICIENCIES. The other technological issue having to do with methods is that if the cognitive processes used in performing the tasks each phase are identified, then current methods have a number of serious omissions [LEFKOVITZ82]. Moreover, there hasn't appeared a new principle in software engineering for over fifteen years, which leads one to suspect that either software engineering theory has come as far as it can (hopefully not), or else a new approach is needed. The fundamental understanding of the principles and how they are used by methods is an important area of research and can impact how well the environment can perform its functions.

On the practical side, currently there are new methods needed in almost every phase of the life cycle, especially the front. For instance, in the specification phase better ways of expressing the specifications, proving their correctness, and being able to execute them are needed [RAMAMOORTHY-84]. In the requirements and design phases, improved ways of capturing a person's conceptual knowledge and elaborating it are necessary [KOO-MEN85]. In the testing phase, testing methods that are directly tied to the methods used to create the information being tested are required [MILLER84]. The management activity requires help too, especially in software size estimation, cost drivers and their attributes, and project dynamics [BOEHM84a]. In the database area, methods to help define multiple overlapping views are needed, as well as ways to ensure timeliness of data, and better performance.

In summary, the methods used impact the quality of the product created, as well as how easily the software engineering environment can be implemented. The next section discusses the technical issues of automation in an environment.

11.3 Automation Issues

Automation has its own set of issues that affect a software engineering environment. The issues concerning the process and the methods used in the environment frame the potential benefits of the environment, while their automation allows the potential to be realized or not. Without automation, a method like SREM could not be used. Automation changes the perspective of what methods can do, and how the user views the use of a method.

Automation makes it possible to perform traceability, consistency, and completeness analysis. Without it, regardless of how integrated the methods, it would be impossible to perform except on small programs. Automation not only allows a method accomplish things that couldn't be done otherwise, but also forces a method to be much more exact, as well as performing the same thing on the user of the method. It is extremely difficult to automate something that is not very well defined. Frenkel [FRENKEL85] reports that using automated specification techniques forced users to be much more exact than those that used manual methods. As one participant in the study remarked, "Talk is cheap."

One benefit of creating a software engineering environment from the top down would be to force the development process to be much more exact. This in turn might help identify and define the methods that are necessary to support the process, which in turn might make automation easier.

ENVIRONMENT TYPES. Automation, in combination with how the methods are integrated, can be used to create a number of different types of software engineering environments. There are basically four types, which can be used in combination to form other types. The four are: closed, open, integrated and strongly typed.

A closed software engineering environment is one where the user is provided a very fixed set of automated methods which can meet the requirements of building the product. It can't be extended or altered short of reissuing the total environment [STENNING81]. An environment built around a methodology would likely be closed. Aside from the ability to do consistency analysis, completeness checks, etc., another advantage from the automation perspective is that products created on one would be highly portable to another closed environment using the same methodology. A disadvantage is that the performance of the environment might be very poor because of the overhead associated with all the method interactions that would take place.

An open environment is one that may be modified or extended at any time. An environment built around methods that were not integrated would be considered open. An advantage, along with its extensibility, is the capability of high performance due to the overhead caused by method inter-action. A disadvantage of open environments is that product portability is usually compromised because it is unlikely that two environments, even if they started out the same, would stay that way for very long. Consistency, completeness, and traceability are also not automatic in an open environment, although automated methods could be made available to perform these types of functions.

An integrated environment is one where all the automated methods work together and share information. An environment built around partially integrated methods is considered integrated. The advantage is some amount of portability of programs is feasible, as well as automatic consistency checks, completeness analysis, etc. How the sharing of information takes place is not predefined. It may be through the database or preprocessors that define interfaces between automated methods. Performance may or may not be good, depending on the number and way methods interact.

A strongly typed environment [MCKAY86] is one that defines a set of values and a set of operations on those values. An environment that uses an object-based viewpoint with methods "virtually" integrated is considered strongly typed. This means that the information is transparent to each automated method. The advantage is high product portability, and a high level of traceability, consistency and completeness checking is possible. Another advantage is maximum flexibility is allowed, as well as the ability to add in more methods. The disadvantage is that its performance may not be that good. The bottleneck is the database that must keep track of which data can be used where. The interfaces, instead of being defined at a macro-level as a monolithic interface, are "carried" with each data object. It is hard to tell if this reduces performance or increases it. Our ideal environment described in Chapter 9, is strongly typed, with user options to make it closed (or open, which severely restricts the capability to perform consistency checking, etc.).

As we've noted, each environment has particular advantages and disadvantages in its use. Each is different in its complexity to build. Closed environments are easy to build, if one has the methodology defined. So far, no one has defined one to cover a full-life cycle. Open environments are easy to build, and most environments today are open. Integrated environments are harder to build because of the partial integration of methods. Again, keeping track of what data can be shared or not makes it difficult on whatever is keeping the record of data usage. Strongly typed environments are easier to build than integrated ones, if the allowable operations on the data by the methods are well-defined. So far, no one has attempted this for a full development model. Partial environments exist in each category, but none that covers the full-life cycle currently exists in any category.

Now, each of the above environment categories can be mixed and matched into a wide variety of environments sub-types. Exactly which kind should be built is highly dependent on the product application being built. Applications with high reliability constraints should probably use a closed or strongly typed environment, where a high degree of product assurance can be supported. Those that don't have as strict a reliability criteria can probably use a less restrictive type like an open environment.

Other considerations might be the level of experience of the users of the environment (closed environments provide alot of guidance in their use, open environments don't), the performance of the environment (open are fast, closed are not) and the time necessary to build (open are fast to build, closed are not).

AUTOMATION AND PROJECT DYNAMICS. Other technical issues concerning the automation of environments concern how well it supports the project dynamics. The automation of the methods should foster communication of information among all the participants in a product development. This communication takes many forms, such as when a designer communicates to an implementer. Is the form of communication verbal or via the methods and documentation or some combination? Automation may serve to actually force less communication between project participants than in the old cases where groups of people might have a discussion about a problem. The environment compartmentalizes the project participants and can shut off communication except through the environment.

Furthermore, if the environment is seen as the arbitrator of problems, then developers may not take the time to do a good job. "Let the environment worry about it" may be the cry of software developers of the future. This phenomena has already started to be noticed in some cases where the use of automation, especially prototyping, has made some developers less disciplined in their approaches to solving problems [FRENKEL85].4

Another issue is that an environment is supposed to lower the entropy or disorder in creating a software product. It must be careful not to increase it as well. One simple way to do that is not to appear seamless to the user, in other words, where the user has to worry about how the components of the environment work together. It can also be as simple as not providing a common user interface to the environment, where the user can't interact with the environment in any logical or coherent fashion. Or it may be just slow performance on the part of the environment, which raises the frustration of the user trying to get a job done.

In summary, automation is very important in attaining the potential benefits of an environment. However, there are many factors that need consideration in selecting which type of software engineering environment is needed and should be built. Moreover, although automation is the factor that makes a software engineering environment possible, it still must support the process model or its usefulness and benefits are degraded.

11.4   Summary

There are many detailed technical issues that require addressing when building a software engineering environment, and in this chapter we barely scratched the surface. Every software engineering environment is a trade off between conflicting goals of the product development. Remember, an environment is a software product, and everything that was described earlier in the book about the problems of building software products holds true for environments as well. If an environment isn't built well and serves its user's needs, the product produced by it probably won't be very good either. Unfortunately, there are not environments around to help build environments. We are constrained by what methods and automation are available today.

But software engineering environments, for all their possible technical problems with integration of methods, supporting incomplete process models, etc., do seem to realistically promise a better way to produce software for large product developments, especially where product assurance is important. The payoffs are high, but integrated and determined efforts are needed to make it happen [BOEHM84b].

Unfortunately, there is the second half of the problem that also must be solved, and that is the reluctance to use new technology in general. The next chapter discusses the problems of introducing and transitioning a software engineering environment into an organization.

FOOTNOTES:

1. This is an area ripe for basic research.
2. In this case, the high degree of integration might be provided by the availability of data transparency. See Chapter Eight for more discussion.
3. Unfortunately the reality is that the user of the product, because he or she isn't there during the development to side with the product, is often the loser.
4. Again, one of the problems with programming is that it is too easy to do, and allows people to be lazy. "Let the compiler find the errors" is how these same sentiments are voiced today.

12. THE FUTURE OF SOFTWARE ENGINEERING ENVIRONMENTS INTRODUCTION & TRANSITION ISSUES

"Come back with your shield or upon it."
— Plutarch, in **Apothegms**

12.0 Introduction

Building software engineering environments might be the easy part. Getting them to be used might be another story. In this chapter we are going to examine just some of the issues of technology transfer and the impacts and ramifications of using an environment in an organization.

As the quote above implies, getting new technology into an organization is not an easy task. Managers complain that developers resist new ideas, while the developers say that the managers don't understand the problem [MYERS78]. If one from outside the computer field were to examine the computing aids and techniques used in the computer field itself, he or she would be amazed at (a) the amount of methods and automation that currently exists, (b) the lack of its use by computer professionals for software product creation, and (c) the fierce determination of those in the field not to use it, yet their equally fierce denunciation of those outside the field for not making use of all the computerized nonsense *they've* developed for them.

This paradox is very difficult to explain. It may be that computer professionals don't like to be "out of control" as it were, any more than a bank manager who is confronted with using an electronic spreadsheet for the first time. Using a software package to do things that you once programmed and understood exactly places a layer between you and the machine. If something goes wrong, you don't know how to fix it, and to a field that attracts tinkerers in the first place, this is not a very palatable situation.

If we multiply an individual's resistance by several dozen for medium-sized software products, and add the normal resistance pattern of any organization to change, there may be a distinct problem trying to get something like a software engineering environment, which will touch everyone's life everyday, in and used. With these few words of encouragement, let's begin.

12.1 Technology Transfer

The first issue we want to discuss is the general problem of technology transfer. Trying to get new technology used has never been easy, and what makes it even more difficult is getting the technology out of the research and toy-problem solving stage into practice. The SEI discussed in Chapter Ten has as its main task technology transfer of technology into DoD. To see what type of task they have, and by implication the difficulties likely encountered in getting a software engineering environment to be used, the following list of issues and discussion was derived from [BOEHM84, MUSA85, REDWINE84, RIDDLE84, ROUSE85, BERGLAND86].

The problems encountered in technology transfer include:

* Technology creation is unstructured, unguided and slow.

There is a split culture between the researchers and practitioners with academicians having different goals than those of practioners. The academicians are after a fundamental understanding of software engineering problems. They work on hypothetical problems, uncovering facts, principles and laws. They also work alone, and publish their findings in technical journals.

Practioners need to improve a particular real situation. If the problem is too hard to solve cleanly, it can't be assumed away. Something has to be done. Practioners work in groups, and need methods that can support that type of interaction. They also don't as a group read the technical journals.

Whether the research undertaken by an academician solves any of the practioners problems is a wild guess. There is no matching of research to problems, except that which is directly sponsored by an industry group.

Therefore, it is not too suprising that it takes an average of 17 years (+/- 2) for a method to move from initial research into practice. Some type of intermediary between the groups is needed.

- There is an explosion in the numbers of practioners.

The number of people in the computer industry has grown phenomenally and should continue to do so for a while longer. The people joining the field do not for the most part have formal training in it which means that even if advanced technology were available, it is unlikely many would understand it without a great deal of training.

- Lack of management commitment to new technology.

We will discuss this in more detail in the next section of the chapter, but there is a firm resistance to new technology being introduced into an organization.

- There must be a low cost for any benefits derived from the technology.

Again we will discuss this in more detail later, but technology introduction must be inexpensive or it won't be introduced.

- Lack of top management software experience.

The computer field is still very young, and the people with computer science and engineering degrees and who have worked all their careers in computer are only in their early to mid-forties. Even with the rapid advancement which marks this field, few in top management are knowledgeable about computers. This lack of understanding contributes to a resistance to try anything new because managers don't understand it.

- Lack of positive experience.

Anyone who has worked on large projects knows how confusing, difficult, and hard it can be. And most people are aware of the high cost of software, and the products that don't work or never worked quite right. Most of the practioners have heard about all the great new technology out there to make their life better, but it never seems to arrive. When it does, it always seems to be oversold.

- Lack of well-developed technology.

It seems that most of the new technology that is transferred isn't completely usable. There are still bugs in it, and it is unreliable. Practioners are users too, and they don't like using anything that doesn't work right as much as anyone. Immature technology that is transferred is worse than no technology in many cases.

- Lack of standards.

It is hard to transfer anything to anyone if they both don't speak the same language, or have a means to translate. This is the state of the industry where there are some standards defined, but not universally accepted.

- Insufficient quantitative information.

What should be transferred? No one really knows. There aren't ways of comparing technologies to see which have potential and which don't. The "worthiness to transfer" is one measure that is desperately needed.

- Lack of a recognized need for a technology.

In many cases a technology isn't used because no one recognizes it is needed. Verification and validation didn't become important until really large software developments became common, and testing wasn't considered a part of software engineering until very lately.

- Lack of formalism in concepts and base theories.

There are a number of principles used in software engineering. We selected seven to define a method. Is that enough, are there more? What makes one different from another? How can the differences be described? These and others need to be answered. A formal foundation of computer science is also needed to give the research and practice structure.

- Proprietary attitude toward software technology.

Software engineering is a business. Companies are not out to advance the state of the art for its own sake but to make money by gaining a competitive edge over their rivals. They also do not want to give it away for free. After all, they paid for it. So much of what is usable technology is kept locked up and not distributed.

SUMMARY. These are only some of the general technology transfer problems a software engineering environment must overcome. Next comes the organized resistance to it.

12.2   Organized Resistance

We won't discuss guerrilla warfare against new technology introduction into an organization because, although it exists, the problem is minor. Dissatisfied workers usually just leave. With the normal turnover rate in the computer field estimated at 20 to 30 percent a year, any problems that occur from individuals have about a one in four chance of disappearing within the year.

The major concern is with those in charge of organizational structures, in other words, the managers. Their longevity in a company is usually longer, and they have the power to change things. Unfortunately, their power to resist things is even greater. Moreover, in the computer industry, managers have become conditioned to resist.

SKEPTICISM. Managers in the computer industry are very skeptical of any new software technology. And they probably should be. As it has been so aptly put, they have seen and heard the prophets so many times before, each crying out that the only thing needed to save them from the demons of high software costs were (take your pick): Compilers, MicroCode, HOLs, Software Engineering, AI; and still they still gaze over the desert and see their bleached bones and wonder who is next.[1] Once a manager has been burned once or twice, he is unlikely to commit too rapidly the next time. You can imagine how their eyes will glaze over when you try to convince them that software engineering environments will do the trick. Just give them a chance!

Managers also know how to count, which tends to increase their skepticism. Let's assume that coding is free. The overall reduction in the total product development only amounts to 10 percent and 4 to 6 percent of the total life cycle costs. First, managers know there is nothing out there that's going to make coding free.

Second, their real costs are people. Saving $1 million by making programmers more productive may seem like a lot, but it only works out to about 12 to 16 programmers. Which on small program developments may mean something, but on large ones where hundreds are involved, well, a manager just is not impressed. A manager not only needs a way to make people more productive, but needs to be shown that whatever technology he or she is going to invest in will permanently reduce the staff level, or at least keep it even.

Moreover, the technology he is buying better not cost him more than he is saving. For instance, when buying a computer system means you are not only purchasing the hardware, and the software that didn't come with it but you absolutely need, but the operator, repair person, etc. Increasing productivity, which allows you to do replace two developers with three or more people isn't always a bargain. Remember also, the replacements' jobs are likely to be permanent, so there is no real way for a manager to maneuver to reduce their costs either.

Managers have become so biased against new software technology that the tradition cost/benefit ratio theory doesn't hold anymore. The cost of introducing and using a new technology must be low, regardless of the benefit [BERGLAND86]. This type of "attitude problem" is further compounded by another called the NIH syndrome.

NIH. The Not Invented Here (NIH) syndrome sometimes looks like unorganized resistance, but is so pervasive in the computer industry that it has to be considered organized. Almost every practioner in the computer field feels that any software they encounter they can, or even more egotistically, they have, done better [REDWINE84]. This attitude is usually expressed in the negative as, "this software is bogus" or more to the point, "this software stinks."[2] When taken to the extreme, it can mean a practioner not using anything but his own tools (which are miserable, if you ask one of his colleagues, who is of the opinion that he could do it better, or did once in high school) which may or may not work.

The use of flowcharts is a prime example of this attitude. No one uses them anymore except at school. Not even the DoD. Why? Because there are better ways of documenting program flow or designing programs. Are these being used? No, because once there is a better way discovered that usually seems enough, and anyway, why bother to learn something new that will only be replaced next year?

The last element really contributes to or abets the NIH syndrome. It always seems that somebody is coming up with a better way, so why can't I?[3] Since programming is relatively easy to do, and programs can be refined ad infinitum, it's easy to see why NIH has taken root in the industry. A person really believes that he or she can do it better. In fact this belief in self is almost a necessity to stay in the field for very long anyway. Spending days and nights tracking down a single bug in a program takes a special (?) person, and when it is fixed, one's pride is high. The industry is still made up of those people who like to tinker, like to spend weekends and nights programming after programming all day at work, and take absolute pride in their creation. "Pride goeth before destruction" might be an appropriate warning for our industry.

But also, we are, as a whole, some of the most severe critics in the world. This has led the field in creating a glut of automated methods and techniques that do many very unique things which either no one needs or needs desperately, but won't use. Overcoming the NIH syndrome is not going to be easy either in an environment where there are dozens of things to ignore.[4]

FEAR OF TECHNOLOGY. Along with the skepticism and the NIH syndrome, there is also fear of using new technology. The attitude might not be expressed as fear, but more in, "Why do I need all this new stuff anyway? Haven't billions of lines of working code been created without the need of _____ ?" [MILLER78]. Trying new technology disrupts the way things are done, and change is never easy to accomodate to. People, as a rule, like stability, and don't readily embrace strange ideas, no matter how novel or useful they appear.

Regardless of its appearance to outsiders, or to the corporate work breakdown structures, software development is still a very informal, person-centered activity [BALZER85]. Use of an imposed discipline, like that advocated by the Japanese Software Factories, in the United States will likely cause great unrest in an programming shop. The word discipline seems to bring out much fear in developers, like they will lose their identities. No product developer, or other human being for that matter, wants to feel his or her work is meaningless. Take away a developer's "right" to free expression through a product development, and one risks this to be perceived as happenning.

Adding to this loss of identity problem is that discipline also means to many a lack of power on their part to control the product's development. They feel powerless to change things, because "that's the way it's done."

Environments may exacerbate the problem as creativity is exchanged for control.

This fear is also expressed by the fact that the introduction of automation into the computer industry may mean someone may lose their job. The computerization of society has displaced workers everywhere, and has caused some hardship. The same thing can happen in the computer field. Who to know that better than the people who caused it to happen in the first place? It use to be that programmers would smugly say during economic recessions that "They will always need programmers." And for the longest time this has been true. The computer industry always was been healthy, even in the bad times. But three things happenned to change this smug attitude. Foreign competition, a recession, and the developers themselves.

Foreign competition in the computer area, especially by the Japanese, has caused many United States firms to either close down or drastically cut back on their workforces. What was once thought impossible took place, and has shaken many in the industry. Second, the computer felt the effects of an economic recession for the first time, where although the industry stayed stable, it did not experience growth. Third, the developers are putting themselves out of business. Research efforts are starting to be directed at practical methods such as environments development to reduce the need for many types of computer personnel. The growth in the number of programmers, for instance, has not continued to follow the trends forecasted in the 1970s, and there has been a debate about whether the amount of shortages stated about software personnel are even true. The combination of these factors makes most people in the industry a little fearful of the future, and introducing new technology on the scale of a software engineering environment which might make their jobs less secure is going to be resisted.

DISINCENTIVES. Another element that adds to the resistance, but more in an unorganized way, are the disincentives involved in using technology like environments. Part of the disincentives lie in the fact that most new software technology serves to satisfy long term goals, not short term ones. The quality of the product may be improved by using environments, but a product won't exist for five to seven years in a large product development. For many managers, they won't be on the project for that long, so why bother going through all the problems of trying to introduce something new.

This issue of long term disincentive also manifests itself in the belief by many managers that they don't want to be the one to introduce something new and unique (and possibly costly) and have it fail. Furthermore, managers often see things like automated methods as a waste. Since they are apt to be unique, they can't be re-used on any other projects. And even if they were useful, the individual project manager isn't responsible for the other projects, and since corporate wide use of standard technologies is not prevelant in the U.S. as it is becoming in Japan, again the reaction is "why bother?"

Another disincentive is that there are really no rewards for saving money on a software product. Costs are high on many developments because, frankly, the United States can afford to waste money. What happens when money is tight is that the product schedule is increased with fewer people assigned to development. Or functionality is removed. Or the product is cancelled. There is no widespread effort to save money or make the software industry efficient in the United States. An excuse has always been that it is hard to predict how much money one saves by using new technology. This is true to some degree. There are no hard numbers on which decisions to make about what is better to use, but there hasn't been exactly a race to find out either.

Another disincentive is that software technology is expensive. Managers look at something like a software engineering environment and react, "Software is expensive, environments are made up of a lot of (untried) software, therefore an environment is going to be very expensive." High cost is a definite disincentive. And as we mentioned earlier, the cost must be low whatever the benefits gained.

Take for instance running simulations or constructing prototypes. For some applications, the cost of doing a simulation is higher than the product development itself. Needless to say, the protoyping doesn't always occur in product developments, and the larger the product size, the more expensive the simulation is required.

SUMMARY. The general resistance to new technology in the computer industry will undoubtably affect the introduction of a software engineering environment into an organization. To better understand how, the next section focuses specifically on an environment's potential impact on an organization.

12.3   Organizational Impacts

A software engineering environment has the potential for radically changing a way an organization does business. To see how, we will first examine how power and control are exerted within an organization, and then examine how an environment can affect them.

ORGANIZATION POWER AND CONTROL. Within an organization, power is spread through the many groups that make up the organizational structure. The power of each group, and the control it exerts on others, is based upon five factors [LUCAS84]:

- Coping with uncertainty;

- Substitutability;

- Workflow pervasiveness;

- Immediacy, and

- Interdependence.

Coping with uncertainty is an organization's ability to cope with confusion or chaos. An organization that can absorb or control uncertainty will have a high level of power.

Substitutability is the ease with which an organizational structure can be replaced. If it can be easily, it will have low levels of power.

Work flow pervasiveness means the extent to which an organization is connected to others. One with many connections should have a high level of power.

Immediacy is the degree and speed of the impact an organization structure would have upon the rest of the structure if it were to be removed. One with a high degree of immediacy would have high power.

Finally, interdependence is the degree to which other organizational structures are dependent upon another one. One that is depended upon by many others should have a high degree of power.

Studies [LUCAS84] have reported that the factor with the greatest influence is coping, followed by immediacy, substituability, pervasiveness, and interdependence.

Coupled with organizational power are factors that influence the control of the software product development. It has been shown that organizational arrangements shape the effectiveness of software practices [SCACCHI84]. This means that organizations with power have a strong influence on how software is developed within an organization. Moreover, decisions made by both managers and individuals in an organization are significantly influenced by the organization's planning and control systems [ABDEL-HAMID83]. Organizations with power will tend to dominate planning.

Finally, the view on how to best develop software also depends on the level in the corporate structure one sits [MYERS78, BOEHM84a, FAIRLEY-84]. For example, upper management believes that productivity can be increased first by improved management techniques, then better working environment and compensation, the education of the personnel, and finally better automated methods. Middle management sees it in the same order but with more emphasis on education and automated methods. However, the developers see the order as automated methods first, then environment and compensation, next education, and finally management.

POTENTIAL ENVIRONMENT IMPACTS ON AN ORGANIZATION. A software engineering environment has a high impact potential on a software development organization.[5] Let's compare the environment's "organizational position" and potential for power against the criteria defined in the previous section.

> **Coping with uncertainty.** An environment potentially can cope with uncertainty to a high degree. In one sense, it is "impervious" to change. If the development changes direction, the environment is there to support it. If new methods need to be added, an environment provides the framework to handle these also.

> **Substitutability.** An environment potentially has an extremely low substitutability factor, especially as the development progresses. Since all the information on the product exists only in the environment, it possess most of the corporate knowledge. Furthermore, it provides the only means to create the product, and therefore it is unlikely that anything but another environment could substitute for it.

> **Workflow pervasiveness.** The environment also potentially has an extremely high workflow pervasiveness factor. All personnel will use it on a daily basis. Their schedules will be planned using it, their ability to create the product is dependant upon it, and even their communication to others are done using it. How the product can be defined is determined by the methods supported by the

environment. Additionally, peoples roles will be determined and supported by the environment. In summary, every organization involved in the software development will be connected to the environment.

Immediacy. The environment potentially also has an extremely high immediacy factor. If it were to cease operation, the development would stop, and probably not be able to continue at all.

Interdependence. The environment also has a potential for an extremely high level of interdepence. Again, all departments will be connected to it and be dependent on its capabilitites.

A software engineering environment has the potential of being the most powerful organizational unit in any organization structure. Notice a subtle point. The members of the environment support organization may not have the same level of power as the "entity" of the environment itself, no more than current Informational Services Departments which provide similar services [LUCAS84]. They don't define the procedures to develop software, someone else in management does. Whoever possesses this authority controls the environment's use and can absorb its power.

If this same group also defines requirements for the building of the the environment, it can maintain its power also. The reason is that the environment provides the organizational structure for the total organization. It defines the roles of the development personnel by determining what kinds of support to provide organization. A software engineering environment will automate the bureaucracy.

Moreover, since the environment can provide visibility into information on all aspects of the development process itself (where trouble areas are, where they may potentially be, the impact of changes, etc.), managers who have access to that information have much power to influence development. A major potential problem is that mangers with access to this information will make decisions all the time trying to "tweak" the development to meet projected development schedules (which in turn may be wrong).

The total aspect of the social processes and dynamics of the product development will be contained in and constrained by the environment. Internal project lines of communication will be disrupted and replaced by those the environment provides.

The social implications on an environment can be staggering. Since no software engineering environment like our ideal model yet exists, it is unknown how much of this will come to pass. However, an environment provides capabilities that have never been provided before, and undoubtably it will have some impact.

12.3 Overcoming Organizational Resistance

Given the facts that a software engineering environment can potentially have a tremendous affect on an organization, and that it probably ranks high on the factors of resistance of software technology, getting it into an organization and used will most likely be difficult. An environment might be placed in an organization as a supplement to or replacement of the current information support system that is there currently. If the environment was originally built to model that particular organizational structure it probably will work as well as the organizational structure allows. If a different organizational structure is supported in the environment than that which exists, then either the environment or organization is going to have to change to make full use of its capabilities.

ENVIRONMENT ACCEPTANCE. The acceptance of a software engineering environment first begins with management. Management must make a commitment to procure or build an environment, and must match the solution provided by the environment against the the problem it is trying to solve. The first questions that need answering are: is the primary problem in developing the project going to be a management one (e.g., the product is pretty standard, no new technology is required, it's just big), or a technical one (e.g., the product has requirements for new types of technologies that haven't been implemented before) or is it some combination of both?

To answer the above questions, more questions [OSTERWEIL81, ANDERSON82, BOEHM84] concerning:

- What specific software applications are likely to be supported in the future?

- What is the product size and likely project staff required?

- What are the quality of environments that currently exist?

- What is the development time for an environment and the product?

- How much improvement to the product will an environment provide over traditional support?

- How much investment is required in training and facilities?

- What are the minimum features that are needed in the environment?

- What is the cost of managing and supporting an environment support organization?

must then be addressed.

If management has made a decision to go with an environment to support the life cycle development, it must back its decision forcefully [BOEHM84]. Motivation and perception are very important factors for acceptance of technology by the development community. If the environment changes the roles of the users, its vital that management support these changes as well. Moreover, every user understands his role in an organization [YEH84], and management risks allienating both users and the groups they belong to if the environment doesn't support them [KOOMEN85]. Their roles can change, as long as they are defined.

ENVIRONMENT INTRODUCTION. To introduce an environment into an organization it will be necessary to coerce the users and various organizational structures into using it. What has to be overcome is what's called the "Gulp Factor" [KERNIGHAN81]. This is the amount of new technology and change an organization can accept before choking. Too much provided at one time will swamp the organization.

One approach to minimize the gulp factor is to build the environment in increments, which allows the users to get used to the idea of having a disciplined approach to building software. This requires, however, for the environment to be built top down (i.e., from the requirements phase out). This has some advantages in that the first groups using the environment will be small, the organizational structure isn't totally fixed, and as the project grows in size, new groups with no defined role can be introduced to the environment as a de facto part of the organization.

If an existing organization is transitioning to an environment, and the product is in development, the task is much harder as the resistance levels are at their peak. The best advice is to introduce environments only on new projects. If this is not feasible, then again an incremental approach is probably best. But the first increment should be the communication support the environment provides. By controlling the communication one can start to control the group social interaction and dynamics. Making the organization dependent on it is a good way to accomplish this goal, and this can be done by making it as attractive as possible. The automation that is added must tie back into the communication system in a very natural way or again, the resistance to using the environment will be too high.

In either case it is crucial that management use the environment. If they become dependent upon it as well, then the chance for successful environment use is high.

12.4   System Engineering Environment

The last thing we want to discuss quickly is the concept of system engineering environments. The software engineering environment we have described in the text is only one aspect of the development process. To be truly complete, we need to consider the current individually defined software and hardware developments as a single entity. The artificial distinction only makes it harder to develop systems. The software development requires knowledge of the hardware throughout its development, and vice versa, in order to put out a good system. By keeping the two separate, there is no communication between the two different development groups, and this is a source of problems, especially at system integration time. Hopefully, in the future the developments will encompass both aspects.

The importance of this can be shown in figure 12-1. The real savings in producing systems are in reducing the cost of the evolution phase. The costs in evolution include both hardware and software, and the development process must model that accurately. Moreover, only by having the information and methods that were used to create the system is there any short-term hope of controlling costs.

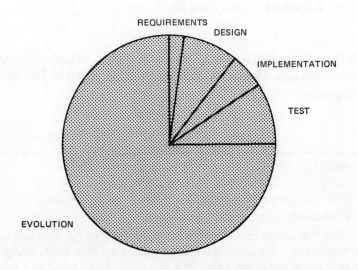

Figure 12 - 1   **Total Distribution of Effort in Evolution Phase**

12.5   Conclusions

In this book we have tried to give a high-level view of what a software engineering environment is, and the processes, methods, and automation that can be used to create one. As we've tried to show in this chapter, building a software engineering environment may not be the toughest problem. Getting it used may be instead. Moreover, software engineering environments can change, and challenge, the way software is created today, hopefully for the better.

What should be the minimum an environment should have? My three wishes are for:

- Information that is transparent to all methods,

- Documentation that is automatically produced,

- A database that executes like the wind.

With those three things, I think I can build the rest of my environment. And one, very last note. People, not technology, build products. This should never be forgotten.

FOOTNOTES:

1. With apologies to [BUCKLEY84].
2. More colorful expressions also abound.
3. Other things that contribute are the commercial innovations and monetary successes individuals have made by doing it better. Apple Computer is a prime example of two individuals who thought they could do it better.
4. We were tempted to rename this the Video Game Snobbery (VGS) syndrome instead. This syndrome, which pervades the general public now and is caused by the computer NIH syndrome, was the attitude young adults displayed as each newer and more sophisticated video arcade game appeared. As each one brought an increase in capability, some magnitudes above the original pong, the reaction became more and more, "Is that all?" They became very jaded to the difficulty in producing these games. Moreover, behind the scenes, the programmers were saying the "I can top that", and further adding to their own demise. Even the press got into the act by calling the SDI "Star Wars."
5. For this section we will assume the environment under discussion is our ideal environment. We also are assuming that the environment will be used for all software development.

APPENDIX

This appendix provides a brief description of the system life cycle model and associated system development cycle. More detailed information is available in DoD-STD-2167, Defense System Software Development, 4 June, 1985.

The life cycle model and associated system development cycle are illus - trated in figure A-1. The software development cycle and related products are illustrated in figure A-2.

SYSTEM LIFE CYCLE. The system life cycle consists of four phases: Concept Exploration, Demonstration and Validation, Full Scale Development, and Production and Deployment. The software development cycle consists of six phases: Software Requirements Analysis, Preliminary Design, Detailed Design, Coding and Unit Testing, Computer Software Component (CSC) Integration and Testing, and Computer Software Configuration Item (CSCI) Testing. The total software development cycle or a subset may be performed within each of the system life cycle phases. Successive iterations of software development usually build upon the products of previous iterations (see figure A-2).

Concept Exploration. The Concept Exploration Phase is the initial planning period when the technical, strategic, and economic bases are established through comprehensive studies, experimental development, and concept evaluation. This initial planning may be directed toward refining proposes solutions or developing alternative concepts to satisfy a required operational capability.

Demonstration and Validation. The Demonstration and Validation Phase is the period when major system characteristics are refined through studies, system engineering, development of preliminary equipment and prototype computer software, and test and evaluation. The objectives are to validate the choice of alternatives and to provide the basis for determining whether or not to proceed into the next phase.

[373]

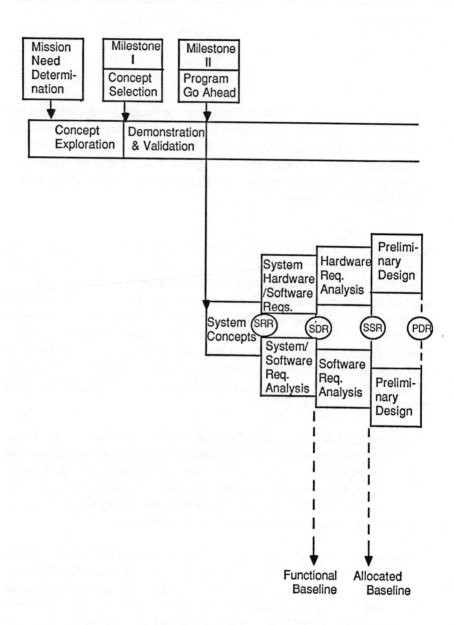

Figure Appendix-1   **System Development Cycle Within the System Life Cycle**

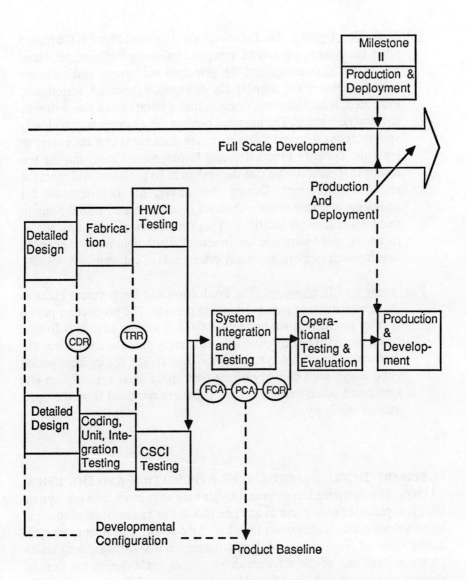

Reviews
SRR - System Requirements Review
SDR - System Design Review
SSR - Software Specification Review
PDR - Preliminary Design Review
CDR - Critical Design Review
TRR - Test Readiness Review
FCA - Functional Configuration Audit
PCA - Physical Configuration Audit
FQR - Formal Qualification Review

Full-Scale Development. The Full-Scale Development Phase is the period when the system, equipment, computer software, facilities, personnel sub-systems, training, and the principal equipment and software items necessary for support are designed, fabricated, tested, and evaluated. It includes one or more major iterations of the software development cycle. The intended outputs are a system which closely approximates the production item, the documentation necessary to enter the system's Production and Deployment Phase, and the test results that demonstrate that the system to be produced will meet the stated requirements. During this phase, the requirements for additional software items embedded in or associated with the equipment items may be identified. These requirements may encompass firmware, test equipment, environment simulation, mission support, development support, and many other kinds of software.

Production and Deployment. The Production and Deployment Phase is the combination of two overlapping periods. The production period is from production approval until the last system item is delivered and accepted. The objective is to efficiently produce and deliver effective and supported systems to the user(s). The deployment period commences with delivery of the first operational system item and terminates when the last system items are removed from the operational inventory.

SOFTWARE DEVELOPMENT CYCLE APPLICATION AND DOCUMENTATION. The Software Development Cycle may span more than one system life cycle phase, or may occur in any one phase. For example, mission simulation software may undergo one iteration of the software development cycle during Concept Exploration, while mission application software may undergo many iterations of the software development cycle during the Demonstration and Validation, Full-Scale Development, and Production and Deployment Phases (see figure A-1).

The phases in the software development cycle may involve iterations back to previous phases. For example, design may reveal problems which lead to the revision of requirement and reinstitution of certain analyses; checkout may reveal errors in design, which in turn may lead to redesign or requirements revision, etc.

Prior to initiating software development during the Full-Scale Development and the Production and Deployment Phases, documented plans
for software development (e.g. Software Development Plan--SDP),
authenticated system, segment, or prime item specifications, and the
OCD typically exist.

In earlier life cycle phases, such plans may not yet exist. The software development plans include descriptions of all organizations and procedures to be
used in the development effort. The system, segment, or prime item specification identifies the requirements of the system, segment, or prime item.
In addition, these specifications identify the Hardware Configuration Items
(HWCIs) and CSCIs making up the system, segment, or prime item. The
OCD identifies and describes the mission of the system, the system operational and support environments, and the functions and characteristics of the
computer system within the overall system. The six phases of the software
development cycle are discussed below.

Software Requirements Analysis. The purpose of Software Requirements
Analysis is to completely define and analyze the requirements for the
software. These requirements include the functions the software is
required to accomplish as part of the system, segment, or prime item.
Additionally, the functional interfaces and the necessary design
constraints are defined. During Full-Scale Development and Production and Deployment, this phase typically begins with the release of
the System Segment Specification (SSS), Prime Item Specification(s),
Critical Item Specifications(s), or Preliminary Software Requirement Specifications (SRS) and Interface Requirement Specifications
(IRS). It terminates with the successful accomplishment of the Software Specification Review (SSR). During this phase, analyses and
trade-off studies are performed, and requirements are made defini-
tive. The results of this phase are documented and approved requirements for the software. Also, at the initiation of Software
Requirements Analysis, plans for developing the software are prepared or reviewed (as applicable).

Preliminary Design. The purpose of Preliminary Design is to develop a
design approach which includes mathematical models, functional
flows, and data flows. During this phase various design approaches
are considered, analysis and trade-off studies are performed, and

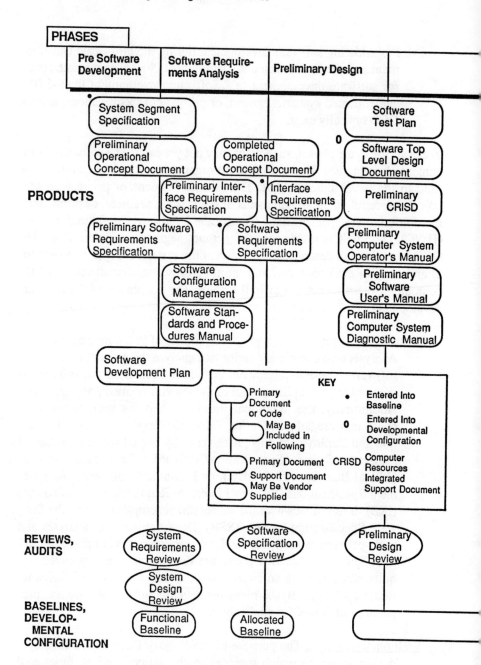

Figure Appendix-2   **Software Development Cycle and Related Products**

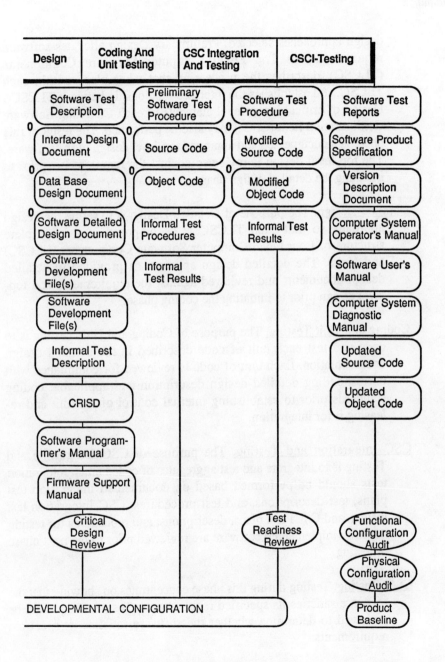

design approaches selected. Preliminary Design allocates software requirements to Top Level Computer Software Components (TLCSC), describes the processing that takes place within each TLCSC, and establishes the interface relationship between TLCSCs. Design of critical lower-level elements of each Computer Software Configuration Item (CSCI) may also be performed. The result of this phase is a documented and approved top-level design of the software. The top-level design is reviewed against the requirements prior to initiating the detailed design phase.

Detailed Design. The purpose of Detailed Design is to refine the design approach so that each TLCSC is decomposed into a complete structure of Low Level Computer Software Components (LLCSC) and Units. The detailed design approach is provided in detailed design documents and reviewed against the requirements and top-level design prior to initiating the coding phase.

Coding and Unit Testing. The purpose of Coding and Unit Testing is to code and test each unit of code described in the detailed design documentation. Each unit of code is reviewed for compliance with corresponding detailed design description and applicable coding standards prior to establishing internal control of the unit and re-leasing it for integration.

CSC Integration and Testing. The purpose of CSC Integration and Testing is to integrate and test aggregates of coded units. Integration tests should be performed based on documented integration test plans, test descriptions, and test procedures. CSC Integration test results, and CSCI test plans, descriptions, and procedures for testing the fully implemented software are reviewed prior to the next phase of testing.

CSCI Testing. Testing during this phase concentrates on showing that the software satisfies its specified requirements. Test results should be reviewed to determine whether the software satisfies its specified requirements.

REFERENCES

ABEL-HAMID, T. and S. MADNICK [1983]. "The Dynamics of Software Project Scheduling." Communications of the ACM, Vol. 26, No. 5 (May).

Ada [1983]. "Reference Manual for the AdaTM Programming Language." ANSI/MIL-STD-1819A, Department of Defense.

ADAM, J. and P. WALLICH [1985]. "Star Wars - SDI: the Grand Experiment: Part 1." IEEE Spectrum, Vol. 22, No. 9 (Sept.).

ADRION, R. et al. [1982]. "Validation, Verification, and Testing of Computer Software." ACM Computing Surveys, Vol. 14, No. 2 (June).

AHO, A. et al. [1986]. "Compilers: Principles, Techniques and Tools." Addison-Wesley Publishing Co., Reading, Massachusetts.

ALBRECHT, A. and J. GAFFNEY [1983]. "Software Function, Source Lines of Code, and Development Effort Prediction: A Software Science Validation." IEEE Trans. on Software Engineering, Vol. SE-9, No. 6 (Nov.).

ALFORD, M. [1978]. "Software Requirements Engineering Methodology (SREM) at the Age of Two." COMSAC '78 Proceedings, pp. 332-339.

------------ [1980]. "SREM at the Age of Four." INFOTECH State-of-the-Art Conference, London 16-18 June 1980.

------------ [1985]. "SREM at the Age of Eight: The Distributed Computing Design System." IEEE Computer, Vol. 18, No. 4 (April).

ANDERSON, G. and K. SCHUMATE [1982]. "Selecting a Programming Language, Compiler, and Support Environment: Method and Example." IEEE Computer, Vol. 15, No. 8 (Aug.)

ANSI [1985]."A Technical Overview of the Information Resource Dictionary
Standard System, Annex 1B, (Draft Proposal)." American National
Standard Institute.

APL [1975]."Department of Defense Weapon Systems Software
Management Study." APL John Hopkins, Report APLJHU SR75-3.

APPLIX [1985]. "ALIS from Applix." Application Summary, Applix
Corporation, Westboro, Massachusetts.

AUGUSTINE, N. R. [1983]. "Augustine's Laws." American Institute for
Aeronautics & Astronautics, New York, New York.

BALZER, R. et al. [1983]. "Software Technology in the 1990s: Using a New
Paradigm." IEEE Computer, Vol. 16, No. 11 (Nov.).

---------- [1985]. "A Fifteen Year Perspective on Automatic Programming."
IEEE Trans. on Software Engineering, Vol. SE-11, No. 11 (Nov.).

BARBACCI, M. et al. [1985]. "The Software Engineering Institute: Bridging
Practice and Potential." IEEE Software, Vol. 2, No. 6 (Nov.).

BASSILLI, V. and A. TURNER [1975]. "Iterative Enhancement: A Practical
Technique for Software Engineering." IEEE Trans. on Software
Engineering, Vol. SE-1, No. 1 (Mar.).

BEHRENS, C. [1983]. "Measuring the Productivity of Computer System
Development Activities with Function Points." IEEE Trans. on
Software Engineering, Vol. SE-9, No. 6 (Nov.).

BELADY, L. and W. LEHMAN [1976]. "A Model of Large Program
Development." IBM System Journal, Vol. 15, No. 3.

---------- [1985]. "The MCC Software Technology Program." ACM
Software Engineering Notes, Vol. 10, No. 3 (July).

BELL, T. et al. [1977]. "An Extendable Approach To Computer-Aided
Software Requirements Engineering." IEEE Trans. on Software
Engineering, Vol. SE-3, No. 1 (Jan.).

BENTLEY, J. [1982]. "Writing Efficient Programs." Prentice-Hall, Inc., Englewood Cliffs, New Jersey.

BERGLAND, G. [1981]. "A Guided Tour of Program Design Methodologies." IEEE Computer, Vol.14, No. 10 (Oct.).

---------- and P. ZAVE [1986]. "Guest Editorial Prologue: Special Issue on Software Design." IEEE Trans. on Software Engineering, Vol. SE-12, No.2 (Feb).

BERSOFF, E. [1984]. "Elements of Software Configuration Management." IEEE Trans. on Software Engineering, Vol. SE-10, No. 1 (Jan.).

BLUM, B. [1985]. "Understanding the Software Paradox." ACM Software Engineering Notes, Vol. 10, No. 1 (Jan.).

BOEHM, B. [1973]. "Software and Its Impact: A Quantitative Assessment." Datamation, pp. 48-59 (May).

---------- et al. [1975]. "Some Experiences With Automated Aids to the Design of Large-Scale Reliable Software." IEEE Trans. on Software Engineering, Vol. SE-1, No.1 (March).

---------- [1976]. "Software Engineering." IEEE Trans. on Computers, Vol. C-25, No. 12 (Dec.).

---------- [1981]. "Software Engineering Economics." Prentice-Hall, Inc.,Englewood Cliffs, New Jersey.

---------- [1983]. "The Hardware/Software Cost Ratio: Is it a Myth?" IEEE Computer, Vol. 16, No. 3 (March).

---------- and T. STANDISH [1983a]. "Software Technology in the 1990s: Using an Evolutionary Paradigm." IEEE Computer, Vol. 16, No. 11 (Nov.).

---------- [1984]. "Verifying and Validating Software Requirements and Design Specifications." IEEE Computer, Vol. 17, No. 1 (Jan.).

---------- [1984a]. "Software Engineering Economics." IEEE Trans. on Software Engineering, Vol. SE-10, No. 1 (Jan.).

---------- et al. [1984b]. "A Software Development Environment for Improving Productivity." IEEE Computer, Vol. 17, No. 6 (June).

BRANSTAD, M. et al. [1980]. "Validation, Verification, and Testing for the Individual Programmer." IEEE Computer, Vol. 13, No. 12 (Dec.)

BROOKS, F. [1975]. "The Mythical Man-Month." Addison-Wesley Publishing Co., Reading, Massachusetts.

BROWN, L. et al. [1984]. "Advanced Operating Systems." IEEE Computer, Vol. 17, No. 10 (Oct.).

BRYAN, W. and S. SIEGEL [1984]. "Making Software Visible, Operational, and Maintainable in a Small Project Environment." IEEE Trans. on Software Engineering, Vol. SE-10, No. 1 (Jan.)

BUCKLEY, F. and R. POSTON [1984]. "Software Quality Assurance." IEEE Trans. on Software Engineering, Vol. SE-10, No. 1 (Jan.).

BUEDE, D. et al. [1984]. "Concept Design of a Program Manager's Decision Support System." IEEE Trans. on Systems, Man, and Cybernetics, Vol. SMC-15, No. 4 (Jul/Aug.).

BURR, R. [1984]. "System Design With Ada." Prentice-Hall, Inc., Englewood Cliffs, New Jersey.

CAIS [1984]. 'Department of Defense Requirements and Design Criteria for the Common Apse Interface Set (CAIS).' KIT Team Report, (Oct.).

CARD, D. et al. [1986]. "An Empirical Study of Software Design Practices." IEEE Trans. on Software Engineering. Vol. SE-12, No. 2 (Feb.).

CHEATHAM, T. [1981]. "PDS, Overview of the Harvard Program Development System," in Software Engineering Environments, H. Hunke (ed)., Proceedings of a Symposium, June 1980, Lahnstein, Germany.

---------- [1984] "Reusability Through Program Transformations." IEEE Trans. on Software Engineering, Vol. SE-10, No. 5 (Sept.).

CHARETTE, R. and R. WALLACE [1985]. "A Methodology for Addressing System Operability Issues." NAECON '85, Dayton (May).

CHARETTE, R. [1985a] "SOEM: Putting Theories Into Practice." Proceedings of the Third International Workshop on Specification and Design, London (Aug.).

---------- et al. [1985b] "Software Engineering Environment Standard Interfaces," Proceedings of the EIA National Workshop, St. Louis (Sept.).

---------- et al. [1985c] "Software Engineering Environment Interfaces: Issues and Implications." NSIA/EIA/AIAA Environment Working Group Report (Sept).

---------- et al. [1986]. "A Unified Methodology for Systems Development." McGraw-Hill, Inc., New York, New York. To be published Fall 1986.

CLAPP, J. [1981]. "Designing Software for Maintainability." Computer Design, pp.197-204 (Sept).

COMPTROLLER GENERAL [1979]. 'Contracting For Computer Software Development.' General Accounting Office Report, FGMSD-80-4, 9 Sept, 1979.

CONRAD, T. and R. CHARETTE [1982]. "Towards Automated Design of Distributed Command and Control Systems." Fifteenth International Conference on Systems Sciences, Honolulu (Jan.).

COOPER, J. [1984]. "Software Development Management Planning." IEEE Trans. on Software Engineering, Vol. SE-10, No. 1 (Jan.).

COULAM, R. [1982]. "Illusions of Choice." Princeton University Press, Princeton, New Jersey.

COX, B. [1984]. "Message/Object Programming: An Evolutionary Change in Programming Technology." IEEE Software, Vol. 1, No. 1 (Jan.).

DASGUPTA, S. [1984]. "The Design and Description of Computer Architectures." John Wiley & Sons, New York, New York.

DAVIS, A. [1982]. "The Design of a Family of Application-Oriented Requirements Languages." IEEE Computer, Vol. 8, No. 5 (May).

DELAUER, R. [1984]. 'Charter for the DoD Software Engineering Institute, 15 June 1984.'

DEMARCO, T. [1978]. "Structured Analysis and System Specifications," Yourdon, Inc., New York, New York.

DEMILLO, R. et al. [1978]. "Hints on Test Data Selection: Help for the Practicing Programmer." IEEE Computer, Vol. 11, No. 4 (April).

---------- et al. [1984]. 'Software Engineering Environments for Mission Critical Applications- STARS Alternative Programmatic Approaches.' IDA Papers P-1789 August 1984.

DIJKSTRA, E. [1972]. "Notes on Structured Programming," Structured Programming, Academic Press, New York, New York.

DOLOTTA, T. et al. [1976]. "Data Processing in 1980-1985," Appendix B. John Wiley & Sons, New York, New York.

---------- [1978]. "Unix Time-Sharing System: The Programmers Workbench.," in Interactive Programming Environments, D. Barstow et al. (ed.), McGraw-Hill, Inc. New York, New York.

ENOS, J. and R. VAN TILBURG. [1981]. "Software Design." IEEE Computer, Vol. 14, No. 2 (Feb.).

FAGAN, M. [1976]. "Design and Code Inspections to Reduce Errors in Program Development." IBM Systems Journal, Vol. 15, No. 3

FAIRLEY, R. [1978]. "Tutorial: Static Analysis and Dynamic Testing." IEEE Computer, Vol. 11, No. 4 (April).

---------- [1984]. "Software Engineering Concepts." McGraw-Hill, Inc. New York, New York.

FERRENTINO, A. and H. MILLS [1977]. "State Machines and Their Semantics in Software Engineering." COMPSAC 77, Congress on Computer Software Application.

FISCHETTI, M. [1986]. "A Review of Progress at MCC." IEEE Spectrum, Vol. 23, No. 3 (March).

FLECKSTEIN, W. [1983]. "Challanges in Software Development." IEEE Computer, Vol. 16, No. 3 (March).

FOX, J. [1976]. "Executive Qualities." Addison-Wesley Publishing Co., Inc.

---------- [1985]. Proceedings of the National Security Industrial Association National STARS Conference Proceedings, San Diego (May).

FREEDMAN, D. and C. WEINBURG [1982]. "Handbook of Walkthroughs, Inspections, and Technical Reviews." Little & Brown Co., Boston, Massachusetts.

FREEMAN, P. and T. WASSERMAN [1977]. "The Context of Design: IEEE Tutorial On Software Design Techniques, 2nd Ed." IEEE Catalog No. 76CH1145-2C

---------- [1982]. 'AdaTM Methodologies: Concepts and Requirements.' Department of Defense Ada Joint Project Office, November 1982.

FRENKEL, K. [1985]. "Toward Automating the Software Development Cycle." Communications of the ACM, Vol. 28, No. 6 (June).

---------- [1985a]. "Report on the Microelectronics and Computer Technology Conference." Communications of the ACM, Vol. 28, No. 8 (Aug.).

GAFFNEY, J. [1986]. "The Impact on Software Development Costs of Using HOL's." IEEE Trans. on Software Engineering, Vol. SE-12, No. 3 (March).

GANE, C. and T. SARSON [1979]. "Structured Systems Analysis: Tools and Techniques." Prentice-Hall, Inc., Englewood Cliffs, New Jersey.

GANNON, C. [1979] "Error Detection Using Path Testing and Static Analysis." IEEE Computer, Vol. 12, No. 9 (Aug.)

GARMAND, J. [1985]. "Data Systems for the Space Station and Beyond." AIAA Conference on Computers in Aerospace.

GLASS, R. [1980]. "Real-Time: The 'Lost World' of Software Debugging and Testing." Communications of the ACM, Vol. 23, No. 5 (May).

GOLDBERG, R. and H. LORIN [1980]. "The Economics of Information Processing, Vol. 2." John Wiley & Sons. New York, New York.

GRIFFEN, W. [1984]. "Software Engineering in GTE." IEEE Computer, Vol. 17, No. 11 (Nov.).

HABERMAN, A. [1980]. "Tools For Software System Construction," in Software Development Tools, W. Riddle and R. Fairley (eds.). Springer-Verlag, Heidelberg, West Germany.

HAMILTON, M. and ZELDIN, S. [1976]. "Higher Order Software- A Methodology For Defining Software." IEEE Trans. on Software Engineering, Vol. SE-2, No. 1 (March).

HASSE, V. and G. KOCH [1982]. "Application-Oriented Specifications." IEEE Computer, Vol. 15, No. 5 (May).

HECHT, H. and R. HOUGHTON [1982]. "The Current Status of Software Tool Usage." IEEE Computer Society's 6th International Computer Software & Applications Conference.

HEITMEYER, C. and J. McLEAN [1982]. "Abstract Requirements Specification: A New Approach and Its Application." IEEE Trans. on Software Engineering, Vol. SE-9, No. 5 (Sept.).

HENINGER, K. et al. [1978]. 'Software Requirements for the A-7E Aircraft.' NRL Memorandum 3876, 27 November 1978.

HENINGER, K. [1980]. "Specifying Software Requirements For Complex Systems: New Techniques and Their Application." IEEE Trans. on Software Engineering, Vol. SE-6, No. 1 (Jan.).

HERD, J. et al. [1977]. "Software Cost Estimation Study: Study Results (Vol. 1)." RADC-TR-220 June 1977.

HESTER, S. et al. [1981]. "Using Documentation as a Software Design Median." Bell System Technical Journal, Vol. 60, No. 8 (Oct.).

HOARE, C. [1984]. "Programming: Sorcery or Science?." IEEE Software, Vol. 1, No. 2 (April).

HOROWITZ, E. and J. MUNSON [1984]. "An Expansive View of Reusable Software." IEEE Trans. on Software Engineering, Vol. SE-10, No. 5 (Sept.).

HOUGHTON, R. and K. OAKLEY [1980]. 'NBS Software Tools Database.' National Bureau of Standards, Washington, D.C.

HOWDEN, W. [1982]. "Contemporary Software Development Environments." Communication of the ACM. Vol. 25, No. 5. (May).

HOWES, N. [1984]. "Managing Software Development Projects For Maximum Productivity." IEEE Trans. on Software Engineering, Vol. SE-10, No. 1 (Jan.).

IEEE [1981]. IEEE Standard for Software Quality Assurance Plans. IEEE/ANSI Std. 730-1981.

IEEE [1983]. IEEE Glossary of Software Engineering Terminology. IEEE Std. 729-1983. IEEE, New York, New York.

IEEE [1985]. Draft Standards Guidelines for an Ada PDL. IEEE PDL Subcommittee.

JACKSON, M. [1975]. Principles of Program Design. Academic Press, New York, New York.

JENSON, R. [1981]. "Structured Programming." IEEE Computer, Vol. 14, No. 3 (March).

JONES, T. [1984]. "Reusability in Programming: A Survey of the State-of-the Art." IEEE Trans. on Software Engineering, Vol. SE-10, No. 5 (Sept.).

KERNIGHAN, B. and J. MASHEY [1981]. "The UNIX Programming Environment." IEEE Computer, Vol. 14, No. 4 (April).

KIM, K. [1983]. "A Look at Japan's Development of Software Engineering Technology." IEEE Computer, Vol. 16, No. 5 (May).

KOOMAN, C. [1985]. "The Entropy of Design: A Study on the Meaning of Creativity." IEEE Trans. on Systems, Man and Cybernetics, Vol. SMC-15, No. 1 (Jan./Feb.).

KRUTCHEN, P. [1984]. "Software Prototyping Using the SETL Programming Language." IEEE Computer, Vol. 17, No. 10 (Oct.).

LAUBER, R. [1982]. "Development Support Systems." IEEE Computer, Vol. 15, No. 5 (May).

LEBLANC, R. and J. GODU [1982]. "Ada and Software Development Support: A New Concept in Language Design." IEEE Computer, Vol. 15, No. 5 (May).

LEFKOVITZ, A. [1982]."The Applicability of Software Development Methodologies to Naval Embedded Computer Systems."Univ. of Pennslyvania Contract #N62269-81-C-0455.

LIENTZ, B. [1983]. "Issues in Software Maintainence." ACM Computing Surveys, Vol. 15, No. 3 (Sept.).

LITVINTCHAUK, S. and A. MATSUMOTO [1984]. "Design of Ada Systems Yielding Reusable Components: An Approach Using Structured Algebraic Specification." IEEE Trans. on Software Engineering, Vol. SE-10, No. 5 (Sept.).

LOSHBOUGH, R. [1980]. "Applicability of SREM to Verification of Management Information System Software Requirements." TRW Report A1, April 1980.

LUCAS, H. [1984]. "Organizational Power and the Information Services Department." Communications of the ACM, Vol. 27, No. 1 (Jan.).

LUDEWIG, J. [1982]. "Computer-Aided Specification of Process Control Systems." IEEE Computer, Vol. 15, No. 5 (May).

MAGEL, K. [1984]. "Principles for Software Engineering Environments." ACM Software Engineering Notes. Vol. 9, No. 1 (Jan.).

MARTIN, J. [1985]. System Design from Provably Correct Constructs. Prentice-Hall, Inc., Engleside Cliffs, New Jersey.

MATSUMATO, Y. [1984]. "Some Experiences in Promoting Reusable Software: Presentation in Higher Abstract Levels." IEEE Trans. on Software Engineering, Vol. SE-10, No. 5 (Sept.).

MCKAY, C. et al. [1986]. "A Study to Identify Tools Needed to Extend the MAPSE to Support the Life Cycle of Large, Complex, Distributed Systems Such as the Space Station Program." University of Houston, NASA Contract NAS9-17010.

MEYER, B. [1985]. "On Formalism in Specifications." IEEE Software, Vol. 2, No. 1 (Jan.).

MILLER, E. [1978]. "Program Testing." IEEE Computer, Vol. 11, No. 4 (April).

---------- [1984]. "Software Testing Technology: An Overview," in the Handbook of Software Engineering, C. Vick and C. Ramamoorthy (eds.). Van Nostrand Reinhold Co., Inc., New York, New York.

MILLS, H. [1976]. "Software Development." IEEE Trans. on Software Engineering, (Dec.).

MIZUNO, Y. [1983]. "Software Quality Improvement." IEEE Computer, Vol. 16, No. 5 (May).

MORRIS, J. et al. [1986]. "Andrew: A Distributed Personal Computing Environment." Communications of the ACM, Vol. 29, No. 3 (March).

MOTO-OKA [1985]. "The Japanese Fifth Generation Computer Systems Project." IEEE Design & Test., Vol. 2, No.5 (Oct.).

MUNSON, J. [1981]. "Software Maintainability: A Practical Concern for Life-Cycle Costs." IEEE Computer Vol. 14, No. 11 (Nov.).

MUSA, J. [1985]. "Software Engineering: The Future of the Profession." IEEE Software, Vol. 2, No. 1 (Jan.).

MYERS, W. [1978]. "The Need For Software Engineering." IEEE Computer, Vol. 11, No. 2 (Feb.).

---------- [1978a]. "A Statistical Approach to Scheduling Software Development." IEEE Computer, Vol. 11, No. 12 (Dec.).

---------- [1985]. "MCC: Planning the Revolution in Software." IEEE Software, Vol. 2, No. 6 (Nov.).

NASSI, I. [1980]. "A Critical Look at the Process of Tool Development: An Industrial Perspective." Proceedings on Software Development Tools, W. Riddle and R. Fairley (eds.), Pingee Park, Colorado March 1980.

NAUER, P. and B. RANDALL, eds. [1969]. "Software Engineering," NATO Scientific Affairs Division, Brussels, Belgium.

NAVATHE, S. et al. [1986]. "Integrating User Views in Database Design." IEEE Computer, Vol. 19, No. 1 (Jan.).

OSTERWEIL, L. [1982]. "Software Environment Research: Directions for the Next Five Years." IEEE Computer, Vol. 14, No. 4 (April).

PAGE-JONES, M. [1980]. "The Practical Guide To Structured Design." Yourdon Press, New York, New York.

PANZL, D. [1978]. "Automatic Software Test Drivers." IEEE Computer, Vol. 11, No. 4 (April).

PARNAS, D. [1972]. "On The Criteria To Be Used In Decomposing Systems Into Modules." Communications of the ACM. Vol. 15, No. 12 (Dec.).

---------- [1974]. "On A 'Buzzword': Hierarchal Structure." Information Processing 74, J. Rosenfeld, ed., North Holland Publishing Company, Amsterdam.

---------- [1976]. "On the Design and Development of Program Families." IEEE Trans. on Software Engineering, Vol. SE-2, No. 1 (March).

---------- [1977]. "Use of Abstract Interfaces in the Development of Software For Embedded Computer Systems." NRL Report 8047, 3 June 1977.

---------- [1985]. "Software Aspects of Strategic Defense Systems." American Scientist 73:432-40, Sept.- Oct. 85.

---------- and D. WEISS [1985a]. "Active Design Reviews." NRL Report 8927, 18 November 1985.

---------- and P. CLEMENTS [1986]. "A Rational Design Process: How and Why to Fake It." IEEE Trans. on Software Engineering, Vol. SE-12, No. 2 (Feb.).

PATSCH, H. and R. STEINBRUGGEN [1983]. "Program Transformation Systems." ACM Computing Surveys, Vol. 15, No. 3 (Sept.).

PETERS, L. [1980]. "Special Issue on Software Engineering," Proceedings of IEEE, Vol.68, No. 9 (Sept.).

---------- [1981]. "Software Design: Methods & Techniques," Yourdan Press, New York, New York.

PLATTNER, B. and J. NIEVERGELT [1980]. "Monitoring Program Execution: A Survey." IEEE Computer, Vol. 13, No.11 (Nov.).

POSTON, R. [1984]. "Determining A Complete Set of Software Development Standards: Is the Cube the Answer? " IEEE Software, Vol. 1, No. 3 (July).

PRESSMAN, R. [1982]. Software Engineering: A Practioner's Approach. McGraw-Hill, Inc. New York, New York.

PUTNAM, L. [1978]. "A General Empirical Solution To The Macro Software Sizing and Estimating Problem." IEEE Trans. on Software Engineering, Vol. SE-4, No. 4 (July).

RALSTON, A. and E. REILLY, eds. [1983]. "Encyclopedia of Computer Science and Engineering, 2nd Ed." Von Nostrand Reinhold Co., New York, New York.

RAMAMOORTHY, C. et al. [1984]. "Software Engineering." IEEE Computer, Vol. 17, No. 10 (Oct.).

REDWINE, S. et al. [1984]. "DoD Related Software Technology Requirements, Practices, and Prospects For The Future." IDA Paper P-1788.

RIDDLE, W. [1980]. "Software Development Environments: Present and Future." Proceedings of the International Computer Technology Conference, San Francisco (Aug.).

---------- [1984]. "The Magic Number Eighteen Plus or Minus Three: A Study of Software Technology Maturation." In DoD Related Software Technology Requirements, Practices, and Prospects For The Future, IDA Paper P-1788.

---------- [1986]. "Software Environments Workshop." ACM Software Engineering Notes, Vol. 11, No. 1 (Jan.).

RIEFFER, D. [1980]. "Software Tool Directory." Rieffer Consultants, Inc. Torrance, California.

RITCHIE, D. and K. THOMPSON [1974]. "The UNIX Time-Sharing System," Communications of the ACM, Vol. 17, No. 7 (July).

ROSS, D. et al. [1975]. "Software Engineering: Process, Principles, and Goals." IEEE Computer, Vol. 8, No. 5 (May).

ROSS, D. [1977]. "Structured Analysis (SA): A language For Communicating Ideas." IEEE Trans. on Software Engineering, Vol. SE-3, No. 1. (Jan.).

---------- [1985]. "Interview: Douglas Ross Talks About Structured Analysis." IEEE Computer, Vol. 10, No. 7 (July).

ROUSE, W. [1985]. "On Better Mousetraps and Basic Research: Getting the Applied World To The Laboratory Door." IEEE Trans. on Systems, Man, and Cybernetics, Vol. SMC-15, No. 1 (Jan./Feb.).

ROYCE, W. [1970]. "Managing the Development of Large Software Systems: Concepts." WESCON Proceedings (Aug.).

SCACCHI, W. [1984]. "Managing Software Engineering Projects: A Social Analysis." IEEE Trans. on Software Engineering, Vol. SE-10, No. 1 (Jan.).

SCHEFFER, P. et al. [1985]. "A Case Study of SREM." IEEE Computer, Vol. 18, No.4 (April).

SEEWG [1982]. "A Software Engineering Environment For The Navy." Report of the NAVMAT Software Engineering Environment Working Group, 31 March 1982.

SHAW, M. [1984]. "Abstraction Techniques In Modern Programming Languages." IEEE Software, Vol. 1, No. 4 (Oct.).

SILVERMAN, B. [1985]. "Software Cost and Productivity Improvements: An Analogical View." IEEE Computer, Vol. 18, No. 5 (May).

SNEED, H. [1985]. "Automated Software Quality Assurance." IEEE Trans. on Software Engineering, Vol. SE-11, No. 9 (Sept.).

SOFTTOOLS [1985]. "IEEE Conference on Software Tools." IEEE Catalog No. 85CH2188-1.

SQM [1979]. "Software Quality Measurement Manual, Vol. II." RADC Report TR-80-109, June 1979.

STANDISH, T. [1984]. "An Essay on Software Reuse." IEEE Trans. on Software Engineering, Vol. SE-10, No. 5 (Sept.).

STANKOVIC, J. [1984]. "A Perspective on Distributed Computer Systems." IEEE Trans. on Computers, Vol. C-33, No. 12 (Dec).

STARS [1985]. STARS-SEE Operational Concept Document (OCD), Proposed Version 001.0, Department of Defense STARS Joint Project Office, 2 Oct. 1985.

STARS [1986]. Preliminary Systems Specification (STARS-SEE), Department of Defense STARS Joint Project Office, 26 Jan 1986.

STENNING, V. et al. [1981]. "The Ada Environment: A Pespective." IEEE Computer, Vol. 14, No. 6 (June).

STEVENS, W. et al. [1974]. "Structured Design." IBM Systems Journal, Vol. 13, No. 2.

STONEMAN [1980]. Requirements for Ada Programming Support Environments, Department of Defense Ada Joint Project Office February 1980.

STUEBING, H. [1984]. "A Software Engineering Environment (SEE) for Weapon System Software." IEEE Trans. on Software Engineering, Vol. SE-10, No. 4.

SUTTON, S. and V. BASSILLI [1981]. "The FLEX Software Design System: Designers Need Languages, Too." IEEE Computer, Vol. 14, No. 11 (Nov.).

SWARTOUT, W. and R. BALZER [1982]. "On the Inevitable Intertwining of Specification & Implementation." Communications of the ACM, Vol. 25, No. 7 (July).

TAJIMA, D. and T. MATSUBARA [1981]. "The Computer Software Industry in Japan." IEEE Computer, Vol. 14, No. 5 (May).

THAYER, R. et al. [1980]. "The Challenge of Software Engineering Project Management." IEEE Computer, Vol. 13, No.8 (Aug.).

---------- [1982]. "Validating Solutions to Major Problems in Software Engineering Project Management." IEEE Computer, Vol. 15, No. 8 (Aug.).

---------- and A. PYSTER [1984]. "Guest Editorial: Software Engineering Project Management," IEEE Trans. on Software Engineering, Vol. SE-10, No.1 (Jan.).

TIECHROW, D. [1974]. "An Introduction to PSL/PSA." ISDOS Working Paper No. 86, University of Michigan.

---------- and E. HERSHEY [1977]. "PSL/PSA: A Computer- Aided Technique For Structured Documentation and Analysis of Information Processing Systems." IEEE Trans. on Software Engineering, Vol. SE-3, No.1 (Jan.).

TIETELBAUM, T. et al. [1981]. "The Cornell Program Synthesizer: A Syntax-Directed Programming Environment." Communication of the ACM, Vol. 24, No. 9 (Sept.).

TRAINOR, W. [1974]. "Trends in Avionics Software - Problems and Solutions." Proceedings of the Aeronautical Systems Software Workshop, Air Force Systems Command.

ULLMAN, J. [1982]. "Principles of Database Systems," Computer Sciences Press, Rockville, Maryland.

VOSBURY, N. [1984]."Process Design," in the Handbook of Software Engineering, C. Vick and C. Ramamoorthy (eds.). Van Nostrand Reinhold Co., Inc., New York, New York.

WALLACE, R. and R. CHARETTE [1984]." Architectural Description of the Ada Language System (ALS)." Joint Service Software Engineering Environment Report No. JSSEE-ARCH-01, Decemeber 1984.

---------- [1986]. "Ada: A Practioner's Guide." McGraw-Hill, Inc. New York, New York.

WALLICH, P. [1986]. "Software, Technology '86." IEEE Spectrum, Vol. 23, No. 1 (Jan.).

WARBURTON, R. [1983]. "The Cost of Real-Time Software." IEEE Trans. on Software Engineering, Vol. SE-9, No.5 (Sept.)

WARNIER, P. [1976]. "Logical Construction of Programs, 3rd Ed.," Van Nostrand Reinhold, New York, New York.

WASSERMAN, A. [1979]. "Information System Design Methodology." Benjamin Franklin Colloquium on Information Science, Philadelphia 11 May 1979.

---------- [1981]. "Automated Development Environments." IEEE Computer, Vol. 14, No. 4 (April).

---------- [1982]. "The Future Of Programming." Communications of the ACM, Vol. 25, No. 3 (March).

WATSON, C. and C. FELIX [1977]. "A Method of Programming Measurement." IBM 1977.

WEINBURG, G. and D. FREEDMAN [1984]. "Reviews, Walkthroughs, and Inspections." IEEE Trans. on Software Engineering, Vol. SE-10, No. 1, Jan. 1984.

WEGNER, P. (ed.) [1978]. Research Directions in Software Technology, MIT Press, Cambridge, Massachusetts.

---------- [1984]. "Capital-Intensive Software Technology." IEEE Software, Vol. 1, No. 3 (July).

WILLIS, R. [1981]. "AIDES: Computer Aided Design of Software Systems," in Software Engineering Environments, H. Hunke (ed.), North-Holland Publishing Co., Amsterdam.

WIRTH, N. [1976]. "Algorithms + Data Structures = Programs." Prentice-Hall, Inc., Englewood Cliffs, New Jersey.

WOLF, A. et al. [1985]. "Ada-Based Support For Programming-in-the-Large," IEEE Software, Vol. 2, No. 2 (March).

WOLVERTON, R. [1984]. "Software Costing," in the Handbook of Software Engineering, C. Vick and C. Ramamoorthy (eds.). Van Nostrand Reinhold Co., Inc., New York, New York.

YEH, R. et al. [1984]. "Software Requirements: New Directions and Perspectives," in the Handbook of Software Engineering, C. Vick and C. Ramamoorthy (eds.). Van Nostrand Reinhold Co., Inc., New York, New York.

YEH, R. [1985]. "Proceedings of the National Security Industrial Association National STARS Conference." San Diego, May 1985.

YOURDAN, E. and L. CONSTANTINE [1975]. "Structured Design." Yourdon Press, New York, New York.

ZAVE, P. [1982]. "An Operational Approach to Requirements Specification for Embedded Systems." IEEE Trans. on Software Engineering, Vol. 8, (May).

---------- [1984]. "The Operational Versus The Conventional Approach to Software Development." Communications of the ACM, Vol. 27, No. 2 (Feb.).

ZELKOWITZ, M. [1983] "Private Communications in Software Engineering Concepts," by R. Fairley, McGraw-Hill, Inc. New York, New York.

---------- et al. [1985]. "Software Engineering Practices in the U.S. and Japan." IEEE Computer, Vol. 17, No. 6 (June).

INDEX